ARTS REVIEWING

Arts Reviewing: A Practical Guide is an accessible introduction to the world of arts criticism. Drawing on professional expertise and a range of cultural reviews from music, film, theatre, visual arts, television and books, Andy Plaice discusses different approaches to arts criticism, with tips on crafting great reviews.

Chapters explore:

- a brief history of arts criticism;
- researching and preparing for an assignment;
- legal and ethical boundaries when reviewing;
- finding your own writing style;
- starting and sustaining a career in arts criticism in the digital age.

The book is underpinned by over 20 interviews with leading practitioners from across Britain, America and Australia. They offer fascinating insights into the life of a critic, including their best and worst career moments and the debates impacting the field of arts criticism. Interviewees include Neil McCormick, rock critic at the *Daily Telegraph*, the *Guardian* theatre critic Lyn Gardner and television critic Mark Lawson (BBC/the *Guardian*).

New approaches to reviewing techniques and writing style are combined with real-world advice from leading professionals in the field, making this book an ideal resource for students and graduates of journalism, cultural studies and media studies.

Andy Plaice is a senior lecturer in journalism at De Montfort University, Leicester, having previously edited local newspapers. As a feature writer and theatre and TV critic, he has written for *The Stage*, *The Times*, *Sunday Express*, *Writing* magazine, *The Arts Desk* and *WhatsOnStage*.

ARTS REVIEWING

A Practical Guide

Andy Plaice

LONDON AND NEW YORK

First published 2018
by Routledge
2 Park Square, Milton Park, Abingdon, Oxon OX14 4RN

and by Routledge
711 Third Avenue, New York, NY 10017

Routledge is an imprint of the Taylor & Francis Group, an informa business

© 2018 Andy Plaice

The right of Andy Plaice to be identified as author of this work has been asserted by him in accordance with sections 77 and 78 of the Copyright, Designs and Patents Act 1988.

All rights reserved. No part of this book may be reprinted or reproduced or utilised in any form or by any electronic, mechanical, or other means, now known or hereafter invented, including photocopying and recording, or in any information storage or retrieval system, without permission in writing from the publishers.

Trademark notice: Product or corporate names may be trademarks or registered trademarks, and are used only for identification and explanation without intent to infringe.

British Library Cataloguing-in-Publication Data
A catalogue record for this book is available from the British Library

Library of Congress Cataloging-in-Publication Data
Names: Plaice, Andy, author.
Title: Arts reviewing : a practical guide / Andy Plaice.
Description: New York : Routledge, 2017. |
Includes bibliographical references and index.
Identifiers: LCCN 2017015807| ISBN 9781138675117 (hardback : alk. paper) |
ISBN 9781138675124 (pbk. : alk. paper) | ISBN 9781315560830 (ebook)
Subjects: LCSH: Arts. | Art criticism.
Classification: LCC NX640 .P59 2017 | DDC 700–dc23
LC record available at https://lccn.loc.gov/2017015807

ISBN: 978-1-138-67511-7 (hbk)
ISBN: 978-1-138-67512-4 (pbk)
ISBN: 978-1-315-56083-0 (ebk)

Typeset in Bembo
by Out of House Publishing

 Printed in the United Kingdom by Henry Ling Limited

CONTENTS

Acknowledgements   *vi*

   Introduction   1
1. The role of the critic   4
2. A history of arts criticism   22
3. Preparation and research   37
4. Writing the review: part one   51
5. Writing the review: part two   70
6. The impact of criticism   88
7. Legal and ethical boundaries   108
8. Everyone's a critic   127
9. Breaking into the business   142
10. The new reviewer: making it pay   159
    Conclusion   174

Index   *177*

ACKNOWLEDGEMENTS

My thanks go to Niall Kennedy, Kitty Imbert and the team at Routledge for supporting this book with such enthusiasm, to my colleagues at De Montfort University, Leicester, and to the arts critics who gave their time so generously for interviews.

Finally, I am indebted to my family: my wife Maria for her love and patience, our sons Jack and Albie (who saw far too much of the back of my head while this book was being written), my father Russell and my grown-up children James and Katie. This book is dedicated to them and to the memory of my late mother Jenny.

INTRODUCTION

Part of being human is the capacity to make judgements about people, places, things and situations, both real and imagined. Experience tells us we are able to weigh up complex data in a matter of seconds on whether, for example, we like someone as a potential partner in life or whether the job candidate who has just stepped into the room might be the one to fill the vacancy.

For critics wrestling with the art they experience we might expect that *critical* judgement is merely an extension of what they have practised since childhood, such as forming taste or understanding a moral code or working out what makes them laugh.

It should be easy, then, shouldn't it? Well, yes and no. The arts critic watches a film or a television show, reads a book, listens to a record, goes to the theatre or gallery and plays a video game, immersed in the experience and programmed to say whether they like it on your behalf. But that is only part of the arrangement. A reader engaged with a film review wants the critic's opinion, certainly, but wants to learn something, too: the quality of the storytelling, the way the film was shot, how it sits in comparison with other movies in this genre or the director's previous work, or even the journey behind making the film in the first place.

All of this forms part of the critic's toolkit, and it can only be of any real use by watching, listening, reading and writing – and then doing it all over again. At the risk of stating the blindingly obvious, I'm assuming you've picked up this book because you love the arts: their power, their richness in form and style, the way they play with our emotions, help make change for the better, bring us together – the list goes on. Whether you're a fan of jukebox musicals or Scandinavian crime drama, whether you're a Harry Potter nut or visit your local art gallery at lunchtime or know every line of dialogue from *Star Wars*, you'll be someone whose life would be weaker without their fix of culture.

I'm also assuming you write about the arts or at least *want* to write about the arts. First and foremost this book is for students and bloggers with some kind of writing portfolio or those about to begin one. Students of journalism will, I hope, find many ideas and tips to improve their confidence and take their arts writing to a higher level; students in traditional arts and humanities subjects like drama and film should also find it useful, especially in the sections that introduce a grounding for *all* journalism, not just arts reviewing.

Professional critics will be particularly drawn, perhaps, to the interviews with their contemporaries – an exciting list of writers who have covered music, television, theatre, dance and more from the early 1970s to the present day – and, finally, I'd like to think the book will be interesting to anyone curious about the strange but wonderful world of reviewing.

Quickly to the beginning: why write a practical guide to arts reviewing? I first taught journalism undergraduates at De Montfort University, Leicester, in 2006, having left the regional press where I'd spent 18 years in total, 14 of those years as an editor but initially as a reporter, where a typical day could mean bashing out an obituary, interviewing a man on the secrets to his prize vegetables and listening to a family threatened with eviction from their home.

In 2013 I created an arts and entertainment course at the university which went some way to satisfying what we observed was a growing demand from students. I'd been a drama student in the north of England and I'd had some experience as a playwright before an accidental switch to newspapers, and so the combination of a love for the arts and for journalism made absolute sense when it came to creating a new course.

The book my students required in underpinning what we were doing simply didn't exist. As far as we could tell, there was a British book some 20 years out of date and an American equivalent, but nothing modern which served as an introduction to all of the arts disciplines. Excellent publications exist with an emphasis on theatre, on music, on film and so on – and some of them are referred to in the chapters to come – but not one book seemed to bring all of those disciplines together.

This book can fill that gap, offering sensible practical advice on arts criticism, and by suggesting ways to get closer to your subject and invigorate your writing. After all, it's the writing that matters. Lazily pick your way around the Internet and you'll soon discover that arts criticism ranges from the dry to the sparkling, from the crystal clear to the deeply murky. In short, a lot of good stuff and a lot of stuff that's quite terrible.

That is not to suggest that print is on a higher level: newspapers were (and remain) guilty at times as well.

But a 600-word review written at speed once the stage lights dim requires good technique and strong discipline, to say nothing of sparking debate with your witty, provocative observations. It's harder than it looks. Most writers will admit to having been faced with their first empty page (or empty screen now, of course) and thinking 'OK, what happens *now*?' – and yet it can be learned. Along with an idea or two to help carry what you want to say, your work must be factually accurate and written with precision.

In the chapters that follow we'll address steps you can take every time you write a review that will ensure your piece can be sustained from start to finish. One common mistake the beginner makes is to start without having any idea of where they're going and then, inevitably, the piece tails off; runs out of steam. How do you find that beginning that will hook the reader? How do you keep them interested while providing the necessary level of facts? I'll draw on my experience as a writer and tutor to supply answers to these and other questions, as well as sharing interviews with a string of critics and bloggers at the top of their game including Mark Lawson, Lyn Gardner, Neil McCormick and Megan Vaughan.

Primarily we're concerned with the disciplines of music, film, television, theatre, books and visual art. You might already be immersed in writing about one of these forms, with half an eye on tackling another: keep reading, then, because patterns will emerge between them, and techniques you learn for one discipline can be applied to others.

One factor that has challenged the norms of arts writing in the century so far – and that shows no sign of relenting – is the impact of the Web. A blessing or a curse? Or somewhere in between? Old-school critics have embraced the realities of online publishing with some success, though the question of how to make it pay remains. They know they cannot operate without some kind of presence on the Web, and most will report they welcome the chance to engage with their readers – in fact, make that viewers or listeners as well, in the cases of a select bunch who have made the leap into broadcasting, podcasting or creating their own YouTube channel.

The field is now wide open: you can run a blog, even a vlog. You can host a website distinct from your portfolio in print or as an accompaniment to it. You can tweet on the hour or podcast once a week – there are no limits to what is possible. Television reviews can be written in advance, primed to be published as the end credits fade or, if you're Neil McCormick, the respected *Daily Telegraph* rock critic, you can write your Coldplay review on your phone while in the crowd at Glastonbury, and have it sent to the artsdesk in London even before you've walked through the mud and made it back to the hospitality bar.

All of this is new and exciting. Indeed the digital explosion of the last 15 years or so means there has never been a more interesting time to think about arts criticism, but what of the elephant in the (chat)room? Arts criticism has been under attack as well, as media players try to adjust to the idea that 'anyone can be a critic'. We will see how creative alternatives to traditional journalism may provide a long-term solution, as well as highlighting how to write compelling arts reviews.

Before sharpening those writing tools, though, we're going to put arts criticism in a historical context and – first of all – discuss what it really means to be a critic.

1

THE ROLE OF THE CRITIC

There has never been a more challenging time to be an arts critic. Delivering to digitally literate readers who expect your thoughts on the play by the time they arrive home is one such challenge, as is meeting the expectations of your over-worked arts editor, who knows that you're both in the firing line should the axe swing again in another round of redundancies. That is to say nothing of the artists, who need and crave your attention, or the fact that the blog you started last year is hitting the spot with your witty observations but hasn't made any money.

The ubiquity of digital content has combined with a downgrading of print – the once superior form has had its face slapped, with tumbling circulations resulting in reduced advertising revenues, which, in turn, has led to job losses and restricted space for arts coverage.

High-profile casualties have included arts writers at the *Daily Telegraph* and *Independent on Sunday* in the UK, and at *Variety* magazine in the USA. An outcry ensued (Kermode 2013) in 2010 when *Variety* cut two of its film critics and one theatre critic from the staff, thinking that readers 'won't notice'. In 2009 *Telegraph* arts staff all came off contract and were put on freelance terms, and in 2013 seven writers at the *Independent on Sunday* were axed as the paper dropped its 'The Critics' section in favour of a rebooted arts section, where it was hoped those same writers would be able to contribute. This was a sign of things to come as the *Independent* printed its final edition in March 2016 and reinvented itself online.

News and sport remain the kings of content in the traditional newspaper, but that is of no consolation if you write about contemporary art and you're at the peak of your powers. Increasingly the arts critic has had to diversify if he or she wants to make a living, though we should not be under any illusion – there are scores of critics eager for business in every town and city – nor should we assume that we are only talking about full-time, professional reviewers.

In reality the number of writers commenting on other people's art as a full-time career was – even pre-Internet – relatively low. Do a quick calculation of theatre critics, totting up the UK's national newspapers from the *Scotsman* to the *Sun* along with its one trade newspaper (*The Stage*), and we have around a dozen or so people, a number drawn from papers without one (like the *Sun*) to those with two or even more (like the *Guardian* or *The Times*). Similar figures can be arrived at for other art forms, though film, music and television would see higher numbers given the wide choice of magazines on offer in addition to newspapers.

The likelihood is that these full-timers are adding value to their roles by interviewing artists or creatives and writing features, sometimes topical pieces sparked by a newsworthy event in the arts but more often than not what the British refer to as a preview and the Americans call an advance. That in itself creates an interesting ethical dilemma for the writer, which we shall explore later on. Lyn Gardner at the *Guardian* said that of her many visits to the theatre in a week – normally five, six or seven – 'the vast majority of those would be things for review but a couple might be that I'm catching up on something that I'm thinking of blogging around, or it's in preparation for a feature'.[1]

Gardner is unusual in that she is on staff and writing full-time for one publication, whereas most freelance critics hop from one title to another (in some cases *across* disciplines as well, increasing their marketability). They might take on other work – teaching, training, writing books – and they possibly write a blog.

So far we have talked about criticism and reviewing as if it is the same thing. Let's establish some ground rules.

A critic or reviewer?

A number of factors lie at the heart of this question, particularly the level of experience of the writer behind the words and the form in which they are published. Many publications offering judgement on works of art – film, popular music, classical music, television, books, theatre, games, visual art, comedy, dance and opera – signpost this kind of writing as 'The Critics' or a 'Critics' Choice' when really the style and format is more rooted in reviewing. So what's the difference?

We associate criticism with scholarly output: Johnson and Hazlitt wrote convincingly about poetry and Shakespeare and other great dramatists from a safe distance. They had reflected on what they wanted to say over a period of time, shaping their argument in the light of what they had experienced in the moment but informed by everything *else* they had read over many years of study. Today's critic should think deeply about the art and evaluate its effect. The ingredients which form that evaluation will be looked at later in the book, though in practice the luxury of this thinking time may not present itself, to a large degree because of points already touched upon such as a shrinking team but also because of a pressure to be *first* with a verdict. The critic will often – though not always – be a specialist in their field, honing their skills over many years of practice, supporting their evaluation in the context of other art they have encountered, whereas reviewing suggests a quicker response. In the broadest sense it does mean something quicker: reaction to a live gig might be uploaded to your blog or your newspaper's website with that last power chord still ringing in the air. Live performance is clearly unique and yet other art forms might happily be tackled in advance – all recorded television, for example, can be viewed and reviewed well ahead of its broadcast by writers allowed access to online streaming.

Let us take stock for a moment because it would be easy to see this as black and white when the reality is far from that: reviewing *is* quick, *is* generally written to a tighter word count than a lengthy helping of criticism but can display many of the hallmarks of criticism in terms of deeper thinking and levels of analysis. As the American author and lecturer Campbell B. Titchener (2005) puts it:

> A *review* is, at its most basic, a report with opinion, but the reviewer can bring so much background to his or her observations that there can be a critical aspect to it.

Michael Billington is regarded as one of the great theatre critics. When he started at *The Times* in 1965, joining the *Guardian* in 1971, the Internet was a world away, and his finely crafted journalism would appear in the next day's edition or the one after that. Nowadays his work is published on the *Guardian*'s website within a couple of hours of curtain call, but we would not dream of calling him anything other than a critic. So why the confusion? Who is who? Is it to do with the length of the piece, the experience of its writer or the esteem in which its publisher is held?

It's all of those things, but it's also influenced by something more simple: first, tradition and second, what trips more easily off the tongue. 'The critics are in!', cries that nervy stage director in his rallying call before press night. 'Can't wait to read their reviews!', says the star (OK, maybe not, but go with it). Nobody says the reviewers are in, can't wait for their criticism. It's just easier the other way, and in any case 'critic' sounds more qualified. People who judge art in print or online may acknowledge that they are writing reviews, but they put 'critic' when it comes to a job title (which seems fair). They are not without ego – and more of that later.

Now we've established what to call them – though whisper it, they've been called much, much worse in private – who are these people?

Profile of a critic

Up until now nobody has designed a qualification of any kind that must be obtained in order to pass judgement on other people's art. All you need is a computer and the willingness to publish.

In his autobiography, the English film star Michael Caine tells an amusing story about his time in the theatre as a young actor:

> Early in my career, I once wondered who became a critic in the first place. In my days in repertory, after receiving a particularly brutal savaging from

the local paper ... I set out for the pub where the journalists hung out and located the drama critic. He turned out to be a spotty youth all of nineteen years old who explained to me that he had been forced to review our show because he had been late into work that week more times than any other reporter.

(Caine 1992, 326)

It had been a punishment. Not really what you want to hear as an ambitious performer but not an untypical situation in the regional press, which, collectively, was a hugely influential part of British life post-Second World War. By 1975, for example, the provincial evening newspaper market accounted for 6.5 million copies sold a day across 79 cities and large towns (Seymour-Ure 1991).

The unique selling point of local newspapers in the pre-Internet age was that they covered just about everything that moved – a paper of record, many of them proudly proclaimed – in a world more innocent, where publishing names and photographs really did shift copies. For the newspaper reporter it meant a fair share of night jobs attending a seemingly unstoppable supply of public meetings and a live performance every now and then. Arts coverage usually consisted of turning up to gigs by local bands on the way up and bigger names on the way down; it involved reviewing books and records sent into the office, which would occasionally cause disagreement because the reporter got to keep the freebie, and it involved seeing drama of wildly differing standards. An editor lucky enough to employ a reporter who *wanted* to watch amateur dramatics or a touring play starring someone vaguely famous would appreciate them; otherwise – as the Caine anecdote showed – it really was a case of avoiding live theatre for the majority of journalists.

This style of reviewing by inexperienced, or even reluctant, observers remains closer to the tradition of reporting rather than criticism, the emphasis being on what happened and who did it rather than any evaluation of what they did. Reporters would show up with the editor's parting words still ringing in their ears: 'Get the names, get the *names!*'

On a wider scale, critics with a national rather than regional outlook have reached their positions from a variety of routes, including listings magazines, job advertisements and stints doing work experience. An Oxbridge education would certainly have opened doors in the past to some forms of arts criticism, helping lead to accusations that the profession was filled by an unofficial club – in 2007 Nicholas Hytner, former artistic director at the National Theatre, despaired at what he saw as 'dead white men' (Hoyle 2007) dominating the field of drama criticism – but that is not to suggest all critics across the arts trod a similar path. Pat Long's history of the *NME* (2012) describes how this much-loved publication became hugely influential, despite employing writers who found real life difficult.

Going on tour with a rock band, sitting in the stalls five nights a week or drinking in the atmosphere of a rowdy comedy club do not fit a nine-to-five lifestyle, and these worlds will attract their fair share of characters.

Ripping up the rule book in criticism currently are bloggers and, catching up fast, vloggers. Writing and talking from the hip, these newcomers continue to challenge the old guard of the printed review with their conversational tone, experimental style and ability to shine a light on the easily overlooked. Plainly, there is nothing new in being new. It could be argued that two of the greatest arts critics, theatre men Kenneth Tynan and Harold Hobson, were doing just that when they went against the grain in the 1950s – Tynan, for example, with his creative, groundbreaking style or Hobson in seeing what nobody else could see: the promise of a truly great playwright in one Harold Pinter.

Arts bloggers use social media to draw attention to their work. Mostly they have no formal training in journalism – which could easily apply to large swathes of professional critics, too – and they are often under 30. Working independently or in partnerships or small groups to produce websites/online magazines, these people have caused a new landscape to emerge. Online critics and bloggers are often motivated in different ways from mainstream writers. Their intention may be to showcase something otherwise overlooked or indulge their total belief in the art form, or at least a movement or genre within that form. If their writing serves to highlight their work, perhaps as a springboard for other paid opportunities, then all well and good.

From the Internet explosion of the late 1990s, the arts world still cannot agree whether it is a good or a bad thing that amateur critics now exist. Is there room for the kitchen-table blogger alongside the seasoned professional? As later chapters explore, it's not so much about whether one is getting paid and the other one not, but the huge shift in power between writer and reader.

Judgement from above

The great editor, writer and essayist Samuel Johnson wrote in 1759 that, 'Criticism is a study by which men grow important and formidable at very small expense.' Popular culture portrays the critic as acerbic and lofty, even relishing the fallout from his words. It is a stereotype but not the full story, just as police detectives spend far more time doing methodical hard graft than they do solving murders. Historically the critic kept his distance from his readers and from the artists whose work he was paid to judge. In the old world of criticism, his pronouncements were made on the artist for the benefit of the reader who may or may not have experienced the artists' work as well and, once published, there was little that either party could do about it.

Sure of themselves and often the products of a classical education, critics post-Second World War were immune from any backlash against their work, arguably removed from the real world in any case and often left to their own devices thanks to editor bosses with a preference for news over culture.

Television reviewing demonstrates this rather well, as pointed out by Joe Moran in *Armchair Nation: An Intimate History of Britain in Front of the TV* (2013, 236):

> The more thoughtful reviewers, like Philip Purser, TC Worsley and Peter Black, had all previously been theatre critics and tended to focus on prestige

programmes like single plays and documentaries, often looking down on the American imports, light entertainment shows and soap operas that most viewers watched.

A few decades later Nina Myskow became the best known of the tabloid newspaper television critics whose editors saw the value of a British readership in love with the idea of watching television and talking about television. Already a respected rock and pop journalist, her appointment as *Sunday People* television critic in 1982 was perhaps a forerunner of things to come as the paper sought to get closer to its readers by more firmly representing the programmes they watched instead of what an out-of-touch reviewer wanted to see.

She told me that upon being offered the role at the *People*, she asked the editor 'What do I know about TV?' 'Well, you watch TV don't you?', he replied. 'A bit', she said. 'Well, you'll be watching it a lot then, won't you?'[2]

Myskow is clear on why her column worked: 'I have what I call a common taste which I think is shared by an awful lot of other people. I did not have lofty views.'[3]

That is not to say Myskow couldn't be brutal in her assessments – she could; and more of that in later chapters – but a style was developing which is closer to what we see now in criticism, of connecting with the reader's world. Figuratively, by watching quiz shows and *Coronation Street*, she sat side by side with her readers rather than perched above them.

In *How To Write About Theatre* (2015), Mark Fisher calls it the removal of 'the top-down school of criticism, with definitive judgements made by the few', to be replaced by 'a more egalitarian system'.

It is a view supported by Mark Kermode, film expert writing for the *Observer* and regular reviewer on BBC radio and television, who says the film critic's word is no longer final:

> Now, there's an active inter-play between critics and their audience … Far from dumbing-down, the input of online contributors has (in my experience at least) caused everyone to sharpen up, for fear of making fools of themselves in public. No longer can a critic operate from a position of ignorance without fear of correction.
>
> *(Kermode 2013, 272)*

Commentators agree that online criticism has been the biggest propeller for change in the dynamic between reader and writer.

The twenty-first-century critic

Later chapters will look at the astonishing rate of change in worldwide arts reviewing in the last 15 to 20 years, with issues including the impact on traditional press and ethical questions arising from the use of social media but, briefly, I want to highlight digital literacy and other qualities as part of a critic's armoury.

The twenty-first-century critic not only has to write the review but shout about it from the rooftops, or at least be encouraged to. Newspaper critics have slowly turned to Twitter, for example, and embraced it in ways perhaps that we – or, indeed, they – might not have expected, while younger writers have, from the outset, used social media as a way of driving traffic to their blogs. Megan Vaughan's theatre blog, *Synonyms for Churlish*, has been widely praised for its edge, its quirky style – producing one review as a series of emojis for example – and its confidence in being able to tackle subjects in a longer form than print allows.

I asked Vaughan about the success of the blog and what she believed it offered readers as an alternative to print:

> That's really difficult to respond to. I agree that it's been successful in some ways, but by most people's parameters of success it's achieved nothing at all. And I'm very aware of how closely it's tied to my Twitter account. I'm not sure it would have been read so widely were it not for my Twitter account acting as gatekeeper. But yes, if we're assuming it has been a success, then I think that success is probably down to a combination of a writing style not usually found in traditional criticism and a sense that my taste is quite 'cool'. It's embarrassing to say this really – telling people that you're cool means that you're instantly not cool anymore – but as certain people started to tune into my taste, it became clear that an endorsement from me was somehow more credible than from an older, more 'traditional', new-writingy critic … but, again, it's hard to know how much of this is due to the blog and how much is due to Twitter.[4]

Writers and journalists comfortable with publishing their own work online are clearly at an advantage compared to the digitally challenged in an overcrowded job market. I will examine this in more detail in Chapters 8 and 9. Critics working for traditionally print-based operations will still file their copy to an arts editor or sub-editor, who will either make that review ready for the Web or pass it to a colleague to fulfil that function. No such luxury for the one-man-band blogger, responsible for checking, uploading and publishing their own work, and only partially so for the website writer working in a virtual office. Whereas she will write and upload the story, source photographs and ensure links are created to relevant content spinning off from her review, she will almost certainly have the benefit of an extra pair of eyes who hits the 'publish' button for the rest of the world to see.

Versatility is key for the twenty-first-century critic, and not only does that involve writing a 600-word review, a 140-character tweet and engaging with readers' comments but also developing a profile both in print and in the real world that underpins your criticism. It can take several forms. At its simplest level, agreeing to a picture byline to be presented as part of your and your publication's brand is now standard practice. We recognise the faces of our favourite critics this way but also from seeing them appear on television delivering criticism as part of a round-table discussion. They may turn up as talking heads on an arts programme casting its eye over a genre of films or a turning point in music history. They may use their expertise as a launchpad for a part-time career writing books, as in the case of Mark Kermode (books about movie obsessives, cinema multiplexes and film critics); drama critic Michael Coveney (biography of Dame Maggie Smith); or radio critic Miranda Sawyer (exploring the midlife crisis).

Digital awareness should be part of the make-up of the modern reviewer but there is more that is relevant regardless of the platform being served. Let us look at the responsibility and the function of the arts critic. What is it they do? What are they thinking about?

Be a reporter

Modern life accommodates an insatiable desire to report and record seemingly everything that happens, from the powerful and important to the desperately banal. Walk around any tourist area at a busy time and you will be hard-pressed not to find someone using their mobile phone to photograph or video the experience. Who needs a memory when you can film every night out, or Facebook reminds you of what you were doing on this day last year?

British television companies of the 1960s and 1970s jettisoned huge quantities of programmes on tape, not just because they were running out of storage space and it cost money to keep collections together but because they had not fully anticipated what would be a fascination for the past. Nowadays the rediscovery of long-lost episodes of shows like *Dad's Army* or *Hancock's Half Hour* will be reported as small triumphs, often thanks to dedicated fans who taped and kept episodes or when an archivist is led to a dusty collection stored long ago in a dead man's attic.

With live performance, as opposed to any kind of art captured in print, on film, on tape or on record, we are reliant on understanding its potency for the people who witnessed it, especially those who wrote about it as a permanent record of what they saw. Tynan (cited in Wardle 1992) said that the purpose of criticism was to 'give permanence to something impermanent'.

Buried within this notion is the idea of the critic as reporter – an important factor easily overlooked – and something we will return to in Chapter 4 when we unpack reviewing and its relationship with news.

Many of us will be familiar with the British punk band the Sex Pistols and their explosive entrance onto the world's music stage in late 1976. Writing this 40 years later, we position the band historically, based on what they did, said and sang. But someone had to be first – to *report* their verdict on the debut single. Cliff White from the *NME* was among the first to review *Anarchy in the UK*. 'I think your record is lousy', he wrote in his column on 4 December that year, as if speaking to them directly.

White's verdict is permanent on a piece of art that is equally permanent, but let us return for a moment to *live* performance from the past that we cannot see, hear, touch or smell. Who has not wondered what Shakespeare's plays were like, as performed in his lifetime or at least in the first 100 years after his death? How were they designed? What style of acting was employed? How did audiences behave? We can – and do – debate what Shakespeare's plays mean to us now, 400 years after they were written, but what effect did they have on his contemporaries?

Little has survived, Stanley Wells suggests, to shine a light on the nuances of performance or to evaluate the significance of a play, but letters, journals and notebooks written by various scholars, doctors or travellers do help us to see how audiences responded to Shakespeare. He writes:

> On the whole, allusions to performances in Shakespeare's time and up to the Restoration tell us more about reactions of audiences than about the theatre and what went on there. They give some indication of the qualities that spectators most valued in actors, and of the emotional impact made by their performances … and they provide clues as to which plays, and parts of plays, were most popular.
>
> *(Wells 1997, 3)*

He goes on to say that in 1610 an Oxford don, Henry Jackson, wrote that in tragedies performed by the King's Men, the players 'moved some to tears not only by their words but even by their actions'. It was, Wells (1997) says, 'an indication that gesture played an important part in attaining tragic effect', and it further strengthens this idea of the reporter in the audience.

With your reviews, think of the art as being live or recorded. Your readers can catch up on the television programme or the album that you consumed, though you may be a day or a week or more ahead of them. The task of reporting its happening is an important one, and becomes even more important for live performance. Distance, time or cost may preclude your readers from experiencing it, too, but they nevertheless want to know about it. Your review is partially a report, partially placing on record that it did happen and this is how you felt.

Be distinctive

At the height of her fame on Fleet Street, the traditional heartland of British national newspapers, television critic Nina Myskow was writing for a Sunday tabloid selling more than 5 million copies a week. The *News of the World* accounted for nearly half of all Sunday red-top sales in the mid-1980s, and it was to there she had switched after a two-year stint on the rival *Sunday People*. Myskow's biting television reviews had earned her a loyal following and catapulted her onto our television screens as a straight-talking panellist on ITV talent show *New Faces*, making her – along with the *Observer*'s Clive James – one of the first critics in the country to make that leap from on the page to on the box.

Her sharp style and distinctiveness helped her succeed, perhaps best summed up with her invention, Wally of the Week, a regular slot on her page which she began at the *People* and took with her to the *News of the World*. She said:

Before I wrote my first column I thought about it quite hard. I wanted to start off by making it distinctive from the rest. I wanted to tap into the idea of what the Americans call a water-cooler moment. Now of course TV is much more fragmented, but when I started there were only three channels and therefore a hugely shared national experience, so that people would know what you were talking about. I wanted to reflect people saying 'did you see how so-and-so made a fool of themselves?' rather than write erudite essays. And that's where the idea for Wally of the Week came. I was merely pointing out what everybody else was saying.[5]

Being distinctive as a critic can be arrived at by reviewing mainstream art in fresh, creative ways, by delivering especially brilliant content or by exploring new areas to excavate. In film, Roger Ebert, alongside his fellow American co-presenter Gene Siskel, came up with a gimmick for their television shows which would stay with them the whole of their careers – a simple but incredibly effective gesture of giving a thumbs up or thumbs down depending on their reaction to a movie. But more importantly Ebert was celebrated for embracing online journalism. In 2010 – three years before his death – Ebert made his 10,000 reviews free-to-view on the website of his employer, the *Chicago Sun-Times*. When the *Sun-Times* adopted a paywall a year later it was keen to tell the world that access to Ebert's work would continue to be unrestricted. Kermode (2013), describing him as 'the most important film commentator on the web', says the publishers were 'clearly sympathetic to Ebert's concern and (more importantly) acutely aware of his role drawing traffic to the site'.

Lyn Gardner notices how first-string critics follow one another around, and 'the bloggers do the same but the more interesting ones are the ones who specialise – for example concentrating on circus. "Why set yourself up to be Michael Billington when he's very good at that already?" Be different', she urges. 'Some of the best blogs do that, like Andrew Haydon on *Postcards of the Gods*. They are writing brilliantly and often in long form or with a different perspective from that of a broadsheet.'[6]

A similar sense of distinctiveness was emerging in television criticism of the early 2000s. Whereas Myskow had targeted mass-market shows like *Coronation Street*, *EastEnders* or the deliciously camp American import *Dallas*, Charlie Brooker, writing in the *Guardian* following the success of his website that produced fake television schedules, was more concerned with 'factory-produced television he called "unentertainment"'. His style was satirical. Shows like *Celebrity Wife Swap* were being 'churned out like sausage meat', he wrote, just to satisfy the enormous hunger of television channels with air-time to fill (Moran 2013).

In an overcrowded market, think about your content and how you can make it distinctive. Is it an eye-catching gimmick, a specialism within an arts discipline where the competition isn't as fierce or a style that instantly sets you apart? Staying true to who you are, be distinctive.

Have an opinion

The opposite of *reporting* on what you experienced, having an *opinion* on what you consumed is central to your role as a critic. Surely nobody could forget to say whether they liked something or not? Normally no, but the reviewer unsure of himself, especially in an environment in which he is unfamiliar, can fall back on those good old reporting skills as a way of ticking off the assignment but minimising the damage. So his concentration is with what happened and the reaction of the audience or crowd. Critics will not agree whether the response by an audience is relevant. 'It's *my* opinion the reader wants, not the people in the stalls', some will say. I would suggest it depends on the context. Comedy, for example, is entirely dependent upon engagement from the audience. A silent, unresponsive crowd will affect the comic's timing, delivery and whole persona – as will a crowd bent on heckling and shouting expletives, for that matter – though performers playing an intense, wordy drama may not fully appreciate the level of warmth coming their way from theatregoers until thunderous applause at the end. Music writers may acknowledge 15,000 voices singing along to that classic ballad and theatre critics may point out the fans who came to the musical dressed in the style of the characters.

It is fair, I think, for a critic to point out that her view went against the grain of the 800 other people in the audience who clearly loved it, but she is not *required* to do so. Equally a critic cannot be expected to predict the commercial potential of a work of art, though sometimes they do. Using the example of Brian Logan's review in the *Guardian* of *We Will Rock You*, the Queen so-called jukebox musical, Mark Fisher says Logan, in his two-star review, was there 'to give his personal evaluation of the production on that night. It's the job of the market to show what's popular; the job of the critic is to say what's valuable' (2015, 27).

The Worldwide Web has changed the way we consume art – e-readers for books, music downloaded onto our devices – and this shifting of the goalposts has influenced the way in which art is reviewed. We watch television differently now, for example, it is not the communal experience it once was, which can affect the reviewer in surprising ways. Worried about viewers who will see the show on catch-up, the critic is at pains not to give away the story or gets bogged down by explaining too much of the premise – and the price we readers pay is a critic forgetting to tell us if it was any good.

Nina Myskow puts it like this: 'You must have strong opinions and be able to express them. Stick to your guns.'[7]

Expressing your opinion is part of a system of finding your voice as a writer, and it is something to which we will return later in the book. The point is not just whether you liked or disliked something, but having the knowledge to explain why.

Critics have a great platform to share their views, but they should use that power responsibly, and we should welcome a wide range of opinions. Neil Norman has been an arts critic for some 45 years, working across music, film, theatre and dance, and he explained it to me thus:

The idea is not to tell people what to think but to encourage them to think more deeply about the work. I love it when critics disagree over the same work – a consensus is rather boring. Much better to raise the debate and get an argument going. It gets everyone involved.[8]

Be responsible

Let us talk more about the responsibility of arts criticism. We are going to focus on five areas which can be broken down into who critics are responsible to, and what they are they responsible for. Specifically we are going to discuss responsibilities to readers, to editors, to artists, to themselves – plus the responsibility of discovering artists, challenging convention and championing individuals, groups or causes.

Above all, the critic's first responsibility is to the reader. That new record, that old film rebooted with a fresh cast – are they worth a look? More to the point, are they worth spending time and money on? You are the eyes and ears of the public for much of the time, given that the vast majority of live art described by you will be out of the reach of your readers. Fisher (2015) points out that publications employ critics 'whose worldview most closely matches that of the perceived readership'. As editor of UK comedy website *Chortle*, Steve Bennett spends time on the road checking out acts and writing about what he sees; guiding the audience is his number-one objective, he says. He told me:

> You're the consumer's guide to what comedy is out there from a position of having seen a lot, so hopefully I can highlight who's doing the interesting and successful work. Lots of comics will say that it doesn't matter what a critic writes as they made the crowd laugh – though to me that's the minimum definition of calling yourself a comedian. My job is to talk about how they go about that, both in giving the reader an idea whether or not they might like that, as well as describing what they bring to the art form – or just take from it.[9]

Iain Shedden agrees. Chief music writer at the *Australian*, Shedden came to the role via his time as a drummer in various rock bands. He told me:

> My responsibility to the reader is to entertain and inform, using my knowledge and experience of the music industry and of music itself, since I am also a musician. I'd like to think that I can also stimulate debate through my opinions. Feedback through the *Australian* and on social media would suggest that is the case.[10]

Your taste, judgement and values are being tested, so you had better not disappoint. At one level your review is a shortcut for someone trying to connect with someone else – perhaps a father wanting to understand more about the paintings or the books that so inspire his son or a dinner-party guest desperately thinking of something clever to say. Beyond these motives there may be readers searching for deeper meanings. For them the review is a gateway to exploring not just the art and the artist but all that surrounds them.

Popular music criticism from the 1970s and 1980s demonstrates the point. The British are more serious about their music than any other nationality, argues Pat Long (2012). At the *NME*, where she was deputy editor, journalists were 'writing passionately about rock music [as] a way of making sure that it was always more than just a commodity: sacrifices of health, sanity and very occasionally even life were made'.

Still with music – though the point remains relevant to other art forms too – it is perhaps easy to think about the digital world merely changing the way we read about artists but actually it is as much to do with how the art is made in the first place. Music writer for the *Guardian* and others, Dave Simpson is also a lecturer in music journalism at the University of Huddersfield. He told me:

> Technology has changed the way we make music: anyone can make a good sounding record/file in their home. For the music critic this means that music is more of an amorphous blob. I find that there is less truly great music and less truly dire music being made. There is plenty at the middle. In practice, this means lots of three-star reviews, and less opportunity to see/hear challenging/strange/awful music … The modern-day critic is less an opinionated voice, and more a consumer guide to help people through the labyrinth. This is not always/necessarily a bad thing.[11]

Artists are human, too. The status and perceived wealth of a writer or opera singer is no measure of how they might feel when their work is given a kicking in print. Perhaps you can recall interviews with actors or musicians who reveal they never read their reviews; equally you may be taken aback when a high-profile artist is particularly stung by what is, to all intents and purposes, some fairly mild criticism. Creative endeavour requires artists to reveal something of themselves, which, at some level, demands bravery. The artist, though, should not be singled out for special treatment; playing Hamlet is tough but not on a par with the pressure facing a surgeon or a soldier in combat. Still, their vulnerability is worth remembering.

What about the critics, then? What is their motivation in all of this? Professional film critics are, according to Kermode (2013), viewed in the modern age 'as being on a par with child-molesters and pension-fund embezzlers in the popularity stakes', while Titchener (2005), with an emphasis on North American print journalism, identifies that in fiction the critic 'is portrayed as being arch, insensitive, arrogant and usually with a hidden agenda'. I do not think we need worry too much about this portrayal. Books, films and television dramas are notoriously weak at reflecting any kind of journalism, for the most part resorting to two-dimensional characters and situations. In my experience critics have a professional attitude and are serious about their work, though – like artists – capable of mistakes.

Titchener adds:

> The reviewer genuinely wants the object of his interest to be successful. This again flies in the face of popular misconception. Colleagues in the newsroom will invariably say 'I love it when you blast someone' … But any reviewer would rather write good things than bad things.
>
> *(Titchener 2005, 28)*

I would go further and suggest that what critics and bloggers want now is art that is not so much labelled 'good' or 'bad', but does it have meaning? Does it stimulate debate? Is it worth my investing in the time and effort to explore what was created? Most critics will, I am sure, enjoy lavishing praise when it is due, but life would be dull without the odd turkey: surely worst-case scenario is a flurry of bang-average attractions?

There is no compulsion for a critic to refrain from saying something harsh, cruel even. Whether *you* have that capacity is impossible for me to judge – perhaps even you don't know yet – and we will examine the extremes of what can be published later on, but what is harder to defend is the artist's despair when their work is misrepresented. Did the critic just fail to get it, or perhaps succumb to a cheap shot? I remember interviewing a high-profile television writer once who still, years later, had not shaken off what a television critic had written about his series, effectively dismissing it with probably what he, the critic, believed to be a clever line. Visibly frustrated – even then – he relayed what his feelings had been when he read the review: 'Thanks, mate, that only took me about two years to write!'

Interpretation is vital. It is a theme touched upon by Libby Purves (2013), the theatre blogger writing under the name *theatreCat*. She had previously worked as chief theatre critic at *The Times* before switching to blogging and, more recently, features and first-person pieces for the *Daily Mail*. On launching her blog in October 2013, she made an interesting pledge:

> Producers, directors, designers and especially actors may sometimes not like what critics write, but they know that we are taking them seriously. Not showing off, not wilfully misunderstanding, not dismissing whole genres or styles because we don't naturally enjoy them. We're watching, trying to get the point, and reporting – as Tynan once put it – 'honestly, accurately and gaily' what it felt like to be in the playhouse on that night.

Sometimes there is no way round it; a plainly negative response to what you experienced is called for and your language can reflect that, so long as it can be justified. Can you imagine saying it to their face? Fisher (2015) imagines the review being pinned up backstage, and I rather like that idea.

There is one person we have not mentioned so far: your editor. Bloggers publishing solo can look away now but even they almost certainly will at some point write for an editor as well. Let us imagine that you do. The variations are probably thus: as a staff writer producing copy for another staffer whose title on this newspaper, magazine or website may be arts editor, sub-editor, features editor or deputy editor depending on the size, emphasis or frequency of the brand; or all of the above but replace 'staff writer' with 'freelance writer'. A third possibility involves unpaid publishing – often online – where writers are writing voluntarily, perhaps as a platform for paid work further down the line (more on this later).

As a critic, being responsible to an editor involves a few simple but important points which can be made very quickly – all of them relevant regardless of whether payment is involved. Essentially, if asked/commissioned to review something then turn up on time (if 'live', of course) and write to length (the word count) at the time that is set (deadline). Writing online does not put pressure on space as it does in print but even so, it is still a good idea to keep to the length you have agreed unless you check in advance with the commissioning desk. Busy editors – no matter how talented – will not mind your review being five words over but they will mind more if it is 50 over or even a hundred. Do not risk your expertly crafted review getting butchered – something more likely, it must be said, in the hands of an overworked editor or one not especially sympathetic to or knowledgeable about your subject.

Your copy must be accurate. Reviewing is opinion based on facts. Any writer taking pride in their work will hate making an error, but we will all make one at some point. Check your work thoroughly before you hit 'send'. Readers will not be shy in pointing out your mistake! The ideal scenario of having time to put the work to one side and then looking at it afresh is unlikely in a fast-moving world, but you can reduce the chance of problems in your copy by following a set of simple rules covered in Chapter 5.

So far we have talked about the critic's responsibility to others but what about to yourselves? Step into the experience with an open mind, not worrying what others think. Neil Norman said:

> The critic's responsibility is to be truthful to his own responses and convey his thoughts clearly and without any due influence from prevailing fashion, PR pressure and fear of seeming to be at odds with the general public and – sometimes – his fellow critics.[12]

Theatre blogger Megan Vaughan touched on an interesting point when she spoke to me about the direct effect that her writing has on *her*. No two reviews are ever the same in what she sets out to do, she said.

> Sometimes it's to celebrate the work, sometimes it's to celebrate one tiny part of the work, sometimes it's to pick at a thread that I could imagine unravelling. One thing is constant, though: that my primary driving force is self-expression and the emotional and psychological effects of writing. On me, not on anyone else.[13]

Discover, champion and challenge

The arts writer has licence to swim against the tide. In Chapter 6 I will talk about some of these factors at greater length but I briefly want to highlight the importance of discovering new talent, challenging convention and championing ideas and causes.

Think how dull the arts world would be if everyone came away from an experience with more or less the same view. Nowadays especially, with pressure pushing editors and writers to produce instant appraisals, it is even more important that critics are able to resist that force. Writing in the *New Yorker*, Amanda Petrusich (2016) argues that 'the idea that the culture is now not merely accepting but, in fact, demanding instantaneous critical evaluations of major works of art feels plainly insane'. Her frustration followed a series of surprise releases of full-length records by Kendrick Lamar, Kanye West and Rihanna, eschewing the traditional route of a promotional campaign for which print publications, editors and critics could plan their coverage.

In fact music is a fine example where critics have stood up for what they believed in, no better exemplified in backing the unknown artist or band and, actually, the more obscure the better. As Pat Long points out (2012), it is something that 'routinely appeals to music critics because it gives them an opportunity to demonstrate in print how much more discerning and attuned they are by picking up on a band that their peers have overlooked or dismissed'. She singles out Nick Kent, the brilliant maverick, who, in his first piece for the *NME* in July 1972, wrote a fresh evaluation of Iggy and The Stooges' first album which had been released three years earlier to bad reviews and poor sales. Kent felt it was the best pure punk-rock ever made and his reappraisal helped to stop the record label from deleting the record. Kent told her in interview: 'I had the best taste of anyone at the *NME*. More than anyone else in music journalism, certainly in Great Britain. I knew the best music that was happening at that time and the best subjects to write about. My instincts were 100 per cent.'

There was no doubt either that two of Britain's greatest theatre critics had not only the wisdom to see special talent where others could not, but the courage to tell their readers. Harold Hobson and Kenneth Tynan were two heavyweights of the 1950s, writing respectively for the *Sunday Times* and the *Observer*. The decade was an important one in British theatre as it sought to reflect the nation's post-war angst, and two playwrights in particular – John Osborne and Harold Pinter – were able to help shape a new style of theatremaking that did not rely on drawing-room settings and clipped English accents. Osborne's *Look Back in Anger* premiered on 8 May 1956 at London's Royal Court Theatre to largely mixed or negative reviews (Shellard 1999).

But Tynan was having none of it, calling *Look Back in Anger* 'the best young play of its decade', and Hobson chipped in, describing Osborne as 'a writer of outstanding promise'.

Two years later, almost to the day, Pinter's *The Birthday Party* opened in the capital's Lyric, Hammersmith, with an even clearer indication from London critics that here was a play to avoid. Pinter's edgy realism laced with a sense of the puzzling abstract was, again, a departure from the well-made play, and Dominic Shellard (1999) in his book *British Theatre since the War* even suggests that the bitterness in the critical reaction was an attempt 'to ensure that this playwright … should be buried without trace'. Even before the end of the first week of the play's run, producers had decided to 'close the production, in the light of the damage to the box office that the dismal notices had wrought'. Hobson went along anyway, as one of 16 people in the audience, and he reported the following Sunday: 'I am willing to stake whatever reputation I have as a judge of plays by saying that … Mr Pinter, on the evidence of this work, possesses the most original, disturbing, and arresting talent in theatrical London.'

Art at its most powerful is difficult and challenging. Every now and then there will be an opportunity to witness somebody or something that is new and distinctive, with something important to say. Often art requires more than one look in order to fully understand what is being said, but of course that opportunity is rarely given. How important it remains, then, that critics are able to disagree.

Notes

1 Gardner, Lyn (19 April 2016), interview with the author.
2 Myskow, Nina (24 June 2016), interview with the author.
3 *Ibid.*
4 Vaughan, Megan (17 July 2016), interview with author.
5 Myskow, Nina (24 June 2016), interview with the author.
6 Gardner, Lyn (19 April 2016), interview with author.
7 Myskow, Nina (24 June 2016), interview with the author.
8 Norman, Neil (27 July 2016), interview with author.
9 Bennett, Steve (11 July 2016), interview with author.
10 Shedden, Iain (27 July 2016), interview with author.
11 Simpson, Dave (27 July 2016), interview with the author.
12 Norman, Neil (27 July 2016), interview with author.
13 Vaughan, Megan (17 July 2016), interview with author.

References

Caine, Michael (1992) *What's It All About?* London: Century, Random House.
Fisher, Mark (2015) *How to Write About Theatre*. London: Bloomsbury Methuen Drama.
Hobson, Harold (13 May 1956) 'A new author', *Sunday Times*; cited in Shellard (1999).
Hobson, Harold (28 May 1958) 'The screw turns again', *Sunday Times*; cited in Shellard (1999).
Hoyle, Ben (14 May 2007) 'Dead white men in the critic's chair scorning work of women directors', *The Times*.
Johnson, Samuel (1759) No. 60. 'Minim the critic', www.johnsonessays.com/the-idler/minim-the-critic/.
Kermode, Mark (2013) *Hatchet Job: Love Movies, Hate Critics*. London: Picador.

Long, Pat (2012) *The History of the NME: High Times and Low Lives at the World's Most Famous Music Magazine*. London: Portico.
Moran, Joe (2013) *Armchair Nation: An Intimate History of Britain in Front of the TV*. London: Profile.
Petrusich, Amanda (9 March 2016) 'The music critic in the age of the Insta-release', *New Yorker*, www.newyorker.com/culture/cultural-comment/the-music-critic-in-the-age-of-the-insta-release.
Purves, Libby (2013) 'theatreCat.com reviews manifesto', https://theatrecat.com/about/.
Seymour-Ure, Colin (1991) *The British Press and Broadcasting since 1945*. Oxford: Basil Blackwell.
Shellard, Dominic (1999) *British Theatre since the War*. New Haven and London: Yale University Press.
Titchener, Campbell B. (2005) *Reviewing the Arts*. Mahwah, NJ: Lawrence Erlbaum.
Tynan, Kenneth (13 May 1956) 'The voice of the young', *Observer*; cited in Shellard (1999).
Wardle, Irving (1992) *Theatre Criticism*. London: Routledge.
Wells, Stanley (1997) *Shakespeare in the Theatre: An Anthology of Criticism*. Oxford: Oxford University Press.
White, Cliff (4 December 1976) 'Conversation piece of the week', *NME*.

2
A HISTORY OF ARTS CRITICISM

The shortest word in the title of this chapter is the most telling: *a* history. No attempt is being made to write *the* history of arts criticism because space does not permit; and that's not to mention the possibility of a whole book on the subject. Arguably a complete account of 300 years' worth of activity across all corners of the globe would run into several volumes. One of the difficulties of exploring different forms of arts criticism is that tracking their progress is far-reaching and yet patterns emerge that make the study of these forms particularly interesting. Indeed, one of this book's aims is to encourage reviewers to stretch their reading into previously uncharted territory.

Good reviews will usually have at least some sense of the artwork's origin – who made it and under what circumstances, what is similar to this piece of work or what is strikingly different. In that respect the book should acknowledge the past. For example, what were the social or cultural conditions that gave rise to a movement or genre that, in turn, allowed critics and criticism to flourish? Attention will be concentrated on the critics: who they were, what their background was and how they prospered. Later chapters will examine how they influenced today's writers, but of course, not even a brief history of criticism can avoid the turbulent changes seen in publishing in the past 20 years, sparked by the digital revolution that influenced the way we work, rest and play.

Changes in taste and technology

One of the recurring themes of this book is a so-called crisis in criticism engineered by a very tangible crisis in publishing, yet it is easy to associate those concerns as being restricted to the present day. It is a bitter irony that a profession facing challenges as a result of the impact of the Internet should lay itself open to what appears to be a new inquest into its demise almost every day – played out online.

But critics have often found change to be difficult. The British organisation the Critics' Circle uses its website to point out worries that its members had in 1923, the content of which is unnervingly similar to many of the issues faced by today's practitioners. S.L. Littlewood, the president of the body at that time, used a members' newsletter to report that:

> Criticism is passing, as many of us know, through a difficult phase. Its field is becoming more and more restricted. There are fewer papers than there were before the war and less space even in these.
>
> *(Cargin 2010)*

The changes critics have seen go well beyond the arrival of the Web but extend to the art they experienced, from shifts in style and tone within their field of expertise to the creation or even collapse of arts and entertainment forms as they knew them. Technological advances may in part account for the critic having to readjust his thinking, as with the move from a silent cinema to the world of the 'talkies', but this might just as easily be explained by the public feeling lukewarm about a kind of entertainment (revues and farces, perhaps) and instead falling in love with another (gritty, naturalistic drama).

Twentieth-century theatre demonstrates this point, fending off a double threat from cinema and, later, from television, long before the Worldwide Web was even a dream. A critic operating in the years before the Second World War would have been keenly aware of the threat posed by the picture palace 'talkies'. Cinema was fresh and exciting, and its influence hit new heights during the war, as Shellard (1999) points out, so that it became 'a national obsession, with three-quarters of the adult population seeking entertainment from films and information from newsreels and between twenty-five and thirty million seats being sold each week'. Drama critic Harold Hobson reported in 1945 that London had lost 12 per cent of its theatres since the start of the war in 1939.[1]

Post-war, the problems for theatrical venues deepened. Now the square box in the corner of the living-room was signalling a new trend – between 1945 and 1959 more than 100 variety theatres went dark for good and, in just a three-year period from 1953 to 1956, the number of provincial repertory companies in the UK halved to around 55 (Moran 2013).

Casualties in theatre were not restricted to London playhouses or provincial companies forced to make cutbacks, but in light entertainment too – specifically the variety theatres once so popular in British towns and cities and the end-of-the-pier shows synonymous with traditional seaside resorts. In the aftermath of the Second World War it was common for variety shows to play twice nightly six days a week, featuring a line-up built around a star comedian or double act supported by singers, dancers and speciality turns. But by the 1970s the appeal of television had indirectly turned many of these venues into bingo halls as a consequence of the decline in footfall. Put simply, the BBC could replicate that show and position it – for free – in your living room on a Saturday night.

More than any other act it was the comedians who had to rethink their strategy. Those who had made it on to 'the box' reaped the rewards, but it did mean that a comic who had recycled his three-minute routine in venues up and down the land suddenly had to find new material.[2] Seaside variety shows could be recreated on screen as well, almost always with the stars who for years had worked their way towards top billing in the country's finest coastal venues. But even as late as the 1990s there was still big money to be made for the most popular live acts – Michael Barrymore and Cannon and Ball in Blackpool and Great Yarmouth, for example – though a slow death had already begun.

The change of emphasis was being reflected in the British entertainment bible *The Stage* throughout the 1950s and 1960s. Traditional entertainment like variety and pantomime as well as that featured in cabaret or working men's clubs was covered in depth. Typical advertisements were a call for female impersonators or a ring-this-number if you need trained chimpanzees who will 'work with anyone'. Sometimes 'tall, lovely girls' were needed or 'glamorous blondes wanted immediately'. In 1959 its writers and critics devoted five full pages a week to news, reviews and advertisements centred on light entertainment – one reviewer that year worrying that singers were not breathing properly as a result of the influence of American pop music. Twenty years later the newspaper was reporting the inability of club venues in the north of England – traditionally a stronghold – to sustain entertainment six nights a week, and ten years after that *The Stage* had reduced its variety coverage by two-thirds.

As indicated earlier, doing justice to the history of arts criticism is difficult in one chapter, but before we look at other important factors in the development of the arts critic and his craft, here are three moments from the last two centuries which highlight how a change in artistic direction can split opinion or baffle even the most respected critics.

Les Misérables

One of the most eye-catching reactions ever seen in British theatre history greeted a 1985 Anglo-French musical produced by the Royal Shakespeare Company. Initially scheduled for an eight-week run at the Barbican in London with hopes for a West End transfer to follow, the show continues to play until this day and has spawned international versions in all of the world's major cities. Historically, the reception given to *Les Misérables* is important for two reasons: most obviously because a majority of first-night critics did not like it or were at best lukewarm, but also because of the debate it would spark surrounding taste and snobbery.

But why should there be such an adverse response to the production? One theory lies with Margaret Thatcher's government of the day which had applied drastic cuts to the arts and encouraged it to turn to the private sector as a solution. Shellard

(1999) points out that 'theatrical activity under the two Conservative administrations of Margaret Thatcher (1979–90) and John Major (1990–97) was characterised by a mixture of financial crises, pessimistic prognoses and a feeling that drama was being forced to justify its very existence'.

Under these conditions the RSC signed its first ever commercial sponsorship deal. Arts journalists did not necessarily approve of such things and were mindful that while it was all very well for the mighty RSC to court private money, smaller and less marketable organisations would not find it so easy. Difficult times meant bad news for new writing as well – at least it did as far as the West End was concerned – and critics would certainly have welcomed more new plays at the expense of a burgeoning market for blockbuster musicals.

Press reaction to this dramatisation of Victor Hugo's novel, with music by Claude-Michel Schonberg, book and original lyrics by Alain Boublil and English lyrics by a former *Daily Mail* television critic, Herbert Kretzmer, was so bad that producer Cameron Mackintosh (2017) feared they were finished before they had even started.

Irving Wardle (1985) in *The Times* wrote that 'the show [includes] spectacle and push-button emotionalism at the expense of character and content', adding that 'talent, energy and money have been poured into the production, only to confirm the general rule that musicals trivialize everything they touch'. The American trade paper *Variety*, with an unnamed London correspondent filing a review, reported that the show was more like opera than anything mainstream audiences were used to and, on that basis, the public was unlikely to trouble the box office too much. He or she added: 'A quality score, impressive singing, superb staging, but lacklustre job of compressing a vast, diffuse classic of a novel add up in "Les Misérables" to a worthy but ultimately under-satisfying specimen of music theatre' (Anon. 1985a).

It was left to the UK's own trade newspaper, *The Stage*, to bang the drum. With a strapline announcing that editor 'Peter Hepple nails his colours to the mast', the review captured a sense that something important had happened. 'To declare unequivocally that "Les Misérables" is the best musical I have ever seen might be going a shade too far', Hepple began. 'But I cannot recall one which has given me so much personal satisfaction.' And whereas *Variety* had bracketed the show's lead, Colm Wilkinson, as being 'competent dramatically', *The Stage* had witnessed a 'remarkable performance'.[3]

A week after its review had been published, *The Stage* went even further and wrote an editorial comment headlined 'The unpopularity of popular shows among the critics'. It began:

> It is strange how musicals seem to bring out the worst in people, particularly critics. A few weeks ago they turned on 'Mutiny' at the Piccadilly, which, as far as we know, is still running successfully. Last week they savaged 'Les Misérables' at the Barbican, which, predictably, is having standing ovations every night and is a hot ticket.
>
> *(Anon. 1985b)*

The writer – presumably Hepple – lambasted 'three pundits' on BBC television's *Saturday Review* for demolishing the show and poked fun at critics for liking musicals as long as they were American. But, he argued, the makers of *Mutiny* and *Les Misérables* had

> accomplished what they set out to do, no more and no less. And this was to provide something which has popular appeal. Unfortunately, popular appeal is something the average critic, in whatever field, can neither understand nor appreciate, though they might be able to do so on hindsight in 50 years' time, when it can be fixed in a socio-historical framework.
>
> *(Anon. 1985b)*

Remarkably, despite a critical backlash, positive word-of-mouth prevailed and ensured an instant demand. On this occasion smartphones and computers were to play no part in driving theatregoers in their thousands to this extraordinary show.

The Impressionists

It was art critic Louis Leroy who coined a phrase to describe this group of groundbreaking painters, one of the most influential the world has known. No compliment was intended, though, when he referred to the work of Monet, Renoir and others as impressionistic. Thanks to the gallery owner who championed their talents, Paul Durand-Ruel, eight Impressionist exhibitions were mounted between 1874 and 1886 but, as Michael Prodger (2015) points out: 'Both public and critics were mystified by what they saw, baffled by the paintings' lack of finish, their bright colours and quotidian subject matter (none of which stopped them coming to look anyway).' One critic even went so far in 1876 as to question the sanity of the artists and, as if that was not enough, felt it necessary to point out that one of them was female. 'Five or six lunatics, of whom one is a woman [Berthe Morisot], have chosen to exhibit their works. These are people who burst into laughter in front of these objects. Personally I am saddened by them' (Prodger 2015).

Orpheus in the Underworld

Jacques Offenbach, the German-born composer, is regarded as an inspiration for great composers and librettists like Gilbert and Sullivan and is even believed to be important as an influence on musical theatre, but that would have been hard to imagine for anyone reading the reaction to his light opera *Orpheus in the Underworld*. The satirical elements in his 1858 work – particularly his poking fun at Napoleon and his government – were hard for some critics to take, but the rage against his production soon turned in his favour. In his book *Operetta: A Sourcebook*, Robert Ignatius Letellier (2015), sees it thus: 'The piece was not immediately successful, but critical condemnation of it, particularly that of Jules Janin, who called it a "profanation of holy and glorious antiquity", provided vital publicity, serving to heighten the public's curiosity to see the piece.'

Starmaker becomes the star

One development of arts criticism in the twentieth century is the elevation of the critic into a personality. A number of factors explain it – the gradual moving of the critic from the background to the foreground as his opinion became required, the fact that competition encouraged writers to share their opinions and their ego, and the fact that other mediums beside print gave a platform for critics to extend their profile.

Bylines – the convention of crediting a journalist with her name above the article – were largely absent from early examples of reporting, recognising that the message was more important than the messenger. 'By Staff Reporter' or 'By Our Correspondent' were the somewhat pointless solutions dreamed up in response to the idea that *someone* must have written it. Arts journalism borrowed from this convention for the most part, and what we now refer to as reviews were closer in style to reporting rather than advocating opinion.

But change came nonetheless. In the medium of film, for example, Kaufmann (1972) suggests that the creation of more 'substantial work' from 1913 and beyond meant the work *had* to be written about, giving rise to greater powers of evaluation. Koszarski (1994) strengthened the theory by noting that early reviews contained little opinion and few bylines. By the 1920s, however, a sense of personality emerged as writers 'used their columns as literary sounding boards for pontificating, amusing, cajoling, or otherwise entertaining their growing readership'.

Editors understand that the best critics are an important part of their commercial armoury. Not only do we expect to see their names adjacent to their work but often their photograph as well; the picture byline is a staple part of the 'furniture' of a page. These photographs can adorn the front covers of publications as well, particularly newspapers when a high-profile arts event has happened. Examine the 'selling area' positioned above or below a newspaper masthead and sometimes situated within these areas, known as 'the boost' or 'teasers', the face of a critic will accompany a cover line promoting his or her 'verdict' inside. The *Guardian* uses this device to great effect with Michael Billington and Lyn Gardner, the *Daily Telegraph* does it with Dominic Cavendish. In the 1980s the *Sunday People* and the *News of the World* made great play of promoting their outspoken television critic Nina Myskow. Indeed if outstanding critics from the distant past were writing for newspapers now – the likes of Dorothy Parker, Pauline Kael or Kenneth Tynan – their picture bylines would undoubtedly be used as selling tools.

What distinguished the best-known critics from others, regardless of whether their photographs were used to complement their words, was the power they carried. One of the most rehearsed arguments of the digital publishing era is that arts criticism has levelled out, no single critic or handful of critics now has the extraordinary weight of influence they had as part of a legacy press. While this is true, it also misses an important point. Today's publishers may use material with 'clickbait' headlines designed to tease and pull the reader in, but critics operating in a pre-Internet landscape faced their own commercial imperatives. Look no further than the leading British music publications of the 1970s, the battlefield for readers consisting of *Sounds*, *Melody Maker*, *Record Mirror* and the *New Musical Express*.

Kings at the NME

The most glamorous and best selling of all the titles was the *NME*, which shifted around 307,000 copies a week in 1964 at the height of the Beatles phenomenon, and ten years later was still selling well over 200,000 (Long 2012). Two of the star writers in the 1970s were Charles Shaar Murray and Nick Kent. As Pat Long recalls in her fascinating history of the newspaper, they embraced the New Journalism movement from the USA which put 'the writer at the centre of the action, combining personal memoirs and experience with reportage'.

It was not unusual for these writers, who penned long-form essays, profiles and reviews, to sign autographs and get attention from female fans. The legendary American music journalist Lester Bangs, writing for *Creem* magazine in the USA, told his readers that having visited the London office of the *NME* he had realised the journalists there were like pop stars who had their photographs published 'so all the young girls in England can see them and get the hots'.

Kent especially, dressed in leopard skin and sporting a feather earring, was behaving like Oscar Wilde, he recalled, and had been catapulted into a lifestyle that thousands of young men at the time could only dream about, which included the practice of touring with rock bands, a sort of ultimate front-line reporting. 'Six months after I joined the paper I was touring with Led fucking Zeppelin', he told Long (2012). 'Labels would do anything to get their act coverage in the paper. Record companies would send bottles of brandy or packages of cocaine to the *New Musical Express* office, or offer to put journalists up in five star hotels in Monte Carlo or New York for the weekend.'

Harold Hobson and Kenneth Tynan

While the most influential drama critics have never enjoyed anything like the perks offered to the rock writers at *NME* (Tony Parsons tells Long he recalls being given a wad of cash as a thank-you to mark the end of his tour with Lynrd Skynrd), they had just as much clout.

In the USA, Frank Rich, nicknamed the Butcher of Broadway, had carved a fearsome reputation for himself covering New York theatre in the 1980s. Unusually, Rich had begun his reviewing life as a film critic before making the switch to live drama. His detractors/admirers reckoned the kiss of death from Rich was enough to close a show early.

No equivalent existed in British theatre, not that its finest critics were without power, merely that the two most celebrated names were more closely associated as positive forces as they sought out new talent, on some occasions completely swimming against the tide of popular opinion.

Harold Hobson's ascendancy in 1947 as theatre critic of the *Sunday Times* had taken shape two years prior to that when his predecessor, James Agate, had found himself in a delicate position, having fled from a male brothel. Agate would have been sacked on the spot had the newspaper's owner, Lord Kemsley, had his way, but was saved by editor W.W. Hadley, who reminded Kemsley 'that this would bring a considerable amount of bad publicity, given Agate's fame' (Hobson 1978, cited in Shellard 1999).

When Hobson did take the seat with Kemsley's blessing – he 'has a daughter', the owner reasoned, and therefore must be 'all right' (*ibid.*) – he encouraged French drama on to the London stage as a possible means to energise home-grown writing and, most notably identified Pinter's *The Birthday Party* as a masterpiece.

Hobson's contemporary at the *Observer*, Kenneth Tynan, was incisive, witty and inventive in his imagery and approach. Critics were, he felt, 'night-nurses at the bedside of good drama' (Tynan 1954a, cited in Shellard 1999)

Tynan championed John Osborne's *Look Back in Anger* in 1956 as 'the best young play of its decade' when others around him had failed to spot its value. With their combined power, Shellard argues, they not only documented the important moments in British theatre in the 15 years following the end of the war, but helped to shape them.

1956: British theatre gets angry

Both Tynan and Hobson stood tall half-way through the 1950s and gave notice to the British theatrical community that it was under-achieving. Tynan, on taking up the drama critic's chair at the *Observer* in September 1954, wasted no time in bemoaning why intellectuals now apparently shunned the theatre in favour of cinema, and why only three new plays were currently being staged among the 27 West End theatres open at the time (Shellard 1999).

Hobson had already signalled his dissatisfaction with post-war drama, as early as 1947 when he joined the *Sunday Times*.[4] 'It was too frivolous, too exclusively upper middle class', he told Dominic Shellard in a 1987 interview. 'It ignored the existence of nine-tenths of the world – more than nine-tenths.' The arrival of Samuel Beckett's *Waiting for Godot* (1955) was the start of an exciting period for the London stage (Hobson raved about its daring shift away from expected forms of presentation), but it was *Look Back in Anger* (1956) that shook the theatrical heartland to its core in its depiction of a post-war, working-class hero and, as Tynan called it, a 'rejection of "official" attitudes'.

Hobson and Tynan were not entirely alone in their support of the English Stage Company's powerful new work, but they were alone in their unequivocal support for it. A critic, identified as 'REL' in *The Stage*'s rather low-key review, saw promise, but other national newspaper writers found it undisciplined or self-pitying. Hobson's and Tynan's support for the play helped establish a new wave of writing, that of the Angry Young Men or kitchen-sink drama, as it was sometimes known, which strengthened its grip for the remainder of the decade and even led to an exciting period in British cinema showcasing talents such as Albert Finney, Julie Christie and Richard Harris.

Critics on the box

The era of black-and-white television of the 1960s unveiled Tynan as one of the first critics to extend his profile from print into the newest medium of television. Arts journalism, including reviews, featured on British television from the 1950s onwards as the medium established itself in the nation's living-rooms. The perception of this style of programming remains that it consisted of black-and-white footage with panellists and presenters locked in earnest discussion as cigarette smoke hung in the air. That is correct, but does not present a full picture. For example the women's programme *Wednesday Magazine* ran in a mid-afternoon slot on the BBC between 1958 and 1963, involving clips from films, round-table discussion and literary readings, as Irwin (2015) suggests, in sharp contrast to other shows for females which focused on domestic competence and good motherhood. *Wednesday Magazine* topics included an interview with Eartha Kitt on the challenges she faced as a black female singer and a debate on the term 'kitchen-sink' drama. Irwin cites an interview producer Lorna Pegram gave with the *Radio Times* in November 1960: 'At first it [*Wednesday Magazine*] was mainly for women but it was born of the conviction that women were interested in more than so-called women's subjects.'

Launched in the same year was the BBC's late-night Sunday arts magazine, *Monitor*, presented by Huw Wheldon, while the corporation's *Film* series, hosted by Barry Norman, mixing news and reviews with a light touch, began in 1972. Other programmes offering criticism, analysis and interviews from a range of commentators were created including *Omnibus* (1967–2003), *Arena* (1975–), *Saturday Review* (1986–90) and *The Culture Show* (2004–) – all at the BBC – as London Weekend Television on the ITV network weighed in with Melvyn Bragg's *South Bank Show* from 1978 to 2010, being revived by Sky Arts two years later.

Critics who began their working lives in print, like Paul Morley and Mark Kermode, found the crossover into television useful and – presumably – enjoyable. More recently a number of critics have found work as 'talking heads' for a flurry of programmes about cultural nostalgia.

A record of the past

Theories surrounding art history which emerged in the USA in the late 1960s and 1970s proposed that 'the art-critic(/historian) does not so much judge art as examine the conditions of judgment' (Williams 2014). As an argument, its essence is more in keeping with values arising from the Internet-driven democratisation of reviewing, and was certainly adrift from the established views, exemplified by James Agate, who in 1922 complained that the role of the critic was changing to a focus on pursuing public taste rather than leading it. He lamented a time when 'the polite world held its breath' until a critic had passed judgement (Fisher 2015).

What the critic judged to be of value, or not, was of course important, but arguably not as important as a record of the artwork being experienced. While art forms like television and cinema cannot boast a long history, for obvious reasons, we do benefit from at least having access to what the chroniclers of eighteenth- and nineteenth-century British literature and drama believed. William Hazlitt, in the early nineteenth century, worked professionally in literary criticism, while in the theatre world Leigh Hunt is regarded as the 'first figure of literary distinction to undertake systematic theatre criticism'. He was just 20 years old in 1805 when he began to write for *The News*, as Wells (1997) points out. Some 85 years earlier, however, Richard Steele's journal, *The Theatre*, had been the first English publication devoted to drama, an opportunity spotted by *The Times* in the second half of the eighteenth century, which increasingly saw the potential for news about plays and players.

For a 200-year period between Shakespeare's career and Hunt's emergence, formal theatre criticism was slow off the blocks – we can only dream of first-hand, first-night reviews of *Hamlet* or *King Lear* – which is one reason why Hunt is so important, as Wells identifies:

> As Hunt is the first, so is he in some ways the best of our professional theatre critics above all because of a literary power that combines apparently objective description with a capacity for imaginative reconstruction which creates in the reader a sense, if not of what it was actually like to be witnessing the performance, at least of what Hunt himself saw, heard, and felt when he did.
> *(Wells 1997, 9)*

Tynan had firmly understood the idea that critics were making something permanent that was impermanent, and his contemporary Hobson, who had studied history at Oxford, told Shellard (1987) that his responsibility to provide a true record 'was a part of the foundation of my work':

> My criticisms, I should say, are records of how I happened to feel at a particular evening at a particular play, that they are the foundation of a historical record more than the passing of a judgment.

Twentieth-century joy

Arts writers of the past hundred years have had the privilege to reflect on extraordinary moments in popular culture, for example film critics charting the rise of the motion picture presented by the likes of D.W. Griffith or Charlie Chaplin. Frank E. Woods had, acknowledges Jerry Roberts (2010), introduced a movie page in the *New York Dramatic Mirror* as early as 1908 and is regarded as almost certainly the first American film critic. The following year (1 May 1909) he told readers: 'Motion pictures are at least gaining recognition as an institution of immense value to mankind.'

Arguably the critics played some small part in charting this development, but what cannot be denied is the importance of the twentieth-century music journalist.

Rock 'n' roll and punk

If rock 'n' roll changed pop for ever, then music journalism was glad of it, too. Riding this cultural wave for decades were a number of British pop and rock magazines, notable in the end for the staying power of the *New Musical Express*.

The *NME* gave a platform to many of the UK's best-known names in music journalism including Julie Burchill, Danny Baker and Tony Parsons. Born in the 1930s to cash in on the national craze for accordion music, the *Accordion Times* merged with *Musical Express* in 1946 but targeted professional musicians rather than fans (Long 2012).

A London music promoter and manager of band leaders, Maurice Kinn, saw the potential of having his own paper and bought the business in 1952. He drew inspiration from the weekly charts published in the USA via *Billboard* magazine, and did the same for the UK, matched with a new focus on performers rather than songwriters, and sales of records instead of sheet music. Bolstered by the charts idea, the circulation of the title, now branded *New Musical Express*, leapt by 50 per cent in just a few weeks.

The music of Bill Haley and the availability of cheap electric guitars was a shot in the arm for the *NME*. By the late 1950s teenagers were buying 40 per cent of all records sold in the UK (Long 2012). While its rival, *Melody Maker*, was kicking Elvis Presley's *Hound Dog*[5] with the equivalent of a one-star review, 'the *NME*'s stance', argues Long, 'cemented rock 'n' roll as a tribal identity set in opposition to the rest of mainstream society, a notion that defined the tone of the paper through punk, acid house and beyond'. Though sales flattened and even dropped in the early 1960s, the emergence of The Beatles helped the *NME* reach record sales of 306,881 in 1964.

NME writers were encouraged to express themselves. Several had come through the route of underground publishing and the idea of being subversive appealed. Music gave talented writers an opportunity to talk not just about tunes, and the charts, and the meaning of lyrics but about life itself. As Charles Shaar Murray put it to Long (2012): 'One of the things [Tony] Tyler used to say was that the *NME*'s not just about the music, it's about all of the things that the music's about.'

In the way that rock 'n' roll ripped up the teenage rulebook, and parents rolled their eyes with a 'whatever next' refrain, worse was to come. Punk rock announced itself on an unsuspecting nation in November 1976 with the release of a debut single by the Sex Pistols, *Anarchy in the UK*. Oddly the *NME*'s Cliff White dismissed the track as a 'third-rate Who imitation' (see Chapter 1), but, as Long reports, editor Nick Logan utilised new recruits Burchill and Parsons 'in a high-profile attempt to reposition the *NME* as the punk rock paper of choice'.

Television gold

Understanding how critics documented the first 50 years or so of television is to understand a wider context involving the suspicion initially levelled at the box itself, plus the changing habits of wealthier families with more time for leisure and relaxation, and the medium's ability to fire the imagination in ways that novels must have done some 300 years before.

Joe Moran, in *Armchair Nation: An Intimate History of Britain in Front of the TV* (2013), superbly captures the public's wonderment at television in the years before the Second World War – the BBC having to reassure viewers that they could not be spied upon (1935) or the fact that the word 'viewer' had not even been thought of, instead early participants in watching television were described as 'lookers in'. No surprise that the term did not catch on. Those 'lookers in' were asked in August 1933 to send an urgent postcard to the BBC, verifying that they were receiving a transmission.

Early broadcasts from 1936 were scheduled for daily one-hour slots (except Sundays) at 3pm and 9pm and some of the drier content consisted of items such as do-it-yourself instruction, a history of inn signs and a selection of people performing animal impersonations. By 1957, however, quality and regularity of broadcast had gone up several notches because a *Sunday Times* study determined that nearly half of working-class viewers were addicted to television.[6]

Journalism responded to television as a serious player at differing speed. *The Stage* added '*and Television Today*' as part of its branding in February 1959, a newspaper within a newspaper which would, its managing director Frank Comerford said, deliver television news and reviews to a fast-growing profession. The cover price of 9*d.* remained in place. Derek Hoddinott edited the section and proclaimed in his first column: 'TV at last, is becoming fashionable.'

Two radio critics were utilised by the *Daily Telegraph* and *The Listener* respectively in the mid-1930s to extend their reach to the visual medium. As Mark Lawson pointed out to me, even after the war Fleet Street was suspicious of the young upstart television: 'There are at least two known examples of TV critics who had to be given a television set in order to perform their task.'[7]

As Moran (2013) acknowledges, *The Times* did not even appoint a television critic until 1966, by which time the critics who *were* engaged in television reviewing had shown their true colours as former theatre critics by concentrating their output on the evaluation of plays and documentaries rather than anything lighter.

The journalists who had greeted television's arrival with disdain would have some explaining to do when the status of the reviewer escalated in the 1970s thanks to consistently large viewing figures for television shows and – in 1982 – the launch of the brand-new Channel 4. Audiences regularly smashed the 20 million mark, ushering in a so-called golden age of programming and a period of time richly dense for reporting, recording and evaluating what was 'on the box'. A flick through the television listings of the late 1960s to the early 1980s provides evidence of popular appeal alongside critics' gold – the shocking racism of *Love Thy Neighbour*

(1972), the Christmas Day *Morecambe and Wise* seen by 28.5 million viewers (1977) and the all-consuming mystery of 'Who Shot J.R. Ewing?' (*Dallas*, 1980). That is to say nothing of the almost constant conversation television was having with itself on issues of morality such as swearing or the depiction of sex and violence – a 1972 editorial in *The Stage* reflected that times were changing and that if television was to keep up, then mistakes would be made along the way.

In this period writers like Nancy Banks-Smith, known for her wit at the *Guardian*, came to the fore, as did Clive James, whose association with the *Observer* gave it 'literary kudos', Moran (2013) writes, adding that there was a belief James's contribution to the newspaper put on an extra 10,000 sales a week. The aforementioned Nina Myskow was hugely important to the energy of the television pages at the *Sunday People* (1982–84) and the *News of the World* (1984–87). Her brief had been to reflect what Everyman and Everywoman were watching.

> These were tabloids with millions of readers and I had to watch TV that mass markets watched and write about programmes that interested them. *Coronation Street* was a must-see and *EastEnders* was introduced during this period, which also became a must-see.[8]

The 1990s signalled a switch of emphasis, reflecting the dominance of reality television on a burgeoning number of channels. The style and the language of those reviews is exemplified in the work of Charlie Brooker, whose column at the *Guardian* from 2000 described the schedules of the day as 'unentertainment'.

Across the Atlantic, *Billboard* had been documenting American television for some years before *The Stage* cottoned on in the UK, with bylined, well-written reviews. In fact as early as the late 1940s many of the main US newspapers switched on to television journalism as the medium became available in major cities. Jack Gould at the *New York Times* and John Crosby at the *New York Herald Tribune* reported and reviewed with great distinction. There was also great scope for syndicated television reviewing, as Brown (2017) points out for *Museum TV*, demonstrating both the scale of the nation and the size of the market.

The style and form of criticism, the platforms it is given, to say nothing of the profile of the critic, have changed immeasurably from that work expressed in previous generations. The present-day reviewer may care to read more deeply around some of these moments in history, but first there is much to be done if you are to become accomplished in the craft, starting with how you prepare and research for your writing.

Notes

1 Harold Hobson's article, 'Number of houses reduced by 12 per cent since 1939', appeared in the *Christian Science Monitor*, 24 November 1945, cited in Shellard (1999).
2 Entertainers had for many generations learned their trade safe in the knowledge that a fresh routine may never be required. That said, even nineteenth-century reviewers were aware of the practice in pantomime and revue whereby comic business originated by a

performer in London would, given time, be picked up and copied in provincial venues, as seen in *The Stage* article, 'Low comedy gagging', 1 November 1880.
3 Peter Hepple's review, 'No need to be glum', *The Stage*, 17 October 1985, was a swipe at the *Daily Mail* review of *Les Misérables*, headlined as 'The Glums'.
4 Harold Hobson joined the *Sunday Times* in 1947 but prior to this had written for the *Christian Science Monitor*.
5 Steve Race's review for *Melody Maker*, 20 October 1956, said Presley's *Hound Dog* was a 'thoroughly bad record' with unintelligible lyrics.
6 The study was conducted by Geoffrey Gorer, a freelance anthropologist, on behalf of the *Sunday Times*, who reasoned that lives were being wrecked and women especially were addicted. Moran felt his conclusions to be 'impulsive'. However, the government's General Household Survey (1976) established that 90 per cent of Britons watched television as their principal leisure pursuit.
7 Lawson, Mark (30 August 2016), interview with the author.
8 Myskow, Nina (24 June 2016), interview with the author.

References

Anon. (2 April 1959) 'Is this singing?', *The Stage and Television Today*.
Anon. (14 September 1972) 'Everybody's standby scapegoat', editorial, *The Stage and Television Today*.
Anon. (16 October 1985a) 'Shows abroad', *Variety*.
Anon. (24 October 1985b) 'The unpopularity of popular shows among the critics', *The Stage*.
Beauman, Sally (1982) *The Royal Shakespeare Company*. Oxford: Oxford University Press, cited in Shellard (1999).
Brown, James A. (2017) 'Television criticism (journalistic)', *Museum TV*, www.museum.tv/eotv/televisioncr.htm.
Cargin, Peter (16 December 2010) 'Difficult times for critics – from the first!', *Critics' Circle*, www.criticscircle.org.uk/history/?ID=106.
Fisher, Mark (2015) *How to Write About Theatre*. London: Bloomsbury Methuen Drama.
Hobson, Harold (1978) *Indirect Journey*. London: Weidenfeld and Nicolson; cited in Shellard (1999).
Hoddinott, Derek (19 February 1959) *The Stage and Television Today*, launch issue.
Irwin, Mary (2 April 2015) 'BBC's *Wednesday Magazine* and arts television for women', Media History 21(2), 162–77, *Taylor and Francis Online*, www.tandfonline.com/doi/full/10.1080/13688804.2015.1025728.
Kauffmann, Stanley with Henstell, Bruce (eds) (1972) *American Film Criticism: From the Beginnings to Citizen Kane*. New York: Liveright.
Koszarski, Richard (1994) *An Evening's Entertainment: The Age of the Silent Feature Picture, 1915–1928*. Berkeley: University of California Press.
Letellier, Robert Ignatius (2015) *Operetta: A Sourcebook*, vol. 1. Newcastle upon Tyne: Cambridge Scholars Publishing.
Long, Pat (2012) *The History of the NME: High Times and Low Lives at the World's Most Famous Music Magazine*. London: Portico.
Mackintosh, Cameron (2017) 'Creation of a musical', *Les Misérables* website, www.lesmis.com/uk/history/creation-of-a-musical/.
Moran, Joe (2013) *Armchair Nation: An Intimate History of Britain in Front of the TV*. London: Profile.
Prodger, Michael (21 February 2015) 'The man who made Monet: How impressionism was saved from obscurity', *Guardian*, www.theguardian.com/artanddesign/2015/feb/21/the-man-who-made-monet-how-impressionism-was-saved-from-obscurity.

Roberts, Jerry (2010) *The Complete History of American Film Criticism*. Santa Monica, CA: Santa Monica Press.
Shellard, Dominic (1987) Interview with Harold Hobson, British Library Theatre Archive.
Shellard, Dominic (1999) *British Theatre since the War*. New Haven and London: Yale University Press.
Tynan, Kenneth (19 September 1954a) 'The second rate', *Observer*, cited in Shellard (1999).
Tynan, Kenneth (26 September 1954b) 'Mixed double', *Observer*, cited in Shellard (1999).
Tynan, Kenneth (13 May 1956) 'The voice of the young', *Observer*, cited in Shellard (1999).
Wardle, Irving (10 October 1985) 'Spectacular boldness', *The Times*.
Wells, Stanley (1997) *Shakespeare in the Theatre: An Anthology of Criticism*. Oxford: Oxford University Press.
Williams, Gilda (2014) *How to Write About Contemporary Art*. London: Thames and Hudson.

3
PREPARATION AND RESEARCH

Before a single word has been written of your thoughtful, incisive review there is much to be done. The depth and direction of that preparation will depend on a number of factors, from the profile of the readership and the motivation driving the review in the first place, to very practical considerations like the deadline and – if it is a live performance – the time of the last train home. More or less chronologically, this chapter will examine what to think when weighing up whether to review a work of art, right through until your fingers reach for the keyboard. Why are some television shows covered but others, seemingly, not? Who decides? What is involved in that decision? How do *you* fit in, either as one of a team of critics or even as a self-motivated blogger who is part of a community and yet answerable to nobody?

The critic should be knowledgeable (not everyone will even agree on *that*!) but how is that knowledge gained? Does the critic need to be able to do what she is talking about? Does it matter if she reads other reviews before writing hers? In short, how to prepare and what to research.

Choosing what to review

In 2015 a staggering 173,000 books were published in the UK. The figure includes fiction and non-fiction titles sold both in print and in digital form only. It does not include self-published books. The year 2015 is highlighted because it offers the most recent figures for the British book market over a 12-month period. To put it another way, well over 3,000 books were published every week.

A fraction of those books would be covered in the arts pages of national and regional newspapers and magazines, though significantly more would garner at least some attention online via well-established websites like *Lovereading.co.uk*, *Goodreads. com* or Amazon. Book bloggers would stimulate interest, as would local radio and higher-profile shows such as Simon Mayo's BBC Radio 2 *Drivetime*, where discussion of one book a week by Mayo and his co-presenter is engaging but is tempered by the fact that the author is sitting next to them in the studio. Still, it all helps in a difficult market – the difficulty being not that the public don't want to buy (they most certainly do), it's just that there are so many choices.

How to choose, then: whether you, the critic, are being paid as a professional staff journalist or (more likely) a freelance reviewer, whether you are writing a daily blog entirely for fun or to develop a portfolio, or whether you are simply sharing a novel you enjoyed with friends on Facebook, the pattern in all of this is the audience. Who will read this review? Who will care enough to stop what they are doing?

Readers of course are in any writer's mind, or at least they should be. What you serve up to them is a matter for you and your colleagues to decide, depending on the system. *The Arts Desk* (artsdesk.com) is a useful example to investigate this further because it blends traditional values of depth of coverage and quality control with newer emphasis on speed of delivery.

A group of Fleet Street critics, disillusioned with arts journalism because of a reduction in budgets and space, launched the site in 2009, intending to operate as a collective with equal emphasis on art forms. No single journalist has complete authority, instead section editors make – and receive – suggestions on what should be picked up. There is no office. I spent about a year writing television reviews for this website at the rate of about one a fortnight, fitting it in with teaching and other writing projects. I exchanged emails with three or four of the editors, one of them regularly, but never met any of them. A contributing factor is that most live in London and I live in the Midlands, but nonetheless the system works perfectly well online.

Once a week the section editor sketched out a list of the programmes he wanted covered for the following week. Usually this was a combination of shows airing for the very first time, familiar shows returning for a new series or shows the team had simply not got round to yet. He may have pencilled in certain names against a show or he may have left it wide open, and then the critics, about nine or ten of us, chipped in with their preference, as well as possibly highlighting something that was not on the list. After a few weeks it soon became clear which writers favoured certain styles of programming and, while a spot of bartering was not out of the question, more often than not the job went to the one who shouted loudest or was quickest off the blocks.

No type of programme is off limits but the *Arts Desk* is clearly aimed at a thoughtful, intelligent readership, hence there is a generous consideration of drama and documentary. Comedy features heavily, and there is room as well for major sporting occasions like the opening ceremony of an Olympic Games. Clearly, the latter has to be reviewed live, with the critic at no advantage to the rest of the nation, but the vast majority of shows are watched a few days before transmission. An *Arts Desk* critic, along with other selected staff and freelance writers working in print and online, will view programmes streamed online via preview sites requiring a password. Providers such as the BBC and ITV each have their own set-up. As well as being able to replay a scene or pause a drama serial for a coffee break, the critic also has access to background on the programme and a selection of approved images.

Some works of art trigger more obvious coverage than others. Major stars or important names connected to the output of books or films, for example, will inevitably lead to a clutch of reviews, and this is strongly linked to the idea (explored further in Chapter 4) of the review as a news event – news both to those we expect to be interested and those consumers not usually aligned to a particular world but drawn to it by this one name or product. The 2016 London opening of *Harry Potter and the Cursed Child* is a fine example, where non-typical theatregoers were desperate for information. Equally a critic can – and sometimes should – push to review a work of art or a form or genre not normally associated with his employer. In the case of live performance we can stretch that to city, region or venue as well.

Along with live music, covering theatre is a challenge when it comes to the sheer distance involved in accessing so many possible venues. London is the theatrical capital of Europe, but its rich array of theatres, from the grandeur of a 2,000-seat auditorium to the intimacy of something like the Donmar Warehouse at just 250 seats, presents a real dilemma – how to do it justice while giving enough prominence to the many other towns and cities producing relevant work. Great theatre can be seen in Sheffield, Glasgow, Belfast, Birmingham and dozens more locations – how can critics, other than those local to the area, possibly demonstrate that? It is a problem, admits Lyn Gardner of the *Guardian*. Being constrained to London at the expense of the regions is entirely possible but editorially unsound. She explains:

> In the 1980s on *City Limits*, the magazine where I started my career, it would be possible to review every single thing that was on a three-week run (our rule) and we ran ten or twelve reviews a week and we could cover it. Now it's ten or twelve opening a night. There is so much more theatre compared to 20–30 years ago so you are making choices of where you go and what you see.
>
> There is a huge responsibility around that. What is reviewed is what is valued in the culture, so if it's not reviewed does that suggest it's not valuable? Should I review this or that, and the reality is that you constantly feel that you are making the wrong choices but you have to make a choice and you have to take responsibility for those choices.[1]

To contextualise Gardner's point, the latest study (Smith 2015) discovered 241 theatres in Inner and Outer London which are putting on professional theatre, dance or opera ranging from large West End venues to fringe theatre above a pub with just 30 or 40 seats.

Over at *WhatsOnStage*, editor Daisy Bowie-Sell has a similar predicament balancing breadth of coverage with budget restrictions. Both the *Guardian* and *WhatsOnStage.com* are hugely committed to theatre news, features and criticism, of course. The former is steeped in heritage as far as print is concerned but has more recently adopted a digital-first strategy, whereas the latter exists only online, so what are their respective set-ups like?

Gardner is at the theatre anything between five and seven times a week. Most of these visits will result in a review but a couple of trips might be motivated by a blog post[2] or a feature that she plans to write or simply to catch up on a production that she feels she ought to see. A list from the arts desk will circulate among the critics as a starting point of what to cover. As chief critic, Michael Billington will get first choice, followed by Gardner herself, who may add suggestions, and then the newspaper's other critics (all of them freelance) covering Scotland, Ireland and the north of England will firm up what they are going to do.

WhatsOnStage has two chief critics: Matt Trueman, who blogs under his own steam as well as writing for a number of leading publications, and Sarah Crompton, formerly arts editor at the *Daily Telegraph*. They are supported by a staff critic, Holly Williams, and an army of some 20 others, including this author. About half a dozen of these write wholly on London productions, while the rest are alive to what is happening in Edinburgh, Glasgow and the English provinces.

How does the system work? Bowie-Sell explains:

> Matt and Sarah have the schedule for the month and they go through it and make their choices. Me and the editorial assistant go through it as well because we think one would be more suited to a particular production than the other. We love them covering shows out of London as well.
>
> We value outside of London as much as within but it costs more to send them out of London than to have a reviewer already there so we have to make a call on whether we can afford it that particular month, whether we send Matt to Liverpool for example because there is a finite budget and we have writers in those regions who we like and who we trust.[3]

The London debate is one that also crops up south of the river at *The Times*. Art critic Nancy Durrant, who also operates as commissioning arts editor on the paper responsible for all visual arts features and reviews and part of the theatre output, is aware of an apparent capital bias but there are mitigating factors:

> It can be an issue with theatre and visual arts because there is so much of it. With visual arts it's slightly self-perpetuating because a lot of the funding tends to leech out in the South-East before it gets anywhere else. This year I have found myself booting Rachel [lead critic Rachel Campbell-Johnston] up and down the country, which is good. I have no doubt that many of our readers who are not based in the South-East will say that the coverage is too London-centric but all I can say is that we are doing our best.[4]

Planning her coverage also starts with a list, but Durrant is at pains to point out that it is done weeks, if not months, ahead, such is the way the art world operates. She will share the list with Campbell-Johnston, who may offer suggestions. 'I will go through the dates for when I need stuff and choose exhibitions that I think readers will want to know about and then allocate slots.'[5]

Professional critics are in the privileged position of seeing or listening to some of the best arts around but the demand on their time is strict. Critics of the past like the great theatre man Harold Hobson would have been 'on call' three nights a week. That is not to accuse him of slacking, but compare that to Gardner's diary, as described earlier, who has additional responsibilities for blogging and feature writing, or Ben Brantley at the *New York Times*, who told me that three or four plays a week is a minimum but that increases at certain times of the year. He adds: 'When I visit London, which I do about twice year, I may see as many as ten plays a week.'[6]

All of it poses the question, with so much to write and so much travel involved, what time is left in which to prepare?

Knowledge, experience and curiosity

The preparation a critic does for reviewing a novelist's new book is not so much whether she reads other fiction by the same author or scans interviews given by said writer but everything she has experienced in the years before she opens the book at chapter 1. For it is not merely the act of reading *this* author's work that matters, but all books, all stories she has encountered that in some way inform the criticism. No need to stop there. Think about the films she has seen, the gigs or the art galleries she has been to that provide extra depth when it comes to writing about the book. Of course, this memory bank of experience, this deeper knowledge, may not surface in the text but the critic *knows* it is there nonetheless. In some small way it may help to shape what she is saying.

Critics and other commentators on the craft of reviewing are often divided when it comes to any perceived advantage that experience brings. Doubters may argue – and it is a compelling case – that the critic should enter into the world of the art with a mind free of prejudice. Is it not more exciting, they may say, that the critic is closer in profile to the consumer: as moviegoer, as listener, as reader? After all, the critic is there to represent her audience, is she not? Again, it is not black and white. Much depends on the objectives of the brand for whom she produces the content and the level of expectation for those who receive it. Niche audiences, for example, would place a greater demand on their reviewer than the majority within a mainstream audience.

But what is the answer? Gardner's view on research before encountering a theatre production is this:

> What one is drawing on is the knowledge you have gained over a period of time. My view is that you need to do enough research so that you are not going to be exposed. *Hamlet*, for instance. You might have seen it 36 times before but it might be interesting to read a review from someone who has never seen it before. It might be *interesting* but they would look stupid if they expressed surprise that everybody dies at the end.

> Treat every play you see as though it's a new play. Sometimes you go and all you have is the press release and that can be written quite cagily. There is a great pleasure in that. If you are going to see a stage version of *War and Peace*, do you have to have read it before? It might be helpful but life is short and what you are reviewing is what is on stage, not the novel. If you go five or six times a week you cannot have read everything or everything around it. There is a huge pleasure in coming at it as if it's new.[7]

It's pleasing when critics are able to reference other work in relation to the work being discussed – not in a way that suggests they are showboating, purely that the background adds a valuable dimension to the review, such as a useful comparison, an amusing aside or an unexpected fact. I like it, too, when they see connections to another art form.

'Unique' is an over-used word, but it may apply to critic Neil Norman. I cannot be sure if reviewing four separate arts disciplines qualifies Norman as unique, but I could not think (and neither could he) of anyone to compare. In his interview with me, Norman spoke at length, reflecting on his evolution from music, to film, and finally from theatre into dance:

> Both dance and theatre are physical performing arts and there is a great crossover between the two. It took me some time to learn how to 'read' dance, especially the abstract stuff which lacks the useful entry point of narrative, but I trusted my instinct and I think I improved as I went on.
>
> The great thing about being versed in more than one discipline is that I can make connections where many cannot. While I may lack the deep historical knowledge of ballet of some of my colleagues, I am aware that they have almost no experiential background in film or even theatre with which to make comparisons. And now that the divisions between the artistic disciplines are eroding – dance/theatre, physical theatre, installations and immersive theatre are now far more common than once they were – my mixed background stands me in good stead. I can see the threads that run between them, if they exist.[8]

Expert knowledge, though, is not something that can be swallowed in the form of a pill, it takes years of immersing yourself in the topic. Inexperienced critics or independent bloggers with a focus on reviewing cannot see their whole careers mapped out in front of them. They may hope to become a trusted voice, but they cannot be certain that it will turn out that way, they all have to take those first tentative steps on a journey towards expertise.

If you are a critic, what might we expect from you?

A minimum requirement is that reviewing on any platform should mean the critic – if he wants to be taken seriously – must read widely, must be curious about his world in close-up but also the wider world beyond the art. Charles Shaar Murray, the rock critic, talks engagingly about the influence of another art form on his music criticism, telling Pat Long (2012) that he 'learned how to describe a rock concert by reading Norman Mailer describing a riot in *Miami and the Siege of Chicago*'.

Furthermore the critic must have a firm knowledge of genre, movement and history along with a clear grasp of current patterns and challenges facing the arts discipline he has chosen to write about. He will be attuned to the cultural, social and political significance of his field. Ideally he will be an expert – or at least have the capacity to be an expert – along with being comfortable in writing about at least one other art form.

A critic working in the field of books and literature, for example, should be clued up on the history of reading, on storytelling techniques and on news surrounding the market – what is selling, what kind of advances writers are seeing and which agents and publishers they are turning to in securing those deals. Comedy critics should have expert knowledge on influential figures both in their own country and be familiar with foreign influences as well. They should understand the psychology of humour, be able to talk about how jokes work and be comfortable with everything from early situation comedy to comedy's relationship with class. Fisher (2015) offers a fascinating episode in 1996 when a theatre director, Michael Bogdanov, publicly attacked critics for what he felt was their shoddy preparation in respect to his RSC production of Goethe's *Faust*. He believed the critics had over-utilised a particular Penguin study guide to brush up on their knowledge, and said it was glaringly obvious when the same words and phrases cropped up in so many of the reviews.

Although writing in discussion of contemporary art, Williams (2014) amplifies this point by suggesting, 'Critics lose credibility if we suspect that they are ill-prepared.'

But is it possible to do *too* much research? To prepare *too* well? Perhaps yes, particularly with the demands placed on one's energy. Nina Myskow does not regret the things she wrote, but does now wonder if her seven-day-a-week approach to watching television in readiness for her reviews was quite necessary. 'I was creating a rod for my own back', she told me, 'so I would watch an awful lot of television, probably far more than I needed to. My life was watching TV.'[9]

Nancy Durrant at *The Times* prepares by reading around the subject she is going to write about, the level dictated by what she knows of the artist already (though it is rare she will not know at least something). 'There is a level at which you can over-prepare', she says. 'I prefer to go into an exhibition not feeling like an expert.'[10]

Critics can't dance

Most of us have seen the kind of comments online at the end of a review that are meant as payback. They go like this: 'Critics? Yeah right. Like to see *him* stand up and make us all laugh.' If intended to embarrass, shame or wound a reviewer who has written something with which the reader does not agree, then it serves as a reminder that the critic himself is vulnerable to criticism, but it also raises an interesting point about preparation for the craft of reviewing, namely, whether the critic can do the thing on which he is passing verdict. Must the know-it-all music critic be able to sing or play an instrument? Should the film critic – you know the one, so full of himself – have the technical skills, let alone the imagination, to be able to make a film? And does it matter anyway?

Another jibe aimed at the critic is that he must have somehow failed as an artist and has stumbled into this dubious trade as some sort of compromise. It smacks of the old saying, 'Those who can, do; those who can't, teach'. While not many people will shed a few tears for a poor, misunderstood critic, the theory is terribly flawed. First, many authors and scholars, and critics themselves, firmly believe that criticism is an art in its own right. It is not a sad, desperate measure by the modestly talented, but something worthy of respect and, as some would point out, even worthy of equal billing with other arts. 'Art has generated art', Wells (1997) suggests, pointing to criticism at its best.

The critic as a kind of jealous, third-rate wordsmith is an argument that also overlooks the possibility that reviewers may actually *want* to do the work they do. Sports writers are often told, 'What a great job you have, to be *paid* to watch all that sport up close!' To immerse oneself in an arts community – watching, listening, experiencing, evaluating and recording – is an exciting, privileged role. And let us not forget the roll-call of critics who did not do too badly as dramatists or other kinds of writers: George Bernard Shaw, T.S. Eliot, Caitlin Moran, Henry James, Dennis Potter, Bonnie Greer, Tom Stoppard, Clive James, Tony Parsons, Herbert Kretzmer. Among the interviewees in this book, Lyn Gardner and Mark Lawson have careers as a children's writer and novelist, respectively.

But what if the critic did dance or play a musical instrument? Iain Shedden, music critic at the *Australian*, was a professional drummer before turning his hand to journalism. He is glad he has that grounding, but added: 'It is by no means a requisite of a music critic to be a musician, I don't think; to have an understanding and appreciation of music is essential, but being able to play is not.'[11]

A less likely scenario, however, is the critic who seeks out theoretical and practical knowledge in the field in which they work, which is why the example of Paul Morley is so interesting. Morley, a heavyweight in rock and pop journalism, had been one of the 1,200 people who had applied for the *NME*'s 'attention hip young gunslingers' job vacancy advert in 1976. He made the shortlist of four and, while he was not offered a staff role, was given freelance work that would prove to be a launchpad for a career writing criticism, articles and books and contributing to television programmes. In September 2008 he took part in an experiment in partnership with the BBC and the Royal Academy of Music. The idea was to see if an experienced critic could learn the basics of playing and making music.

The subsequent BBC Four documentary shown the following summer, *How to Be a Composer*, asked a number of searching questions. With access to the best tuition, Morley (2009) wrote: 'Would it make me a better critic, or mean that I lost the ability to generate and arrange my decisions, effectively ruining me as a critic and music writer?' Recognising the need of the documentary form, that a narrative must convey a sense that something has been learned, that is exactly what happened to Morley, who 'began hearing music in a new way' towards the end of the process.

Critics with inside knowledge of the creative arts provide an interesting dynamic; their personal accounts may bring an added richness to their commentaries yet we should not stray too far from the underlying point that art is shared experience and that to record its effect, to evaluate why it works or does not quite work is the job of an informed writer – whether they have ever *practised* that art is not the be-all or end-all.

Free tickets for the reviewer: who pays?

Until now we have been concerned in this chapter with choosing what to review and how we might prepare, either as a reaction to that choice or over a longer period of time. Once we have made our selection we experience the art differently depending on whether it is live or recorded. Recorded for this purpose relates to television, film, music to play as a download or on CD, computer games and books in printed or digital form. Accredited critics are given free access to this content by the relevant producers of this material or their representatives.

Likewise with live events, invited critics receive complimentary tickets to attend concerts, theatre, opera or dance. Often a plus-one is part of the arrangement, but this is not guaranteed, especially when there is particularly strong interest in the event. A free programme will be thrown in with theatrical productions and drinks will be organised for the interval on an official press night. All of this is tantamount to bribery, surely? What else might the critic be entitled to?

It really comes down to fairness and common sense. I have attended many press nights for plays and musicals, both big-budget professional productions and, in my days as a reporter, church-hall shows where they sell weak orange squash in plastic cups. Theatres want you, the critic, to be there and so – within reason – will go out of their way to make your experience a happy one: a seat or seats with a good view, a programme, photos in advance, wine or a fruit juice (or, sadly, squash) in the interval and so on. It is quite common now that theatres outside of London will shift their performance times as well to accommodate the needs of critics returning to the capital, where they live and work. So 7.45pm, a typical performance time, is more likely to be switched to 7pm so that the critics can catch the last train. Transport, as previously discussed, is a thorny issue for London-based critics keen to spread their wings beyond Watford.

Lyn Gardner recalled the difficulties of reaching a production of a play called *A Shepherd's Life* at Theatre by the Lake, Keswick. She was keen to go but the venue was 18 miles from the nearest railway station and so an agreement was reached that one of the marketing team would collect her and then drive her back afterwards. She praised the play in her four-star review – was there a danger that the welcome she was given might colour her view?

> It did not and would not influence what I thought about something any more than you have a free ticket or two free tickets if you wanted them and a glass of wine in the interval. Everyone involved understands that. My view is a pragmatic one – better to get it reviewed. Being paid, for example by a theatre, and being facilitated is different.[12]

That seems a fair interpretation. Indeed I have attended press nights where a venue offers a second production for critics. In this instance the 7pm main attraction is preceded by a separate performance at 2pm in the studio space, followed by a hot meal on the house at 5pm. Again, would that push the critic to be a bit kinder? I suspect not, given that all those present were experienced practitioners, but it is not a set-up that finds favour with everyone.

Megan Vaughan's theatre blog, *Synonyms for Churlish*, is heralded by many as one of the brightest and best around. Her views are strong. Although her blog was on hold when we spoke while she considered her next move – more on that later – she takes the unusual stance that publications, websites or blogs should pay for their own tickets, reasoning (as a professional arts administrator) that budgets on shows are tight and getting funding secured for the subsidised arts is difficult.

> I don't believe in passing the costs of criticism on to artists because I believe that artists should be kept out of the economic transactions of criticism as much as possible. A commercial newspaper asking a subsidised theatre company to effectively pay for their critic to attend is a fucking rotten practice. And, personally, I choose to pay for my tickets because it keeps my relationship to the work as simple as possible. Considering I'm struggling with the psychology of crowdfunding donations, getting a ticket from a theatremaker would've just torn me up inside.[13]

So far we have made a distinction between live and recorded arts, pointing out that music has a foot in both camps since it can be enjoyed in the moment or recorded on vinyl, on CD or as a digital file, whereas other arts are one thing or the other. There is another art form worth exploring, however, and that is the exhibition, notable because it has – or at least it *can* have – elements that are both recorded and live. The art exhibition or museum exhibition is recorded in that it is defined by the space in which you see it, the way it is structured and the fact that you have little control over when you see it (you cannot persuade your local gallery to open up its doors at 3am, for example, but you could open up a book then). But the exhibition is partially live, too, in the sense that a change to the content or way it is presented or the order in which you see it can happen from one day to the next. With performance art, of course, the element of live action is much more obvious. This sense of visual art as a live experience is also interesting, given that a member of the public can encounter the exhibition as part of a group, as part of a couple or on their own. It is quite possible that at quiet periods you may be the only person viewing the artworks at that moment. While it is not wholly impossible that you would be the only audience member to arrive at the opera or for the play or concert, it is wholly improbable.

Art and museum exhibitions allow critics to prepare and research for their reviews in two clear ways. A launch event will be organised a long time in advance of the exhibition opening – it could be months ahead – and its purpose is to stimulate interest in the media and create news stories or features for journalists and critics. A press viewing will usually be the day before the exhibition opens to the public. Nancy Durrant said:

> The idea is that people will publish their review the next day or put it up online straight away. I will often ask if me or my critics can get in as early as possible – sticking to whatever embargo there is – to give someone as much time as possible to write it.[14]

Watch, listen, write

How you engage with the art you are reviewing does of course depend on whether you are in an auditorium with 2,000 other people or in the comfort of your own home. An album affords you the opportunity to hear it as many times as you wish; similarly with a book. Although with a book you are unlikely to have the time or the stamina to start it all over again the moment you finish the last page, it is possible to read knotty passages, or even chapters, one more time as a way of seeking clarity. And as we have discovered, the online streaming of television allows critics in this field to replay the scene as many times as they like.

Deadlines at least partly dictate how many 'spins' a record will get before a reviewer places his fingers on the keypad. Iain Shedden explained to me:

> With album reviews I have no set rule about how many times I will listen to one, but at least a few hearings. It depends on deadlines. I have been known to re-evaluate my rating of something after more listening.[15]

Jude Rogers, live gig reviewer for the *Guardian* and the *Observer*, and senior lecturer in journalism at the University of Gloucestershire, agrees that a judgement can change. She formerly reviewed albums for *Q* magazine, and I asked her about when the reviewer is able to get her hands on a copy of a record.

> That depends. When high profile acts like Radiohead or Rihanna release an album out of the blue, the reviewer's listening at the same time as everybody else. If you're writing for a music magazine, you get the album a few months before release, but you often only have a week with it, at the very most. This makes reviewing difficult – and often hopeless long-term, because everyone's opinions change! I have given records four stars that I've not listened to much again after a rush of interest. I've given things two stars that I've ended up really liking over time. It's an imperfect business![16]

For a lot of music writers, it is not just about how many times they listen to an album, but *where* they listen to it – if nothing else because they want to replicate how fans might engage with it: on the train, in the car, at the kitchen table, on a walk in the woods. Then the level of research raises other questions. Marvin Lin, editor-in-chief of the website *Tiny Mix Tapes*, provides some insight on this in an interview for a book edited by Marc Woodworth and Ally-Jane Grossan, *How to Write About Music* (an excellent source for students wanting more specialist knowledge). He said:

> It's crucial for me to immerse myself in the music first, then, depending on the artist, do as much research as possible by reading interviews and articles. This research is not only for fact-gathering purposes, but also to understand how meaning is created and reinforced throughout the media, how publicity might have affected how people are writing about the music in question, and whether or not it aligns with my personal beliefs.
>
> *(Woodworth and Grossan 2015, 20)*

The safety net of another listen must be reassuring for the album critic, though no such luxury is afforded her when she is half-way into a gig – artists tend not to repeat a song on request just because the reviewer didn't quite catch it. For the critic, then, or indeed any writer covering live performance, how you adapt in that moment is largely down to the specifics of the show and what you and/ or others feel is appropriate. Contrast for a moment the difference between an arena concert bulging with 10,000 fans and an intimate acoustic set where you are so close to the stage you are practically on it. Some writers might feel that tapping away on their smartphone, making notes or dreaming up hooks they will later use in their review is perfectly acceptable; they may even be writing their copy there, in the moment, taking full advantage of the immediacy of the Web and filing the piece while that last power chord hangs in the air. Others might suggest the phone is an intrusion – even at a rock concert – and on that basis they will feel the same way when it comes to the more intimate gig. Writing in a notebook may work better, and certainly so in a theatre auditorium where phone use is strictly off limits. I know this to my cost, having been put in my place by an usher at a variety show of all things – despite my sitting at the back, the light from the phone shining on my notebook, but it was still worthy of a yellow card. I usually restrict my note-taking to a few scribbles in an A6 notebook: lines of dialogue, key words or phrases, scraps of ideas that jump out at me in the moment. I do shorthand, so that helps, but not too much material, as writing in the dark is not recommended, and later on, at home, the results will disappoint. I used to write quite a lot of notes, perhaps anxious (wrongly, as it turned out) there would not be enough to say. Now, most of these scraps of notes will lead to nothing, certainly nowhere near the finished review, but there is a comfort knowing *something* has been written down. The most important point – and an obvious one – is to properly watch and listen. The best notepad of all is your memory – key moments, images that could spark an idea, the feeling of what it was like to be there, watching that play, on that night.

As Luis Sanchez points out in *How to Write About Music* (Woodworth and Grossan 2015, 47), 'If I do take notes on a show, it's usually right after, in a mad scramble before the mood wears off, and the notes mostly consist of impressions, passing thoughts, and as thorough a set list as I can remember. It's more important for me to put something about mood and atmosphere before it wears off.'

Reading other critics' reviews

Thanks to the Internet it is increasingly possible to read a review of a work of art that you are going to write about and publish. Whether you are tempted to look depends on your personal set of values and the practicalities of your deadline – for example, you might want to think about the wisdom of spending too much time weighing up your competition and what they have written when you still haven't filed *your* piece. Lyn Gardner at the *Guardian* has this to say:

> There is a generation of critics that go 'Oh no, I would never want to read a review before I do mine.' But it's not an exam, you are writing your response to something so there is no right or wrong. I would not particularly seek them out but I would always seek them out afterwards.[17]

I would share that view, though others – particularly emboldened by social media – would suggest that a review is the start of a conversation, almost a living entity open to change and development – very different from the idea of permanence that Tynan wrote about. Personally I would rather avoid what someone else has written until my review is filed. I don't want my thinking to be muddled by other noise, to worry that I have missed the point or been wide of the mark with the stars at my disposal. Similarly, reviewers like to keep their powder dry when it comes to engagement with other critics, such as in the interval of a play.

In reflecting on what to write about for our readers, we have considered their tastes and interests. We have thought about the effort and costs involved in reaching this art, particularly travel, if indeed it is to be experienced as a live event. We have thought about the knowledge required to evaluate the work, the level of preparation required for the specific task balanced against the practicalities of everything else we have to do in a limited amount of time. Finally we have considered how to see it or hear it when the moment comes. With our notes, our ideas and our memories, there can only be one thing left – it is time to write your review.

Notes

1 Gardner, Lyn (19 April 2016), interview with the author.
2 In April 2017, budget cuts led the *Guardian* to cancel Gardner's contract to write 150 blogs a year. *The Stage* critic Mark Shenton (2017) wrote that it was 'distressing news' as

Gardner covered topics away from the mainstream and attended 'more theatres around the UK than any other critic I know'.
3 Bowie-Sell, Daisy (25 April 2016), interview with the author.
4 Durrant, Nancy (7 September 2016), interview with the author.
5 *Ibid.*
6 Brantley, Ben (11 August 2016), interview with the author.
7 Gardner, Lyn (19 April 2016), interview with the author.
8 Norman, Neil (27 July 2016), interview with the author.
9 Myskow, Nina (24 June 2016), interview with the author.
10 Durrant, Nancy (7 September 2016), interview with the author.
11 Shedden, Iain (27 July 2016), interview with the author.
12 Gardner, Lyn (19 April 2016), interview with the author.
13 Vaughan, Megan (17 July 2016), interview with the author.
14 Durrant, Nancy (7 September 2016), interview with the author.
15 Shedden, Iain (27 July 2016), interview with the author.
16 Rogers, Jude (19 October 2016), interview with the author.
17 Gardner, Lyn (19 April 2016), interview with the author.

References

Fisher, Mark (2015) *How to Write About Theatre*. London: Bloomsbury Methuen Drama.
Long, Pat (2012) *The History of the NME: High Times and Low Lives at the World's Most Famous Music Magazine*. London: Portico.
Morley, Paul (12 July 2009) 'Critic to composer', *Guardian*, www.theguardian.com/music/2009/jul/12/classical-music-becoming-a-composer.
Shenton, Mark (14 March 2017) 'Pulling Lyn Gardner's blog is another nail in the coffin of arts journalism', *The Stage*, www.thestage.co.uk/opinion/2017/mark-shenton-pulling-lyn-gardners-blog-another-nail-coffin-arts-journalism/.
Smith, Alistair (2015) *London Theatre Report*. London: National Theatre and the Society of London Theatre.
Wells, Stanley (1997) *Shakespeare in the Theatre: An Anthology of Criticism*. Oxford: Oxford University Press.
Williams, Gilda (2014) *How to Write About Contemporary Art*. London: Thames and Hudson.
Woodworth, Marc and Grossan, Ally-Jane (eds) (2015) *How to Write About Music*. London: Bloomsbury.

4
WRITING THE REVIEW
Part one

Picture the ideal arts critic: immersed in their chosen field, with an appreciation of and a fascination for practitioners of the past. This critic speaks knowledgeably about landmark events, placing them in context with other moments – even moments not necessarily within their own area of expertise – and marries all of that knowledge to a firm grasp of what is happening now. This critic can write and talk about local, national and international developments. This critic has the benefit of 20 years' experience in the business and yet has the bright-eyed enthusiasm of an absolute beginner. He – or should that be she? – writes so well it makes you long to dig deeper into what they've put on the page or screen. It makes you want to share it with a friend, or simply smile, nod or even shake your head in defiance but the writing has gripped you anyway. This critic writes so well, the review not only fizzes on the page, it practically burns a hole in it. This critic is clever, relevant, funny, insightful and brave, sparking debate and providing a useful service to his or her readers on how to spend their money and time. This critic is accurate and fast as they go about their business recording, reporting and evaluating all that they see and hear.

This critic could be you.

But stop.

Before that can happen, you are going to require a skills-set that will enable you to adapt to different situations, different platforms for producing content. In the next two chapters we reveal the components that go into writing a review as well as analysing extracts of criticism produced by leading practitioners.

Objectives and expectations

Whatever the circumstances of the review you are about to write, it is a good idea to take stock of your objectives and the objectives of those who made the work.

Indeed, these intentions should also be considered in light of the expectations that others have when they read your copy. More precisely, there are three interested groups of people – the readers, of course, then the editor who commissioned the work and finally the artists and others responsible for the work (producers, investors, production staff, public relations agencies and so on).

First of all, you. In all probability you want your review to be read and appreciated, perhaps even to ruffle a few feathers. In 2013 the *NME*'s Mark Beaumont infamously rated the new Tom Odell album as a zero out of ten with this justification: 'He'll be all over 2013 like a virulent dose of musical syphilis, pounding and warbling away at every Papal election and Bradley Wiggins finishing line. Be warned, you can't unhear it.'

But critic Simon Price, quoted in the *Independent on Sunday* (Rawlinson 2013), labelled the move 'cowardly' and other writers felt the zero score was there to attract attention. As a comparison the *Guardian* and the *Observer* both felt it had merited three stars, while the *Daily Telegraph* went one better.

The Odell example may be extreme, but the point remains that anyone publishing a review does so to create an impact, just as the artist does. What else is an objective? Your purpose is to inform and illuminate. Evaluation comes into play as well – how does this work compare with others that are similar in theme or style or even made by the same people? What *value* should be placed upon it? Entertaining the reader is equally key; some of your readers – probably most – will not see or hear the art you have written about, but they read your page anyway. As television critic Mark Lawson explains, the ideal review

> is a piece that can be read with enjoyment both by those who have seen the work under discussion and by those who haven't. It's for this reason that inflected précis – spiced with wryness, warmth, scepticism or moral outrage – has become the dominant voice of TV criticism.[1]

In discussing arts reviewing with many practitioners during the course of writing this book, it is clear that one point easily overlooked is the *need* to write about what inspires them. Rock critic Neil McCormick calls himself a 'writing machine',[2] while the theatre blogger Megan Vaughan describes her compulsion thus:

> Sometimes it's to celebrate the work, sometimes it's to celebrate one tiny part of the work, sometimes it's to pick at a thread that I could imagine unravelling. One thing is constant though: that my primary driving force is self-expression and the emotional and psychological effects of writing. On me, not on anyone else.[3]

All sorts of reasons may explain why a reader is reading your review about something they possibly won't see: they are weighing up their options, they have heard people chat about this and here is a way not to be left out of the conversation (they really do not have time to watch another box set), they stumble across your article via links from other websites or because the newspaper was left open at this page, or they have read your work before and like it.

Importantly, your objectives as a reviewer of an artwork should be weighed against those of the artmaker. To briefly return to Odell – ambushed by the *NME* for producing a 'decently bland album' – was this 'offensively dull piano pop' so bad it deserved zero in a rating out of ten? The reviewer may have hated it (he has every right to say so if that is the case), but his displeasure could have been measured in the context of what it was that Odell was trying to create.

Mark Lawson picked up on this theme when recalling his reaction to the bawdy comedy *Mrs Brown's Boys*, a BBC television show filmed in front of a live studio audience, which was not his 'kind of thing' but one which he nevertheless felt compelled to review favourably thanks in part to a system he attributes to Esther Rantzen, the distinguished BBC journalist. Rantzen's very sensible advice is a variation of theories explored by the Italian writer Manzoni.[4] Lawson explained:

> Advice I was given as a young critic by Dame Esther Rantzen has always stayed with me. The role of a critic, she said, was to answer two questions: 'What is this show trying to do? And how well does it do it?'
>
> The great advantage of that approach, which I still try to follow, is that it prevents a critic becoming a prisoner of personal taste or politics, especially useful at a time when citizen criticism can tend too easily towards the polarities of 'I'm loving this' / 'Who commissioned this shit?' If more critics had applied the Rantzen Formula to *Mrs Brown's Boys*, they would not have been so bewildered by its huge success.[5]

Expect the unexpected

What better way to get readers coming to your online review than via clicks from a news story that you originated? As this book tries to demonstrate, one of the critic's prime responsibilities is that of a reporter. So when an arts event takes an unexpected turn, you need to be ready. The beauty of live art – concerts, gigs, stand-up comedy, performance poetry, dance, opera and theatre – is that every night is different, and occasionally those differences are highlighted by an interesting twist. Most obviously this comes in the form of something going wrong, but it need not be the case.

Broadly we can group the possibilities as outlined in the sub-sections that follow.

Audience behaviour

Who can say with any certainty how 900 people will behave if they are put in seats in the dark and asked to sit there for two hours? This is a good thing for reviewers who like to write about spectators. But all the same, a sense of perspective is crucial, as low-level chatting in a 50-seat studio theatre will cause more disruption than an argument in an arena jammed with 20,000 comedy fans. Famously, the late British actor Richard Griffiths berated West End and Broadway audience members on three occasions in total for using their mobile phones in the middle of performances of *The History Boys* and *Heroes*.[6]

Our love affair with our phones – even at the theatre – might provide useful copy for the news pages of the quality press, but increasingly it is a real worry for theatre management. In 2013 James McAvoy brought a performance of *Macbeth* at Trafalgar Studios to a halt to ask an audience member to stop filming him. Two years later Benedict Cumberbatch's portrayal of Hamlet garnered nearly as much attention for his angst at phone-obsessed fans as it did for his work in the Barbican production. He addressed fans at the stage door, pleading with them to curb their behaviour while the play was in progress, as the constant barrage of filming was having a detrimental effect on him and others. It was 'mortifying', he told them (Hauser 2015), adding that 'I can't give you what I want to give you – a live performance, rather than on your phones.'

In his column in the same year, *The Stage*'s senior theatre critic Mark Shenton reported an incident where actor Patti LuPone confiscated a mobile phone from a woman who was using it during a performance of an off-Broadway play. She returned it at the end of the show. 'We are losing the battle against mobile phone usage in the theatre', Shenton (2015) wrote, citing the need for greater awareness of why such behaviour is unacceptable and urging zero tolerance against the worst offenders.

Long before mobiles had become a way of life, I reviewed a professional dramatisation of D.H. Lawrence's *Sons and Lovers* in a provincial English town. Audience profile was essentially a combination of over-50s and some teenage girls from the local high school. Tension had been building from the start, with said girls giggling inappropriately in a play not big on laughs. A knot of mature women out for the evening were having none of it. With their calls for the girls to get a grip falling on deaf ears, an astonishing conclusion prevailed when – early in the second half – one of the women got up from her seat, fixed a stare on the teenagers and told them to go. The bewildered actors halted the play as these women proceeded to give the girls a slow hand-clap until the shame of it was too much, and they left. My review clearly had to focus on this moment, in part admiring the pluckiness of the older women but also wondering if it might have been handled in a way that spared the teenagers such a public humiliation. This was clearly unexpected, and it was certainly news.

Illness, injury, death or fire

Developing a news sense is a useful tool for the critic, not only in helping to bring alive their review but also for the added bonus of suggesting (and perhaps even filing) follow-up news stories or features. Bloggers are likely to wear all of these hats, of course (the opportunity to write in different styles can be part of the attraction), while writers operating within small teams online or in print may be asked to double up and help out with the feature or news story arrived at as a consequence of their review. Critics with dedicated news reporters on staff will be happy that an arts event is in the news while enjoying the fact that the story will almost certainly cross-refer or link to their page. Tweets they send shortly after the performance has finished will also help to direct readers to their work.

Live performance is unpredictable, and this is a valuable truth as far as arts journalists are concerned. Performers of all kinds have the capacity to trip, fall or be taken ill, just as any of us may, but to do so with a critic in the house is doubly unfortunate – though potentially it paves the way for an understudy to step in or for other creative solutions to be found. In April 2016 rock singer Axl Rose, frontman for Guns N' Roses, broke his foot during a warm-up gig prior to a greatly anticipated money-spinning tour, thus presenting clear news potential for reviewing. First-night critic Corey Levitan, writing for *Billboard*, grabbed the opportunity with this opening sentence:

> When the partially reunited original Guns N' Roses performed its first arena show in 23 years on Friday night in Las Vegas, singer Axl Rose was completely immobilized by a foot injury.

Having been wheeled onstage at 11.57pm, Rose tapped his one good foot to the beat and sang from a throne which he had borrowed, says Levitan (2016), from Dave Grohl, the Foo Fighters star who had broken *his* leg only the year before.

While this book was being written, Sheridan Smith took extended leave from her West End role in *Funny Girl*. Seizing her chance as female lead Fanny Brice, 26-year-old understudy Natasha J. Barnes made everyone sit up and take notice, so much so that during her second, longer stint at replacing Smith, who was suffering from exhaustion, critics made a return visit to the show. They had loved Smith, and now they loved Barnes as well. Dominic Cavendish (2016), for the *Daily Telegraph*, said in his five-star endorsement that this was 'the stuff of fairytales' and that Barnes was not 'just a serviceable stand-in, she's a sensation in her own right'. News reports, television appearances and features about Barnes as well as that of the life of an understudy duly followed. A star was born, an angle was created.

Amid the overnight success stories, the arts and entertainment world is packed with serious, occasionally tragic episodes where musicians, comics and others inadvertently find themselves making headlines for all the wrong reasons. Comedy greats Eric Morecambe and Tommy Cooper died about a month apart in 1984 having collapsed on stage, the latter during a live television broadcast, while *Carry On* film star Sid James had also succumbed to a fatal heart attack performing at Sunderland Empire in 1976. Television actor Gareth Jones never recovered from the heart attack he suffered during a live recording of *Armchair Theatre* in 1958.

Janette Tough, better known as Wee Jimmy from The Krankies double act, did survive but sustained serious injuries, including a fractured skull, slipping at least 10 feet from a pantomime beanstalk in Glasgow. But perhaps the most poignant of all of these cases involves that of Jane Little, principal bass emeritus with the Atlanta

Symphony Orchestra. Reportedly the longest-serving musician in the world, having spent more than 70 years with the orchestra, she was 87 years old when she collapsed and died on stage in the closing seconds of a final encore during a concert in May 2016. The song they were playing at the time was *There's No Business Like Show Business*.

Critics get two bites at the cherry when reviewing live art and the unexpected happens – but in order to capitalise on the news potential of the situation, it is best that they are there, doing their job as agreed. I am reminded of an extreme response to being asked to review a play and the consequent dismissal of the reporter who neglected his duties. I was given a chance in journalism at the end of the 1980s after the previous junior reporter was sacked. Asked by the editor to review an amateur dramatic society's performance at a local theatre, he had no intention of staying beyond the first half. His plan was to watch the first act, get enough in his notebook – including the names of the players and production staff – then retire to a pub for the rest of the night. What he could not predict was that moments after he left, a backstage fire started to spread, causing serious damage to the venue and the play to be abandoned. Oblivious to this breaking news even as he arrived for work the next morning, the young reporter was encouraged to try a different career when his editor discovered he had missed the story of the week!

Artists behaving differently

There is nothing new in artists behaving in ways that will attract media attention for all the wrong reasons. It might involve the slurring of words or having an old-fashioned pop at the crowd. The digital age takes their unexpected forays to new heights, though, with the capacity for anyone who is there to record the misdemeanour on social media – often instantly and using video as well if the environment allows it, such as at a pop concert. The bigger the star, the greater the news potential.

The remarkable case of actor Laurence Fox is included here but so easily could have come under the section about audience behaviour. Starring alongside Tom Conti in *The Patriotic Traitor* in March 2016 at the Park Theatre in north London, Fox, fellow cast members and presumably some of the audience as well had been bothered by a man muttering, heckling and eventually swearing at one of the characters (played by Fox). Two lines from the end of the play, Fox stepped out of character, turned to the man and said, 'I won't bother telling you the story because this cunt in the front row has ruined it for everybody.'

Hannah Ellis-Petersen's news report for the *Guardian* (2016) added: 'Conti said that incidents of audiences talking, commenting and heckling during live theatre were becoming increasingly common as people had become so used to watching entertainment on screens.'

In this example and others like it, critics can flex their feature-writing muscles in a number of ways.

Pitch ideas to commissioning editors about artists who make public outbursts, both justified and unjustified. What other interesting examples can you find? Cast your net beyond the current age and see what riled the stars of yesteryear. What is harmless banter between a comic and a crowd, and when does it become uncomfortable? The discomfort starts to make it newsworthy. Use your piece to explore whether social media actually encourage singers and rappers to court controversy. Get a range of interviewees to argue a case for and against. In the example of Laurence Fox, his actions were supported by his colleagues. Use this incident to debate the behaviour of theatregoers. Where does the convention come from that – aside from laughter – we should more or less be quiet? How do audiences behave in other countries around the world?

Openings, intros and angles

Beginning a chapter section on the importance of beginnings rather cranks up the pressure, yet the point does serve to remind that arts criticism is an unforgiving arena. Capturing – and sustaining – the reader's attention is paramount, as scores of alternative examples of content immediately present themselves to anyone with Internet access. Let us look at some ideas for making your openings stand out to your readers.

Arts journalism is rooted in truth, just as news reporting is; the gallery exhibition you experienced has a number of facts as its cornerstones which are the 'news' part of your criticism. Your evaluation of the experience is another vital layer to the review, and we can come back to that in a moment. For now, let's stick with the facts. News writing is powered by a set of questions which can be applied to all stories, even the more mundane ones. They are sometimes referred to as the Five Ws (who, what, where, why and when), though I prefer to label them as the Six Ws, adding the all-important 'how' question into the mix. No prizes for correctly pointing out that 'how' does not begin with 'W' but neither does irony, and that's why it's easy to remember. With our art exhibition example, *who* is the artist, *what* have they created, *where* is the work being shown, *why* have they made it and *when* can it be seen? *How* they have made it/exhibited it/publicised it – and there is your set of Six Ws.

But facts alone do not make news as we know it. Information must be arranged in some way so as to make it a story. This editorial solution is an angle – literally the slant or the direction in which you present your story.

A grounding in news reporting, though not essential and certainly not commonplace as so-called traditional routes into journalism become less frequent, builds a deep understanding of the importance of angles – particularly useful when news reporters are working to tight deadlines and often juggling half a dozen stories at any one time. This sense for an angle is something we can all develop, though, because – blissfully unaware that we already have the basics – it is something we have practised our whole lives. To demonstrate the point that instinctively we know about angles, I ask my first-year students to think about their own lives and the stories they share, be that the sharing they do on Facebook with their community of friends and family or a 20-second burst of conversation in a crowded corridor before the start of a class. Restricted by time and space, they already have quite a sophisticated grasp of choosing the best angle, based on life experience so far. Journalism has not taught them this – instead their friends have, who stop listening if their story is dull.

In their second week of studies, we underline this point with a quick exercise that not only works as a lesson about storytelling but also as a great ice-breaker. Does everyone have a phone with them today? Of course they do. Their task, then, is to call someone they know and get that person to relay a story that has happened to them in the last few hours or days. Typically one or two students are ahead of the rest and immediately they phone a friend, parent or sibling. Instantly it cajoles the others and soon there is a cacophony of 24 simultaneous interviews taking place. There is chatter, laughter, a series of rapid questions and furious note-taking. Free from the pressure to find a *great* story, an *important* story (rarely does this happen), they are able to deliver on the real point of the exercise, which is to gather a story that may or may not be published but at the very least can suggest an angle to the student:

- a woman was late for work after she needed AA assistance to get her car started;
- a block of student accommodation was evacuated in the early hours after a tenant set off smoke alarms while making toast.

There is nothing earth-shattering with either of them, though the car breakdown is of some interest to the woman's immediate set of friends and family, while the toast incident may have some potential for a student newspaper or website, particularly if this is a common occurrence (hungry and drunk can lead to consequences). With stronger stories, students learn that more than one angle now presents itself. In this respect, news is no different from writing a review: how do you possibly choose? The answer may depend on one or more of the following: your target readership, your editor's preferences, your own level of confidence, or what is most straightforward because time is pressing.

Once the angle has been established, a sentence or opening paragraph to convey that thought is required, and that is your introduction or 'intro'. Intros are crucial for catching the eye of the reader, as well as for clues about the tone and mood of the piece. Here are six suggestions on how to find an intro for your review.

A single image or moment or line of dialogue

The unpredictability of live theatre is caught magnificently in David Jays's review of *She Loves Me*, a 2016 production at the Menier Chocolate Factory in London of a musical set in 1930s Budapest. What happens when a mouse (not part of the cast, just to be clear) walks onstage? Jays (2016) uses this one moment to drive the narrative of his whole review:

> The Menier, near London Bridge, is an intimate theatre. So it must be painfully apparent to a leading man giving his all in a big musical number when the audience has its attention forcibly diverted.

Jays sets up comic tension by telling us straight away that this is a small theatre and indicating that something went awry. He goes on:

> [Mark Umbers] was bringing out his best patter, high notes … He was almost certainly rather good. But there was a mouse – where? There on the stair – and we couldn't look away. People jumped in their seats, pointed. Someone squealed. The mouse didn't hang about (oh, everyone's a critic) and, reluctantly, we all turned to smile politely as Umbers closed his song with a sustained note. Live theatre is the best.

For music critic Jude Rogers, the memory of a defining image came to her rescue while struggling to write up a Bruce Springsteen gig. Working from 6am for a 9am deadline, she had so much to say about how Springsteen was revered that it was getting in the way of the previous night's concert. She always uses 'the pub test', she told me, as a springboard for an angle, and remembering the test jolted her review into life:

> A fan had come to the gig dressed as Father Christmas and held up a request for the band to do *Santa Claus Is Coming to Town*. They did, and brought him on stage with them – in the middle of May! That had been the first thing I told my husband on the phone after the concert. It was a great, unique detail about the gig, and I realised that that detail could make the review come alive. The thing that grabs your attention first is often the thing that can grab other people's attention first.[7]

And the intro in question:

> On an unseasonably damp night in Manchester, in a soulless football stadium, Santa Claus is coming to town. 'You gotta help us out, man,' burrs Bruce Springsteen as Father Christmas is brought out of the crowd: a fan holding his request on a piece of cardboard, as many have done successfully over the years. E Street Band guitarist Steve Van Zandt stands back from the mic he usually shares with his bandleader, leaving a gangly bloke in red fancy dress 'making a list, and checking it twice' next to rock's kindest superstar.

(Rogers 2016)

An observation or an idea prompted by the work

The art critic Eddy Frankel begins his *Time Out* review of Yuri Patterson's installation *User, Space* with a striking realisation that some of us spend too long at work, specifically the office in this example:

> Forget your home, your family, your friends, forget it all. The office is where we spend our lives, it's where we see our days dribble past, miserably, endlessly, relentlessly.
>
> *(Frankel 2016)*

Frankel does not for one moment believe that everything beyond the office may as well be cast aside, but his exaggerated reaction absolutely underlines the argument that too much time there renders our lives pointlessly grey. He expands this idea in his second paragraph, and, at the same time, provides useful information about the artist:

> In young London-based artist Yuri Pattinson's installation, the modern office is cast as a dystopian, derelict, steel-and-glass tomb. It's like a future look back at how we spend our days, and it makes for grim but addictive viewing.
>
> *(Frankel 2016)*

The overall effect

Reporting from the front line almost, the impression might be that it was stunning, mesmerising, innovative, an absolute waste of money. This approach is often very news-centred, the critic firmly wearing her reporter's hat. The intention is to be direct, no urge on this occasion to conjure clever imagery or lay the groundwork for a short essay. See how Jenny Gilbert (2016) for *The Arts Desk* swiftly reassures us with her verdict on *The Red Shoes*, a new work at Sadler's Wells, London, from the celebrated choreographer Matthew Bourne:

> Anyone expecting a knockout punch from Matthew Bourne's latest creation is in for a let-down. His hotly anticipated take on Powell and Pressburger's 1948 film, unlike his *Swan Lake*, is not going to send anyone out into the night weeping into their hankie. Nor is it likely to turn unbelievers into ballet fans, and yet it is probably his best piece of work to date.
>
> *(Gilbert 2016)*

David Mellor, a former arts minister, writes about opera for the *Mail on Sunday*. He wastes no time with this assessment of *The Nose* at London's Royal Opera House:

> Wow, what a show! The evening belongs to the Australian director Barrie Kosky. He turns Shostakovich's problematic pig's ear, *The Nose*, into a silk purse, with a razzle-dazzle production that even his fellow Aussie showman Baz Luhrmann would be hard put to better.
>
> *(Mellor 2016)*

Context

This involves what an artist/maker has done before, how this work links with other books/films/shows/plays/performances, etc., why this work is important, what is happening in the world (either the arts discipline itself or the wider world). Compare two intros highlighting Lenny Henry's award-winning role in *Fences*, a 2013 London production of August Wilson's play about a Pittsburgh garbage man who had once been a baseball star. Writing in *The Times*, Libby Purves's four-star notice (2013) suggests this leading man can now enter an unofficial club for elite theatre actors. The review is brightly written and inventive in its form, and Purves makes her statement while drip-feeding important information along the way: 'This is it, Lenny Henry – three strikes and you're in! *Othello*, *Comedy of Errors* and now this: the stand-up 'n' sketch image evaporates as Henry joins the ranks of great stage actors.'

It is an unusual start, directly addressing the actor, which immediately captures our attention (and presumably Mr Henry's, assuming he is minded to read such things), as well as keeping us on our toes with a reference to baseball. We are reminded of Henry's two previous successes following his rebranding as a serious stage actor, and that his previous persona as a comedian is – for now at least – on the back-burner. In labelling his style of comedy as an image – 'stand-up *'n'* sketch', rather than the more formal *and* – there is just a hint that its status is some way down the pecking order compared to this new, elevated position as an important actor.

Michael Billington in the *Guardian* (again four stars) takes much the same route as Purves, though plays a straighter bat:

> Lenny Henry has won his spurs as a Shakespearean actor in *Othello* and *The Comedy of Errors*. Now he takes on the titanic role of Troy Maxson in August Wilson's *Fences* which won a Pulitzer Prize in 1987 and which is part of a ten-play cycle about the African-American experience. Given that James Earl Jones created the part, there are some big boots to fill and I can only report that Henry confirms he is an actor of massive presence and emotional power.
>
> *(Billington 2013)*

The critic may draw inspiration from how an artist's work connects with previous work or how the content stacks up against something similar, but potentially there is an even bigger picture to consider, and this is to place the artwork in the context of what is happening in the world – both in the literal sense of topical events on a global scale such as war or political unrest (interpretations of Shakespeare, laden with big themes, may be viewed entirely differently in the wake of a government scandal, for instance) or something more localised like a musical addressing street crime in the city where the production is made. Either example requires the reviewer to consider what the artist/creative is trying to achieve. Where art is made in direct response to an event, these intentions may be clear, though this is far from guaranteed, while art can be coloured by changes in circumstances. David Bowie's death two days after the release of his final album, *Blackstar*, is a case in point.

On 11 January 2016, the day after Bowie's death, the *New York Times* commented:

> Only now, with hindsight, does the scope of Mr Bowie's oracular farewell become clear: His latest works were haunting, conflicted and not entirely subtle – both the Off Broadway show he co-wrote and a new song are named *Lazarus*, for the biblical figure brought back from the dead.
>
> *(Coscarelli and Paulson 2016)*

The story as a lever

Where narrative is important to the artwork – plays, novels, television drama and film most obviously spring to mind – describing the story can be a useful tool for the reviewer. This, as Fisher (2015) identifies, 'can help the reader get a sense of what's at stake and can be especially valuable for new and unfamiliar work'.

Here is *The Times* television critic, Andrew Billen (2016), jumping straight into story and character in his four-star review of BBC Two comedy *Motherland*: 'Julia is not a mother who keeps a constant eye on her children. She is a mother who tolerates them in her peripheral vision.' Not only does the intro show an expectation of motherhood turned on its head but sets up the comparison that Billen wants to make with a firm favourite on television, BBC One's *Outnumbered*, in that this show is 'not about the kids'.

Reviewer's personal relationship with the work

Equally this may be the genre or style, or musician or writer, for instance, 'I've never understood Shakespeare'.

Matthew Bond, film critic at the *Mail on Sunday*, owns up to his prejudices but manages to park them in time to write this intro for a four-star review:

> *Nerve* (15) didn't sound like my sort of film at all, what with its story of assorted unhappy American teenagers getting caught up in an addictive online game of dare that tempts them to take ever greater risks in exchange for money and fame.
>
> *(Bond 2016)*

The late A.A. Gill, television critic at the *Sunday Times*, pulls off a similar trick with his take on *Naked Attraction*, a rather odd Channel 4 game show where contestants get to date someone by revealing their bodies in a competitive way, literally bit by bit. Given two pages to develop his argument on this show along with three other programmes, Gill (2016) begins: 'I never thought I'd want to hear what Malcolm Muggeridge and Mary Whitehouse thought about today's television ever again, but *Naked Attraction* did it for me.' Gill fantasises at the prospect of Muggeridge hosting a late-night talk show where Whitehouse,[8] the queen of 1970s prudery via her National Viewers' and Listeners' Association – Gill is quick to remind us that she once gave Jimmy Savile 'an award for family entertainment' – could tell us why it should come off our screens. Gill puts the boot in by concluding that *Naked Attraction* is a 'cynical exercise in objectifying bodies, from a channel that would have a fit of righteous vapours if you suggested that it broadcast Miss World'.

Sometimes, of course, reviews can mix and match two or even more of these entry points. Jenny Gilbert's *The Red Shoes* review merges a straight-to-the-point report with a comparison between Bourne's latest and earlier work. Or take this example from Camilla Long, film critic for the *Sunday Times*, writing about *Fantastic Beasts and Where to Find Them*. 'It is five years since the last Harry Potter film', she begins, before adding that this movie – based on a 2001 spin-off book by J.K. Rowling – is 'intensely unambitious' (2016). But it is in revealing her own relationship with the franchise that Long's review kicks into another gear. 'I've long wondered what defines her world, but this confirms my suspicion: all it is really is deep, dribbling nostalgia.'

The six suggestions for finding an angle for your review are exactly that – suggestions. There may be variations on these examples discussed or entirely different ways of unlocking an idea. All reviewers are different, and you will be different as well: borrowing ideas, adapting them, stumbling upon your own, but made different because they find a reader through the experience that only you have had. I spoke in some detail with Neil McCormick, rock critic at the *Daily Telegraph*, on how he finds his angles – a subject made all the more interesting because of the changes forced upon review writing by digital technology. He said:

> I watch for a few songs, waiting for an angle, trying to get a sense of how I might tackle it, then start taking notes on my phone in quite well-formed sentences. The down side is that as soon as I am writing, I am no longer really in the moment. I'm moving back and forth between looking up at the stage and down at my phone (meanwhile half the audience are looking at the stage through their phones). My mind is working at a furious rate and I am siphoning information – what fits into the thrust of my review and what doesn't? At a certain point, you really have to commit to and follow a particular idea, and if something happens later in the gig that contradicts that idea, it can present a conflict. Very often, the last paragraph you write might become the opening, and half of what you have written during the show gets ditched.[9]

Your angle is found, your intro is safely in the bag as well – perhaps it is eye-catching, almost demanding to be read; perhaps it is more intriguing than that, a suggestion that keeps the reader hanging in there for more. Either way, your angle and intro propel the review forward and yet there are other, important components which also cannot be ignored.

Other components for your review

The art form you are writing about will largely dictate the components available as you begin your review. Put simply, a $100-million movie creating employment for hundreds of people will offer more scope for criticism than a stand-up comedian's 30-minute riff on his childhood, or a debut novel or indeed other mostly non-collaborative arts projects. Note, the movie is not necessarily more important than the novel or the stand-up routine, it is merely that the reviewer's senses must be alert to a wider set of possibilities. (Commercial logic kicks in as well given that more readers are interested in the film than the comedy routine and more readers have the opportunity to see this movie rather than catch the comic at a local venue).

Let us look at where the similarities and differences lie. While emphasis may be shifted depending on the readership being targeted, there are some broad principles at play.

In film criticism the names of the director, the key actors involved and possibly the scriptwriter too are going to be of interest to readers. They will want to know what rating the movie has been given and its running time (97 mins; 2hrs 25 mins and so on).

Story is hugely important. As we discussed earlier, an outline of the story can be given but it does not have to be in full and it should certainly not give away the ending. Is it an original screenplay? What do we know of its providence? There may be potential here to talk about how the film came to be made ('director X and her 15-year refusal to give in when Hollywood's elite turned it down'). It may be adapted from a stage play, from a novel or even inspired by a work of non-fiction. It may be a sequel or – more likely in recent years –a prequel; it may be a reboot of an earlier, much-loved film, prompting the questions how does it compare and why bother anyway? Possibly it is a true story. If so, is this a faithful reconstruction or have liberties been taken with the source material?

Film is a director's medium. Their input – impressive or less so – is a significant contributor to why good actors can flourish or flounder. How well have they told the story? Is the film visually interesting? What about the casting? *Sunday Times* critic Camilla Long does not hold back in her assessment of Ewan McGregor's first outing as director, overseeing an adaptation of Philip Roth's novel *American Pastoral*:

> What kind of mindless arrogance has driven McGregor to choose one of America's greatest modern works as his debut, putting himself in the role of

one of its most iconic characters? He can't even get the hair right, let alone the tone, the themes or the casting.

(Long 2016b)

More than any other art form, readers like to know about the cost of making movies. Other costs interest them as well – the six-figure advance paid to a politician for their memoirs, a controversial commission for a new sculpture or the investment in a 13-part transatlantic television series – but not on the same scale as big-budget movies made by major studios. What do the viewers get for a $100-million investment? Here the critic can discuss the stunning locations and incredible special effects. The flip side to all of this, of course, is a low-budget, independently made film whose charm captures the eye of critics, not least for its refreshing storytelling and beautiful performances.

Critics reviewing stage plays and television drama or comedy are interested in many of the areas relevant to film. The director's vision and – especially with theatre where a familiar text is being returned to – their ability to interpret work in a fresh, exciting way is just as important to the overall quality as the merits of a great script. Georgina Brown, drama critic for the *Mail on Sunday*, notes how Michael Longhurst's 'lavish revival' of *Amadeus* at the National Theatre '37 years on, has a very different emphasis' from Peter Hall's world premiere of Peter Shaffer's play, which 'deliberately muted the music' of Mozart. In one sentence she says something interesting about a new interpretation, along with informing us about the subject of the play, the key creative personnel both now and in 1979 and, if that was not enough, quietly reminds us that she knows about the original staging. Brown's observation (2016) that Longhurst 'rather pointlessly' stages *Amadeus* 'as a sort of play within a play, starting off with the actors warming up backstage pre-performance' is balanced by the 'spine-tingling' effect of having around 20 young musicians on stage at all times, 'sometimes helping with scene-changing but usually making music'.

Acting does of course score highly on the critic's checklist but it would be wrong to suggest it dominates the thinking. With less experienced reviewers especially, making the actor or performer central to the piece is a common response, and not without some justification, as Titchener points out:

> The reader feels he or she knows about acting, even if he or she has little understanding of how it is done. Thus, the critic and reviewer begin their approach to drama with the contradiction that their readers know acting, but not the theatre.

(Titchener 2005)

Part of the test, part of the leap beyond 'this was good acting' or 'this was poor' is to drill deeper into how or why something worked. How has the stage actor invested in her characterisation? What makes this performance come alive? Is there a truthfulness to it and, if so, what moments particularly signpost this effect? (This is not to suggest necessarily that the acting style is naturalistic.) Consider the actor's suitability for the role and his presence on stage. Are we drawn to him even when he isn't speaking? How does he move or use his body to add depth to his characterisation?

Opera critic Kate Kellaway, writing in the *Observer*, is acutely aware of a performer's presence on stage, as demonstrated in this reference to Renée Fleming, who 'has a rare quality – absolute relaxation on stage. It is a star thing: she is comfortable in her body, secure in her glorious voice.'

The voice cannot be ignored. Neither can the space in which the performers use their voice, as some seem to fill even the largest auditoriums with sound and you still feel there is something left in the tank. Others sound tinny, perhaps even muffled. (In television drama this has been particularly newsworthy in recent times, with complaints of actors mumbling their lines as they search for the ultimate in naturalism.) With theatrical performances I am always interested in how actors listen to one another. Do we feel the characters are hearing these words for the first time?

Aside from the performances, other aspects of a production require thought. It would be unusual not to give at least some indication of how the play or musical was staged, so considering stage design is important. Designers work very closely to achieve the director's vision and – certainly with more innovative work – their input can be crucial in shaping this vision. A set that works wonders within the limitations of a tiny space is as worthy of mention as the most spectacular revolving sets that light up a major musical.

See here how Andrezej Lukowski (2014) achieves such an example, writing about the National Theatre production of *The Curious Incident of the Dog in the Night-Time* which switched from its Cottesloe Theatre home to the West End:

> Bunny Christie's design was neat at the intimate Cottesloe, but blown up for a big stage it's awe-inspiring, her huge mathematical grid flaring with life at every turn: maps, cities, trains, constellations – the wondrous strange workings of Christopher's mind, pumped into something exhilarating by Adrian Sutton's electronic score.
>
> *(Lukowski 2014)*

Which brings us to music; either orchestrations or incidental music may be noteworthy alongside sound effects, costume and lighting. Elsewhere the theatre itself can sometimes provide an impetus for the critic in the sense of the feel that the space gives us, for example how it lends itself to a certain kind of production above others, or perhaps the effect that a new or refurbished building has on its community.

Critics of fiction, aside from points already discussed surrounding the context of the book, may want to concentrate their review in six key areas: story, character, use of language, emotion, the reader and point of view.

First, the story. What is this book about? Without giving everything away, what is the narrative that drives it forward and what are themes being addressed by the author? Even in a longer review, you will not have space – or inclination – to assess every character, but the main character, and possibly one or two others, will be of great importance. How are these people brought to life? Are they recognisable as being real? Who do you like/dislike and why? What makes these characters interesting (or not)?

Central to a work of fiction is the way the author uses language. Your job as a reviewer is to evaluate the prose for its style and richness. Does the novelist describe something familiar in a way you have never encountered before? Or does this sketch of a dark winter sky have a predictable ring to it? These long descriptions may be slow but we embrace them for their vividness and for the way they influence the pace of the narrative. Equally sentences might be snappy. Why is this so? Supported by a heavy leaning towards dialogue, this may be entirely appropriate for a fast-paced thriller about an innocent man on the run.

Who the book is for should also form part of your thinking – what kind of reader did the novelist have in mind? And what does she want them to feel? The emotional response to a book may be vital in deciding its success, as is the point or points of view chosen by the writer. A first-person approach would be, 'For ten years I wrote to you and tried to call you but got nothing in return. It was clear you wanted me out of your life.' A second-person point of view is, 'You ignored my letters and telephone calls for more than a decade. You made it quite clear you wanted me out of your life.' Third person: 'She ignored Diana's letters and telephone calls for ten years. It was clear she wanted her out of her life.'

First-person point of view is especially effective for intimacy, atmosphere and suspense. A second-person viewpoint is unusual, often associated with thrillers or literary fiction. Third-person point of view provides options, for example seeing through one character's eyes, multiple viewpoints where more than one character is the narrator or an omniscient point of view (in this approach the author sees and knows everything about all characters). The point of view may switch in a novel between first person and third person, and the critic should be aware of these techniques.

Music criticism is as much about feelings as it is about lyrics or melody; the emotions evoked in the reviewer should never be far from the core of the piece. In late 2015 a YouTube video surfaced in the news showing how a piece of classical music was making a young boy cry, a boy who had never heard such music before. Nothing could demonstrate the point so convincingly (see Anon. 2016).

Writing in the *New Yorker*, critic and journalism lecturer Amanda Petrusich (2016) says she repeatedly asks her classes how a song moves them and how it makes them feel. 'Sometimes a student will have to shift an album around in her life a little before she can really figure this part out: take it out for a walk, eat dinner with it, share it with a buddy.'

Recorded music – along with books and to some degree television and film, which are catching up – is a portable art form which influences when and where we listen to material. We cannot summon a company of actors to recreate their play for us in the second-class carriage of a train but the music you desire is just a few clicks away as you depart from the platform or, indeed, as you walk, drive, work or relax.

On the reader's behalf you are looking out for lyrics: what is memorable? Perhaps they are cryptic. What offers insight into the artist's state of mind? Perhaps the songs are linked thematically; either way, you should aim to discover how and why these songs were written, where they were recorded, whether the recording techniques used are interesting (especially to knowledgeable readers), who produced the tracks and – especially with solo artists known for experimenting with style and even personnel – who are the musicians featured on the tracks. If instruments were used beyond the ordinary, tell us about them and how they were utilised. Have other musicians influenced these songs? Ultimately, what is it about this music that you feel you have to share with your readers?

Notes

1 Lawson, Mark (30 August 2016), interview with the author.
2 McCormick, Neil (17 October 2016), interview with the author.
3 Vaughan, Megan (17 July 2016), interview with the author.
4 Alessandro Manzoni's 'three questions' for the critic (1819) are dealt with in Fisher (2015).
5 Lawson, Mark (30 August 2016), interview with the author.
6 Performing *Heroes* at Wyndham's Theatre, West End, in November 2005 Griffiths told a woman whose mobile phone had gone off for the third time, 'Is that it, or will it be ringing some more?' A similar problem had arisen the previous year while he performed *The History Boys* at the National Theatre.
7 Rogers, Jude (19 October 2016), interview with the author.
8 Mary Whitehouse, an art teacher, launched the Clean Up TV campaign alongside Norah Buckland, the wife of a Staffordshire rector, at Birmingham Town Hall in 1964 (Moran 2013). Asked what she thought of Kenneth Tynan's use of the F-word on a television programme about 18 months later, she replied that the critic should have his bottom smacked.
9 McCormick, Neil (17 October 2016), interview with the author.

References

Anon. (1 December 2016) 'A 2-year-old heard Beethoven's Moonlight Sonata for the first time, and his reaction will make you cry actual tears', *ClassicFM.com*, www.classicfm.com/composers/beethoven/news/2-year-old-beethoven-moonlight-sonata/.
Beaumont, Mark (15 June 2013) 'Tom Odell review, *Long Way Down*', *NME*, www.nme.com/reviews/album/reviews-tom-odell-14533#MckyYSovvfwzV017.99.
Billen, Andrew (7 September 2016) '*Motherland*, review', *Sunday Times*.
Billington, Michael (27 June 2013) '*Fences*, review', *Guardian*.
Bond, Matthew (14 August 2016) 'Second screen', *Mail on Sunday*.
Brown, Georgina Brown (6 November 2016) '*Amadeus*', *Mail on Sunday*.
Cavendish, Dominic (13 May 2016) 'Natasha J Barnes is every bit as good as Sheridan Smith in *Funny Girl*, review', *Daily Telegraph*, www.telegraph.co.uk/theatre/what-to-see/natasha-j-barnes-is-every-bit-as-good-as-sheridan-smith-in-funny/.
Coscarelli, Joe and Paulson, Michael (11 January 2016) 'David Bowie allowed his art to deliver a final message', *New York Times*.

Ellis-Petersen, Hannah (10 March 2016) 'Tom Conti defends Laurence Fox over heckler rant during play', *Guardian*, www.theguardian.com/stage/2016/mar/10/tom-conti-defends-laurence-fox-heckler-rant-theatre-the-patriotic-traitor.

Fisher, Mark (2015) *How to Write About Theatre*. London: Bloomsbury Methuen Drama.

Frankel, Eddy (2016) 'Yuri Pattison: User, Space', *Time Out*, www.timeout.com/london/art/yuri-pattison-user-space.

Gilbert, Jenny (16 December 2016) '*The Red Shoes*, Sadler's Wells', *The Arts Desk*, www.theartsdesk.com/dance/red-shoes-sadlers-wells.

Gill, Adrian Anthony (31 July 2016) 'And robot geeks shall inherit the earth', *Sunday Times*.

Hauser, Christine (10 August 2015) 'Benedict Cumberbatch to fans: No cellphones, please', *New York Times*, www.nytimes.com/2015/08/11/arts/benedict-cumberbatch-to-fans-no-cellphones-please.html.

Jays, David (11 December 2016) 'Hungary for love', *Sunday Times*.

Kellaway, Kate (1 January 2017) 'The dramatic force of farce', *Observer*.

Levitan, Corey (4 September 2016) 'Guns N' Roses rock Las Vegas reunion concert despite Axl Rose's broken foot', *Billboard*, www.billboard.com/articles/columns/rock/7326476/guns-n-roses-reunion-t-mobile-arena-axl-rose-broken-foot-slash-duff-mkcagan.

Long, Camilla (20 November 2016a) '*Fantastic Beasts and Where to Find Them*, review', *Sunday Times*.

Long, Camilla (13 November 2016b) '*American Pastoral*, review', *Sunday Times*.

Lukowski, Andrzej (July 2014) 'The National Theatre's joyously clever West End blockbuster', review of *The Curious Incident of the Dog in the Night-Time*, *Time Out*.

Mellor, David (30 October 2016) 'This Aussie has the nose for a hit!', *Mail on Sunday*.

Moran, Joe (2013) *Armchair Nation: An Intimate History of Britain in Front of the TV*. London: Profile.

Petrusich, Amanda (9 March 2016) 'The music critic in the age of the Insta-release', *New Yorker*, www.newyorker.com/culture/cultural-comment/the-music-critic-in-the-age-of-the-insta-release.

Purves, Libby (28 June 2013) 'Lenny Henry proves a tour de force: A great actor is born', *The Times*.

Rawlinson, Kevin (19 June 2013) 'Hello, *NME*? I'd like to complain about your Tom Odell review. Why? I'm his dad', *Independent*, www.independent.co.uk/arts-entertainment/music/news/hello-nme-i-d-like-to-complain-about-your-tom-odell-review-why-i-m-his-dad-8665499.html.

Rogers, Jude (26 May 2016) 'Bruce Springsteen and the E Street Band review: The magic and madness go on', *Guardian*, www.theguardian.com/music/2016/may/26/bruce-springsteen-e-street-band-review-etihad-stadium-manchester-river.

Shenton, Mark (10 September 2015) 'Hell's bells, switch off that phone', *The Stage*.

Titchener, Campbell B. (2005) *Reviewing the Arts*. Mahwah, NJ: Lawrence Erlbaum.

5

WRITING THE REVIEW

Part two

In the last chapter we highlighted the importance of opening your review, preferably made possible by a strong angle and an introduction that compels the reader to continue. These points are an essential requirement for effective reviewing for good reason, yet their impact is devalued if the rest of the article falls apart because of a weak structure. The kind of framework you choose for your review is at the core of this chapter, along with other important components such as language and developing your voice as a critic, and even the small matter of meeting that deadline.

Why structure matters

Structuring your review is to think about the beginning, middle and end; any form of storytelling (and your review is to a large extent the story of how you engaged with an artwork) requires a framework. For a moment let us go back to the beginning. You know about finding angles for your criticism, that key message that must be told – remember the example of shouting out to a friend across a busy street or, if you are the music critic Jude Rogers, her 'pub test' theory. Essentially it is the same thing: what's the *best* bit to say about this work?

The directness of your angle may be mirrored throughout your review, or you may adopt a more indirect approach. There are plusses and minuses for both.

Some reviews are direct, almost news-like in the way they are presented, following the pattern of an inverted triangle where information is revealed in a descending order of importance. In news-speak this is sometimes referred to as a WHAT triangle, where W stands for what happened, H for how it happened, A for amplify the facts so far and T will see the reporter tie everything up at the end.

In Larry Bartleet's review of *Fantastic Beasts and Where to Find Them*, written for *NME.com*, the technique for a direct statement is clear to see:

> Since this utterly delightful spin-off was announced in 2013, it's been anticipated as a grown-up answer to Harry Potter. In its unflinching approach to political and personal tragedy, grown-up it is – but in some ways J.K. Rowling's script will also be more enchanting to your inner kid than the Potter films ever were.
>
> (Bartleet 2016)

Immediately we are in no doubt that the critic is on side with the film – it is 'delightful' and it is at once grown-up and yet appealing to the child within, even more so than the original series of films.

It should come as no surprise to learn that Lynn Barber (2016), known for a searing honesty in her celebrity interviews, adopts a tell-it-like-it-is manner for her *Sunday Times* review of a new book about singer-songwriter Paul Simon. Check this out for a bold intro:

> Paul Simon is easy to admire, difficult to like, and this biography certainly doesn't help. It is basically a cuttings job dressed up in bewildering prose.

With this eye-popping start, Barber then structures her review in a simple, chronological order, gently pointing out that if we are fans of Simon then we will know this stuff anyway. Summarising the author, she describes where Simon grew up, his childhood meeting with Art Garfunkel and their musical partnership, stardom and simmering dislike for one another. We learn about disputes over copyright and Simon's complicated relationship with the actress and writer Carrie Fisher before this parting shot in the last paragraph:

> Simon is a fine musician so listen to his music rather than grappling with this wearisome book.

In short, Barber makes a statement about Paul Simon and observes that the book is not useful, develops an argument to support that claim and signs off with a similarly stinging sentence.

Compare the instant praise foisted upon *Fantastic Beasts* and the clear dislike of the biography with a different approach altogether. Sam Wollaston's structure for his *Guardian* review of ITV crime drama *Unforgotten* pulls us in – literally – with mystery and a great joke. Here is the intro:

> The River Lea, north-east London, and a dredger is doing its thing. Dredging. Oh dear, I think I know where it's going, this being the return of Chris Lang's crime drama *Unforgotten* (ITV). Yes, here's a suitcase, pulled from the mud after God knows how many years. The workers prise it open ... Jesus! Did you pack this yourself, sir?
>
> (Wollaston 2017)

He manages to establish some facts – the title, television network, name of writer and genre – as well as setting up the premise of the second series before he hits us with a rather risqué but clever punchline. But Wollaston's sense of urgency is different from the previous example. He wants us to take our time with his overview, confident we will stick with him.

Apart from one fleeting reference to the lead actors being 'excellent', Wollaston spends the next 325 words establishing two main points:

- that the groupings of characters whose lives we are introduced to (he briefly describes them) are apparently unconnected;
- that something emerges which shows there *is* a connection; it creates tension in the review and propels us to watch.

Only then, in the final two paragraphs, does Wollaston show his hand and tell us exactly what is on his mind:

> I like so much about *Unforgotten*. That it is not trying to be too smartarse (*Sherlock*?) clever. Or Scandi-bleak. Cassie and Sunny aren't tortured geniuses with dark secrets ... They are credible, real and, refreshingly, they are really into what they do ... I am excited to find out how it all weaves together, to see the completed picture. I also care.

From an opening where we are not sure which we way the critic will go, Wollaston's flippant demeanour gives way – if only momentarily – to something much more vulnerable. His approach, although indirect compared to the immediacy of Bartleet's review, is nonetheless well organised, there is nothing accidental about this structure. Williams (2014) may have visual art in mind but her advice is equally suitable for other forms of reviewing when she urges that 'logical order should be preserved at every level – a single sentence, a paragraph, a section, your whole text'. 'Prioritise information', she suggests, so that key information 'goes at the end, or front – don't bury it in the middle.'

Why language matters

Those of us who have been trapped in a room while a particularly dull work-based presentation muddles its way to a half-hearted conclusion via a checklist of clichés, unnecessary detail and painful in-house jokes will know the feeling. 'Thank you for listening: are there any questions?' Well, yes, why could you not have communicated this in a way that kept me engaged and saved me half the time? Why did you feel the need to tell me all that detail I neither understood nor will ever use? Like the presenter armed with PowerPoint, your job as a reviewer is to keep people reading by matching your terrific points of view in an impressive written style. Part of that deal is to get the language right.

Precision

Students who are inexperienced in writing about the arts can sometimes get frustrated with a common line of feedback on their work which asks, what does this *mean*? They kick themselves that they have left the sentence dangling, open to misinterpretation. They were so sure they had got it, but one crept through.

The reviewer's objective should be to write clear English. That is not a limited ambition, because it does not suggest she should *only* stick to simple sentence construction, devoid of any flourishes, or simple ideas for that matter, but it does encourage a fondness for precision. Precise writing is the key; readers are busy with many other choices of what to do in that moment and they will not wrestle with your clumsy prose.

Williams (2014) argues that twenty-first-century art is 'experiencing a phenomenal boom, with the demand for written accompaniment raised to fever-pitch'. Reacting to the explosion, more and more copy is being produced by critics, bloggers, editors, students, publicists, auctioneers and so on, and yet 'much contemporary art-writing remains barely comprehensible. Banal and mystifying art-writing is a popular target for ridicule', she writes.

Why should it be that way? Williams offers the proposition that the task of writing about this work is a more advanced task than is initially recognised. 'The cause of much bad art-writing is not so much pretentiousness, as is commonly suspected, but a lack of training.'

Failure to train may be one reason, but I would add to it an argument that 20 years' worth of words written worldwide online will also take their toll. Let me put that into perspective. While the Internet has enriched our lives, and hundreds of excellent websites and blogs have sprung up to cover the arts, some of the writing is lazy, error-strewn and disjointed. Space is limitless online. There are practitioners who take advantage of that with beautifully crafted long-form arts writing but others see it as an invitation to say even more, safe in the knowledge that the discipline required for print does not apply to them. I suspect they know, too, that readers are more forgiving of inaccuracy in online journalism than in print journalism.

Lazy writing

Notice how sometimes words and phrases have more than their fair share of attention. Overly used words are only noticeable to diligent readers. How many times have you noticed a reviewer attempting to engage you with a forced question, along the lines of 'You've probably been waiting for this film your whole life, right?' Or just as bad, 'This film's got the lot: a great story, beautiful people, incredible car chases and the best soundtrack you'll hear in a long time – what's not to like?'

Especially when writing to a deadline, it is easy to find yourself using these and other stock phrases. Avoid them.

Shortcuts and jargon

As a rule the more specialised the readership or audience, the more likely it is that the reviewer will use language to reflect that relationship. Niche audiences will pick up on shortcuts, which may come in the form of slang, jargon or knowing references to background or backstory.

One element of reviewing which can alienate readers is use of jargon. First, let's clear up the differences between technical language and jargon – the former is often necessary for any piece of arts writing that scratches beneath the surface. Jargon suggests a more negative connotation, and – unless the platform is deeply specialised – should be avoided. As can be seen from the following, among several similar comments on a forum on *Talk Classical* website, it is a trait that worries readers:

> Unfortunately some writers on music seem intent on using jargon that goes way above the heads of most listeners, even quite experienced ones. I'm not sure what's the reason, is it just being pretentious, e.g. trying to impress the reader with the writer's (supposed?) knowledge? Is it to shut some listeners out (e.g. elitism, highbrow attitude). I really don't know.
>
> *(Anon. 2012)*

Describing the moment

Quite the opposite of shutting people out, your potential to describe what you see and hear as a critic is a powerful tool and should be used to breathe life into your copy. When an art installation or a painting stops you dead in your tracks, what is it that you see, that you feel? When pop superstar Beyoncé has a crowd mesmerised by her talent, can it be described in a way that is both accurate but also fresh and inventive? It is here that the critic becomes important, both as eyewitness and as writer.

Precise writing based on a powerful experience can be a great system to truly engage your readers.

Williams (2014) sums it up as thus: 'Knowledgeable, unexpected use of language in response to a single, well-chosen artwork instantly elevates your writing out of the doldrums. Vague words, swirling aimlessly around an artwork, die on the page.'

To illustrate the point I have turned to Michael Billington, one of the most respected of all theatre critics, and someone particularly strong at reporting what he saw. His 2015 series for the *Guardian* website revisited what he felt to be the ten best performances he had seen on stage in a career spanning more than 50 years. At number nine on his list was Mark Rylance, a most exciting, charismatic actor, and the character study he chose was Rylance's Johnny 'Rooster' Byron in Jez Butterworth's brilliant play, *Jerusalem*. On the topic of the actor's physicality, this is how Billington saw it:

> Offstage, Rylance is a relatively slight man with delicate features. As Byron, he transformed himself into a strutting, muscular figure with the weight of a human cannonball.
>
> *(Billington 2015)*

I saw the production and agree that Rylance's physical transformation was fascinating. He wasn't just walking but 'strutting', Billington recalls, evoking the walk of a man completely in control of his land, but the description is doubly interesting because, married with 'muscular figure', it is as if the language itself is prancing across the page. This muscularity made Rooster not just heavy but having 'the weight of a human cannonball', suggesting recklessness or an unpredictable quality that is exciting to watch on stage.

It is a given that the best reviewing uses language in fabulously compelling ways; let us not forget that it is a critics' job to entertain if nothing else. Look at this playful sentence from Sarah Ditum, reviewing a new Jilly Cooper novel, *Mount!* The novelist is best known for her stories about the 'horsey rich':

> For ten novels now, she has extracted frothy, filthy entertainment from the lives of the rich and randy in the fictional (and fittingly named) county of Rutshire.
>
> *(Ditum 2016)*

A triple helping of alliteration in one sentence might not be to everybody's taste, but the world Cooper imagines is over-the-top anyway, and Ditum's response does not seem out of place. She does not stop there. Leading character Rupert Campbell-Black isn't just unfaithful to his wife but – as 'a magnetically caddish shagger' – his 'penis has slipped the straits of matrimony'.

In reviewing any artwork, strike the right balance in how much description to give. You want the reader to have a vivid sense of what you experienced, but, at the same time, not to the extent that they feel you have lived it for them. There is so much to think about. With music, say, you are not merely concerned with the sound but the feelings those lyrics and melodies produce. What about the way the song was made, including the instruments used? That guitar part at the core of the track: did the sound swell or soar? Think about the agility of the fretwork, a sense of urgency or anger. Did it sound dirty, clean or fuzzy? It was coming at us through the speakers – growling, maybe screaming; you get the idea. To tell us the guitar work was 'excellent' serves little purpose: in what way? By whose standards? What was it about the playing that so impressed?

Humour and wit

On the basis that arts reviewing is partly an entertainment, the facility to make the reader laugh or smile, to impress them with your wit, is one to be valued. It can go too far. The American theatre critic John Simon revealed in a 1997 interview with

Davi Napoleon (1997) in *Paris Review* that he had once gone overboard in a notice for *Stop the World I Want to Get Off*, starring Sammy Davis Jnr. 'If I say so myself, it was rather funny. The editors of New York passed it around to one another and all of them fell over in their chairs laughing, after which they said, "we can't print that".'

In descriptions, wit is often married with the words 'sharp' or 'razor-like' – a clue that it might cut through something, or *someone*. A thick skin may well be a requirement for an artist on the receiving end of your witty put-down – and of course there is a compelling argument that professionals are fair game. Over the years there have been wonderful moments of wit in print. Ned Sherrin brought many of them together in his book *Cutting Edge* (1984). Two are worthy of mention here. James Agee, dispatching a review of *Tycoon*, wrote that, 'Several tons of dynamite are set off in this picture – none of it under the right people'; while Sherrin reminds us that Robert Cushman in the *Observer* said of Peter O'Toole's Macbeth that 'his performance suggests that he is taking some sort of personal revenge on the play'.

Of course humour does not have to involve being cruel or funny at someone's expense. Your clever observation may bring a wry smile to the lips of the reader but harms no one. Your sense for the surreal has the reader laughing unexpectedly, but – once again – nobody gets hurt. Billington's account of new West End musical, *The Girls*, by Gary Barlow and Tim Firth, has a delightful play on words when Billington (2017) explains that 'the musical works beautifully because it suggests the calendar was a way of vanquishing private demons' – the well-known true story on which the film, play and (now) musical is based uses a Yorkshire Women's Institute naked charity calendar as its starting point. 'These women', Billington adds, 'strip to conquer', which works perfectly well for readers who are not aware of the Goldsmith play[1] and even better for those who are.

But with today's emphasis on online journalism and social media, it is no wonder that your funny comment about that big-for-his-boots novelist can have a life long after the review would normally pass its sell-by date. The temptation to do it is understandable. But what if you are upstaging the work of art you were asked to write about? What if you bump into that artist who was the butt of your joke the following week? The artist had it coming, you may say. And you may be right. In fact none of this may affect you in the slightest and you will do it anyway. Good luck with being funny!

Swearing

Any assessment of the language of reviewing will inevitably arrive at bad language – that is, to swear or not to swear. It comes down to three factors and, depending on who you write for, one of these factors or even all three of them will influence what you do:

- the tastes of your editor
- the values of your readers/listeners/viewers
- your own personal tastes.

Size or reputation or reach of the publication you write for is necessarily an indication of how far to push things. British middle-market newspapers are cautious in their use of swear-words, and certainly so in their arts and entertainment journalism. Red-top tabloids are similarly nervous of offending – despite a stereotype that they strive to do the opposite – while there is no such restraint in the more liberal quality press (at one time labelled 'the broadsheets' though it is no longer a straightforward description), such as the *Guardian* and the *Observer*. The *Independent*, now online-only since early 2016, would also fall into this category. In publications like these strong language – including the F-word – is far from compulsory but neither is it a rarity, and this especially applies to music reviews, where a critic may focus on lyrics or so-called banter between a singer and crowd at a gig. You can add theatre to that list as well, where critics may write about colourful language in the dialogue or even, on occasion, as part of the title: Mark Ravenhill's *Shopping and F******* a case in point.

Smaller-circulation magazines, especially those independently owned, and specialist titles aimed at lovers of rap or rock, for example, will have a liberal sprinkling of swear-words. Websites and blogs will tend not flinch at publishing swear-words. Video reviewers who swear at the camera bring another dimension to the debate, raising an interesting question as to whether hearing the word increases its impact versus the permanence of print.

As with using colourful language in any setting, the context is everything. I have no qualms about including 'bad' language in my reviews if it serves a purpose – such as a representation of the text – and as long as it fits within the editor's boundaries. If in doubt, ask if the word or phrase really adds something to your review. What would be lost if it wasn't included? Part of your job is to report, but there is always a line that can be crossed. Local newspapers would not thank you for the F-word you overheard in the fifth row of the am-dram you reviewed, but most readers understand that what causes outrage in the columns of the *Anytown Chronicle* would barely raise an eyebrow on *Death Metal Weekly*.

House style

If the website you have started writing for does not offer its style guide more or less straight away, then ask if they have one. An indication of how professional this outfit is can lie in the answer you are given. While the site may not pay its writers, if it wants to be taken seriously then it will have a style guide – even a basic one. The house style is the way a newspaper, magazine or website ensures there is consistency with English usage. Most obviously for critics this can involve the way titles of works are presented:

Harry Potter and the Philosopher's Stone
'Harry Potter and the Philosopher's Stone'
Harry Potter and the Philosopher's Stone.

All three are valid. There is no rule as such, simply to say that consistency is the most important point. Words like 'a', 'it', 'of', 'on', 'the' are not usually capitalised unless appearing at the start of a title or after a colon.

As with titles, dates can catch you out as well. Any choice from Monday 17 May 2013, to Monday, 17 May 2013, to Monday May 17, 2013 could be correct. You can add to that list a decision about eras. For example, take this sentence, '*The Secret Diary of Adrian Mole, Aged 13¾* was a publishing sensation in the 1980s.' Notice the plural use in the date; decades are plural, not possessive – no apostrophe is required. But if you were writing less formally about things that happened in that decade then it's a case of 'the 80s' or 'the Eighties'.

Job titles, at least those associated with the arts, are normally lower case. So we have 'director Stephen Daldry', 'producer Cameron Mackintosh' or the 'stage manager' or 'musical director'. But plays featuring a government scandal may include fictional representations of the 'Prime Minister' or 'Foreign Secretary'. (Note it was a *government* scandal, rather than something specific about those running the country right now – *the* Government.)

Acronyms, inevitably, will come into the critic's eyeline. The BBC and ITV need no special introduction when writing about television (and the same can be said about the RSC in theatre or MGM in the movies) but acronyms are usually spelled out, and at the first instance is best. Ultimately the target readership will be your guide in deciding what to do, but, as a quick overview, a specialist or quality publication will not feel the need to explain what ENO is, while a mid-market/generalised title will spell out that it is the English National Opera.

Some journalists find matters of style more accessible than others. How much should you know? As a freelance writer you ought to be aware of the basic requirements in style for the editor who commissions you. It is unrealistic to suppose you will be an expert in all of these systems, especially if you have half a dozen or more major clients, but the more you know, it will help the sub-editors and will do your reputation no harm. Check out some of the different style guides available online.

Style need not be a big deal, but it becomes one if the rules are not followed. Remember: consistency is king.

The voice of the critic

Imagine a squad of reviewers, locked up together for 13 weeks while they and their superiors see if they have what it takes. Unable to phone their parents and denied regular sleep, their schedule consists of round-the-clock talking about – and thinking about – the films they will see and the art galleries they will visit when they are ready to enter the 'field'. As we address elsewhere in the book, no training camp exists turning out ready-made reviewers fresh from the rigours of wall-to-wall arts criticism in theory. To become a confident, competent critic making a useful contribution to the arts world in which he operates, the reviewer must develop his style. Many articles or books on the subject will refer to this as finding your voice.

This involves accepting who you are as an individual – all of the things from your background that make you who you are, like your family, education and the way you were raised – and tapping into the character traits, beliefs and circumstances that apply to you now. It involves reading as widely as possible, not just in your specialised area if you have one but further afield, as well as different forms and styles. Clearly, you are going to be a writer so you had better be writing, ideally every day, and for aspiring reviewers wanting experience and exposure there is no excuse not to have a blog.

Individuality is very apparent in some of the best and most successful critics from the current time and from the past. Television reviewer Nina Myskow was one of the best-known journalists in Britain at the peak of her powers, having cultivated a style that did not always win her friends but certainly got her attention, not to mention a pay rise. More recently A.A. Gill, who shared his television reviewing duties for the *Sunday Times* with dining out as its restaurant critic, was – until his death in December 2016 – notorious for his scathing put-downs. The obituaries remind us of unjustified attacks on various actors and presenters but also the bother he got himself into as a food critic by not very nice things said about Cleethorpes or the Isle of Man.

Readers like the unpredictable nature of such writing ('what *has* he said *this time*?') and editors like it for commercial reasons – copy sales, clicks, advertising revenue built around it – but it is a fine line to tread. As with a star footballer worshipped for mazy runs and spectacular shots, his manager knows that the star player will sometimes give the ball away in crucial areas or even trip over his shoelaces. With greatness, comes risk.

Some may see this kind of voice in criticism as egotistical. Up to a point, perhaps it is. Fisher (2015) places Gill under the heading of critic-as-entertainer. Julie Burchill (pop culture) and Jeremy Clarkson (motoring) would also come into this bracket, he says. 'The pop culture, television and cars act as a jumping-off point for whatever else is on their minds. They are very present in their writing.'

The point about finding your voice is just that, in that you *find* it, you do not *manufacture* it. This is not like wearing a hat, you are not pretending to be someone. Nancy Durrant felt strongly about this when we spoke:

> You need to find your own voice. That takes time and you must not try to create it but identify it and then you might want to accentuate it, otherwise it's not really your own voice. As a critic you need it.[2]

First person or third person?

Critics are split on whether first or third person should take precedence in their reviews. As we saw in Chapter 2, the emergence of online reviewing – particularly blogging – has helped to shift the acceptance of the convention of the third person. A reluctance to break away from this style stems from the influence of news reporting, where the story matters most, way above and beyond who wrote it; indeed an afternoon spent in the archive room at a newspaper office will reveal the matter-of-fact way in which articles were presented in the past, very often anonymously or sometimes by 'Staff Reporter'.

Inexperienced student critics will, in their first week or two, insert the phrase 'I think' into their reviews but these words are struck out by the tutor with the comment that we, the readers, understand that you think this. Readers know it is part of the deal where you tell us some things that are on your mind. Sometimes reviewers avoid the decision altogether and adopt a second-person approach: 'You are taken into the darkest corners of the director's extraordinary imagination, and you are scared. You find yourself laughing nervously when…' But this is just annoying, and the readers will have rumbled you anyway.

Simplicity is best. Some reviews are best served by the critic keeping herself at a safe distance and offering an authoritative third-person notice. We are reminded of her skill, her insight, her sharpness of mind rather than any distraction surrounding the drink she knocked over in the interval. Being present in the review (the 'I' word: *I was moved*; *I was gripped*; *I woke up with a start thinking about this song*) is permissible – and can work very well – as long as it serves a purpose. The review is not about you.

In fact let us tweak that last statement: the review is not about you but you can be involved in it as long as it can be justified. It would appear that some television critics – more so than any other kind – think that their national newspaper column is a platform to talk generally about them. Reviewing three programmes per column is a popular format, but so many spend the first third of the page being side-tracked before getting to the main event, inevitably leaving less space for intelligent analysis of the work. Good ones are still out there, but too many rely on lazy anecdotes and cheap shots dressed up as something they are not.

As you flex your critical muscles, try writing two versions of the same review – one in the first person, the other in the third. Which one is more effective, and why? If your first-person response is a more genuine, satisfying read that helps you to be distinct in a noisy, crowded digital market then you may be on to something, otherwise a third-person review is a perfectly good solution.

Tense … and then relax

Ask an inexperienced group of students about the review they have just read as part of a class exercise and the majority of them will be unsure about which tense the text was in that they have just read. Perhaps that is a good thing – perhaps they were caught up in the quality of the journalism – but as they get more familiar with unpacking the components that go into making a review they will become increasingly rehearsed at spotting past or present tense.

Whether you opt for past or present will be coloured by who you are writing for, the art form you are covering and the effect you want to create. The popularity of present tense cannot be denied. There are good reasons why critics employ it, none more so than a feeling that the words carry you into the moment the art was created or even that the art is still current, as with a play where the production may run for a number of months. The natural immediacy that present tense offers the reviewer is a powerful tool, but a distinction should be made. Present tense is not a universal choice for arts criticism. Occasionally the past tense is preferred, and it can also be the case that a critic bounces between the two in the course of a single review.

One separation to be made is the distinction between live and recorded art, but even here the landscape is blurred. Live performance (theatre, dance, opera, comedy and concerts) sees a preference for the present tense. Examine *Mail on Sunday* music critic Tim de Lisle, in the thick of the action, reviewing a Pet Shop Boys gig (2016), where 'it begins with circles and lines dancing on a vast video screen, and slowly adds a third dimension to end up with big bouncing balloons and banks of lasers, wheeling through the air like starlings'. Or catch Dominic Maxwell in *The Times*, troubled by a comedy show in Edinburgh from spoof news reporter Jonathan Pie:

> It's outstandingly boring ... It's hard to see what the joke is, though. This is staged as a mock Children in Need charity event that John Barrowman has pulled out of. We duly sit through Pie doing links to camera, before turning to his captive audience and venting spleen at us. Why? It doesn't add up.
>
> *(Maxwell 2016)*

Then there is Nancy Durrant, in a woodland writing about sculpture. But hang on, is sculpture live? Visual art sometimes has a foot in both camps as far as live or recorded is concerned – the artwork itself may be permanent but here, in the woodland example, it is a changing experience for the visitor. The weather will change and so will nature, from the time that Durrant saw the exhibition in August, through to November when it was due to end. This is her reaction in the present tense:

> [Rania] Ho wittily references the location with her version of a public fountain – an unremarkable bucket that suddenly and unexpectedly bursts forth at odd intervals with a dramatic and completely out-of-proportion 20m gush of water.
>
> *(Durrant 2016)*

Books, films and albums – clearly permanent works of art, not living and changing – also stay in the present tense. Here is Melanie White, writing in the *Literary Review*, on Ann Patchett's novel *Commonwealth*:

> The book takes a good while to warm up. Patchett spends the first third of the narrative laying its foundations – a necessary evil, with so many characters to delineate – until she has built up enough material to be able to explore her central theme. This sense of delay is exacerbated by a surfeit of unnecessary detail.
>
> *(White 2016)*

As for the past tense, classical music concerts are an area where this preference is displayed. The *New York Times*, *Sunday Times* and *Daily Telegraph* all offer strong examples of critics who are most interested in what *did* happen – this may be reflected in the fact that the concerts are often one-off events but, in any case, there is a sense here of the critic calling on her skills and values as *reporter* as well as someone who delivers an opinion.

Sent to Hamburg in Germany for the opening of a brand-new concert hall, the *New York Times* writer Corinna da Fonseca-Wollheim (2017) reports that the inaugural concert 'opened with the slender, pliable tone of a single oboe – the instrument to which other players tune in halls around the world'. While present tense fits perfectly with theatre, the authority that past tense lends itself to the world of classical music seems equally sensible.

And so to television reviewing, which is consistently inconsistent when it comes to a choice of tense. At the *Los Angeles Times*, Lorraine Ali favours present tense while looking at dark British drama *Taboo*, but past tense is the preferred route for many writers, including Deborah Ross at the *Mail on Sunday*, while specialists at *The Arts Desk* are among a band who utilise both within a single review. As someone who wrote regularly for this well-regarded website for about a year, the style takes some adjusting to but, once learned, works very well; one of the benefits is that it reminds you – the writer – not to dwell for too long on plot development. Essentially the system works like this: if it is drama, for instance, refer to plot development in the present tense and your reactions to the show in the past.

As with any point involving style, most readers will be blissfully unaware of every nuance to your work, but you will be, as will other professionals and some readers engaged at a deep level. Consistency matters most.

Too good, too bad: the dangers of extreme reviewing

Several of the critics I spoke to report that the majority of artworks they experience sit somewhere in the middle when it comes to quality. Here is music critic Dave Simpson:

> I find that there is less truly great music and less truly dire music being made. There is plenty at the middle. In practice, this means lots of three-star reviews, and less opportunity to see/hear challenging/strange/awful music.[3]

A potential consequence of this is the temptation for reviewers to go overboard with work at either end of the spectrum, perhaps to get more people clicking through to their page or even as an antidote to the perceived monotony of three-star experiences. Good, responsible reviewers will evaluate the work truthfully as they see it; to do otherwise risks their integrity and leaves them vulnerable to attack. Here are some points for you to look out for when you go red hot or icy cold.

Outstanding work should be labelled as such. Particularly if you are going against the grain of what your peers may think, your endorsement leaves you a little more exposed than you were before – but how dull the world would be if every reviewer was in agreement. It is exciting when a critic falls in love on the page; it happens on rare occasions, so enjoy it.

Some of the work you see will not make the grade, and you need to say that to your readers. But again be wary of how far you push your dislike for the piece. Let us be honest, it is easier to stick the boot in than to provide balanced insight into the failings – and successes – of a piece of work. Deadlines can be a factor in how you respond. A heat-of-the-moment review penned an hour after seeing a live show might be recalibrated were you to write it the following morning.

Be prepared for your killer lines to be lifted and used in unexpected ways. Watch your words being recycled in front of your very eyes in newspaper adverts, on Facebook, on Twitter, on publicity profiles created by agents or public relations professionals and even on the sides of buses. In fact, as you grow more accustomed to the practice you will even be able to predict the lines that are borrowed.

Critics reviewing live events face an entirely different challenge. Although impractical to quiz each member of the audience on what they thought, these critics will at least get some sense of the feeling of the crowd – a feeling denied the reviewer of a book, for instance, who will not read the pages in unison with 50,000 others. Press nights at the theatre can foster a giddy reaction in the stalls, especially with comedies and musicals. The excitable crowd can partly be explained by fans of the show being there – for example with a musical that attracts a hard-core following like *Legally Blonde* or *Wicked* – and by friends and family of the performers, always willing to cheer more wildly or laugh a little louder along the way. Their reaction should not influence yours, but it is worth bearing in mind before you say too much about that 'first-night standing ovation'.

Star ratings

It seems that people interested in the arts who least like star ratings are the people who apply them. As shorthand, the star rating system is a great device: using a minimum of space it offers an eye-catching summary of an artwork. Readers find star ratings user-friendly, editors tolerate them and PR executives lap them up when there are enough of them to shout about. Four stars bring happiness and relief; five stars open up a whole new set of possibilities. Three is a matter of perception: artmakers on the receiving end talk of it in terms of 'only' three, whereas the reviewer, weighing up the level of ambition with the work for instance, may see it as a positive. One or two stars? Suddenly the critic is irrelevant and had better prepare because they will come under fire online and on Twitter.

But reviewers often find that the need to think in terms of stars is rather restrictive – or that too much energy is required for something quite shallow. Is this a three-star performance in a four-star show? Sometimes you will read a review that has the hallmarks of a four-star experience but only three to show for it – or vice versa.

While readers understand the clear signals that a one-star or five-star notice brings, the borderline territory of three continues to confuse. Some would believe it to mean 'good', others might say it is an 'average' presentation, and this is where the critics themselves get frustrated. A brand-new musical, an experimental album that is a departure from what the artist would normally do may 'only' garner three stars but, given the extent of the ambition, three is arguably an endorsement that this is worth seeing/hearing; it is not *perfect* but the strengths outweigh the weaknesses.

Fisher (2015), from the perspective of a drama critic, suggests the review itself could play against the stars, accentuating any positives in a two-star notice or highlighting weaknesses where four have been awarded. His rule of thumb, that the number of stars should represent the quality of the *production* where a revival of a play is concerned, and the quality of the playwright's *ideas* in relation to a new play, is an excellent suggestion for theatre, opera and dance but would be less effective with other art forms: books are reviewed only the once, for example, upon publication and a similar situation exists with film.

The perception that three stars equates to something rather average or only reasonably good is unfortunate, and is not helped by a lack of definitions published in review sections. *The Stage* does do it, but this is unusual.

The ubiquity of star ratings means that any break from this format is instantly interesting. One novel approach is that from YouTube film reviewer Catherine Reitman whose Breakin' It Down channel uses variations on her surname to indicate her reaction to a movie ('Reit On', 'So Wrong It's Reit', etc.). Elsewhere Libby Purves's blog *theatreCat* has fun with the name by awarding mice instead of stars.

Press 'send': the final piece of the review jigsaw

For all the watching, listening, thinking and talking you will do about the artwork you have experienced, ultimately only one thing matters and that is to submit your review to the right person at the right time.

Ideas will come to you as you watch or read or listen to whatever you are reviewing, but those ideas are not fully formed yet. Only in the process of writing do you fully work out what you think. So what happens next? After a concert or play, you are likely to have a car or train journey home, and therefore time to reflect – though not long. National critics often write on the train, whereas music reviewers may even write into their phones while the gig is still in progress. Either way, even if there is a print outcome for what they do, most reviews of live performance will be online by midnight or by 10am the next day.

That is the case for theatre reviews I have done for *WhatsOnStage*. To compare, I have been given a couple of weeks to read hefty non-fiction for the *Daily Express* and a week's or a few days' warning to write up a television show for *The Arts Desk*. How long do other critics get to craft their latest assignment? Mark Lawson, former BBC Radio 4 presenter, combines television essays and reviewing for the *Guardian* along with features and obituaries. He said:

Very occasionally I will still review a heavily embargoed final episode or controversial show 'live off-air' for *Guardian* news which, we should always remember, is how the pioneers of our profession, in the time before video-recording, did all their work.

For one of those rare live overnight reviews – or an unexpected obituary – I would have as little as 45 minutes and never much more than 90 minutes. When the deadlines are more known or leisurely, I ideally like to spend four to six hours on a piece of 1,000–1,200 words. Ideally I write at home, but deadlines are destiny. I wrote a 2,000-word obituary of Sir Terry Wogan either sitting on the floor of a train, or in a station café at Manchester, while returning from doing a theatre review in Leeds.[4]

Neil Norman takes an opposite view and avoids writing at home where possible. The *Daily Express* and *Stage* critic favours study areas or cafés at London libraries and museums, and has no issues about producing work in public spaces. He said:

> For an overnight review I will probably make notes on the Tube on my way home and then write it up immediately. For a dance review I usually have until 9am the morning after the show so I would set it up the night before and do a first draft then polish it in the morning … I do a quick first draft without referring to my notes then check my notebook for any salient details before doing a final edit. I would try and get a review of 350 to 400 words completed in an hour or 90 minutes. On rare occasions I have managed to write one in under 15 minutes though I wouldn't recommend it.[5]

The rock and pop journalist Neil McCormick talks in Chapter 8 about his almost improvised method of working with live reviews, but here he describes those moments when, essentially, the review is done but there are still passages to iron out, phrases with which to tinker. I worked once with a colleague who found it difficult to let go of the copy he wrote (in those days it was a case of physically printing a document and filing it in a tray). His hand would hover over the basket until, finally, the paper dropped from his grasp; then, ten minutes later, he would be back, ferreting among a now bigger pile of stories as there was just 'one more thing' he needed to check. This merry little dance could go on all day if somebody didn't stop him.

McCormick's concern to get it right is healthier and warranted, given the size of the task, his readership and the pace at which he is working. He likes to sit somewhere at the end of a gig and 'write and shift sentences about' but inevitably finds himself being moved on by staff looking to clear the venue; that few minutes of head-space is vital in order to firm up his thoughts.

> Then I'll press send and, of course, immediately regret it and think there is something else I could have said, or a way to put it better. When I get home, I read it back online and often find myself thinking, wow, that gig sounds great, I wish I'd been there.[6]

Anyone who has ever written to be published can take heart from McCormick's point that a better version of the sentence might present itself the next morning. Too bad. Perfect journalism does not exist because a deadline is never too far away, and arts journalism is no different. Whether you are given two hours, 12 hours or a few days to produce your review, you have to deliver.

Practice does not make perfect, but it certainly helps you improve. Simple, logical steps will help you establish a system to deliver your work on time, and to a professional standard:

- an angle that drives your review forward, gives it a sense of purpose;
- an intro that catches the reader's eye: a surprising statement, unusual image, sense of intrigue, clever observation, perhaps;
- a clear viewpoint (even if your feelings are mixed on the quality of what you experienced; at least argue the good and the bad);
- an understanding of what was being attempted and, ultimately, whether it reached that level;
- an opinion rooted in fact; journalistically it must be sound – this happened, these people took part, this exists and so on;
- a use of English free from error and clutter;
- a determination to write something that will make your readers think, and entertain them too.

Keen students of criticism can improve their craft so easily now. Blogging, to name one example, provides a platform to post a review two or three times a week if they wish. With so much content on the Web, it is a straightforward exercise to watch a television programme, listen to a new album or read a book and then compare your review to that of others on a range of platforms and in differing styles.

Is yours as good as or of a similar standard to the best? What works in your version? What are its weaknesses? Which talking points did the reviewer come up with that you overlooked? How did they use language, vary the pace? Repeat the exercise many times until your writing becomes clearer to read and more fluent to produce. Step out of your comfort zone and review styles, genres and even art forms that are not your first choice. Notice how techniques borrowed from book reviews can inform your television criticism and vice versa.

And then just write, and write some more. Some reviews will come more naturally than others, the ideas and the words flying from your brain to the keyboard; others need to be cajoled but you will get there. Inspiration may get you started; thereafter it is you, your computer and a commitment to finish. Whatever happens, make a start. A blank page is in no hurry.

As Neil McCormick says:

> There is no such thing as writer's block. It's a fiction invented by fiction writers, a glorified name for procrastination (even if it feels real to the individual crippled by it). Journalists write for a living and work to deadlines. In all my

years in this profession, I have never, ever heard of a journalist saying to his or her editor, 'Sorry, can't get the copy in today, I've got writer's block.' When in doubt, just start writing. One word after another. That's the way you get things done.[7]

Notes

1 *She Stoops to Conquer*, Oliver Goldsmith, 1773.
2 Durrant, Nancy (7 September 2016), interview with the author.
3 Simpson, Dave (27 July 2016), interview with the author.
4 Lawson, Mark (30 August 2016), interview with the author.
5 Norman, Neil (27 July 2016), interview with the author.
6 McCormick, Neil (17 October 2016), interview with the author.
7 *Ibid.*

References

Anon. (4 January 2012) 'Musical jargon', *Talk Classical* website, www.talkclassical.com/17316-musical-jargon.html.
Barber, Lynn (20 November 2016) 'Not so simple Simon', *Sunday Times*.
Bartleet, Larry (14 November 2016) '*Fantastic Beasts and Where to Find Them*, review', *NME.com*, www.nme.com/reviews/movie/fantastic-beasts-and-where-to-find-them-review.
Billington, Michael (13 April 2015) 'Great performances, Mark Rylance in *Jerusalem*', *Guardian*.
Billington, Michael (21 February 2017) '*The Girls* review, Gary Barlow gives *Calendar Girls* a classy musical makeover', *Guardian*, www.theguardian.com/stage/2017/feb/21/the-girls-review-gary-barlow-calendar-girls-phoenix-theatre.
da Fonseca-Wollheim, Corinna (13 January 2017) 'The first concert at the New Elbphilharmonie in Germany', *New York Times*.
De Lisle, Tim (31 October 2016) 'West End swirls', *Mail on Sunday*.
Ditum, Sarah (September 2016) 'Horse play, review of *Mount!* by Jilly Cooper', *Literary Review*.
Durrant, Nancy (26 August 2016) 'Plugged in to new Chinese art', *The Times*.
Fisher, Mark (2015) *How to Write About Theatre*. London: Bloomsbury Methuen Drama.
Maxwell, Dominic (26 August 2016) 'Edinburgh comedy: Jonathan Pie', *The Times*.
Napoleon, Davi (1997) 'John Simon. The art of criticism, no. 4', *Paris Review* (Spring), issue 142, www.theparisreview.org/interviews/1282/john-simon-the-art-of-criticism-no-4-john-simon.
Sherrin, Ned (1984) *Cutting Edge*. London: J.M. Dent.
White, Melanie (September 2016) 'Private lives, review of *Commonwealth* by Ann Patchett', *Literary Review*.
Williams, Gilda (2014) *How to Write About Contemporary Art*. London: Thames and Hudson.
Wollaston, Sam (6 January 2017) '*Unforgotten* review: For once, a crime drama that avoids being *Sherlock*-clever or Scandi-bleak', *Guardian*.

6
THE IMPACT OF CRITICISM

The anger in his voice was plain to hear. In May 1956 the theatrical impresario, Jack Waller, addressed a congregation of actors, backstage staff and showbusiness peers to celebrate the 500th performance of his production of Philip King's smash-hit farce *Sailor, Beware!*. But what should have been a joyful occasion at the Strand Theatre in London turned on its head when Waller took a swipe at what he saw as the enemy – the critics. His outburst was in reference to his other show which had opened in town only a few days before. *Wild Grows the Heather*, a musical based on a J.M. Barrie play, had effectively been beaten up in print.

Perhaps Waller's own input as co-writer of the music was partly behind his bad mood, but either way he took aim: 'They don't want the theatre to live', he said, as reported in *The Stage* on 17 May. 'These critics, who come along and stab the theatre in the back and are allowed to say what they like have no love for the theatre.'

The phrase 'allowed to say what they like' possibly suggests his deeply buried view of the artsmaker–reviewer hierarchy. *Wild Grows the Heather* opened on 3 May at the London Hippodrome, and its critical kicking – *The Stage* itself labelled the show old-fashioned and corny in its 10 May review – was in stark contrast to the excitement surrounding John Osborne's *Look Back in Anger*, which premiered only five days later. Again, perhaps this stoked his mood. While praise was by no means unanimous for the groundbreaking Royal Court play, at least critics found it interesting and new. Waller was furious that his show was apparently loved by the first-night audience, 'but the critics I am speaking of hadn't the decency to acknowledge even that'.

Waller's attack did not go unchallenged. Responding with a letter in the next edition, drama critic Stephen Williams argued:

> I am amazed at a seasoned impresario falling back on such outworn and childishly nonsensical abuse. Does Mr Waller seriously believe that a man

would spend three or four nights each week of the best years of his life in the theatre, studying every aspect of its art … if he had no love for the theatre? Does Mr Waller seriously believe that a critic, who depends on the theatre for his income and for the major part of his enjoyment in life, wishes it to die?

(Williams 1956)

The critic's job, he went on, was 'to encourage with all his might those who serve the theatre worthily and to attack those who degrade it', before pointing out the irony of Waller's comments being made at a party celebrating 500 performances of a West End success: 'He was not reported to have thanked the critics for their share in the success of that play. Of course not: if a show fails it is because of the critics; if it succeeds, it is in spite of them.'

Wild Grows the Heather closed after just 28 performances.

The story illustrates the emotional pull of presenting and judging any kind of art form, particularly when people's livelihoods and reputations depend on it. While it is unlikely that the situation would have been managed in quite the same way today – imagine the terror on the publicity agent's face as the modern impresario launches into their attack – the sentiments are, I am sure, not too far adrift from how some recipients of criticism still feel. Why is this person judging me and my work? What qualifies them to do so? Why is the enjoyment of everyone else present not being reported? Yet Williams's response typifies the thankless task of the critic, hinting at a lack of appreciation and even the often-heard jibe that if they were any good at whatever it is they appear to be pronouncing judgement on then they'd be doing it, wouldn't they?

In publishing your work, the critic or blogger takes a precarious walk on a tightrope. One false move and the dangers are a-plenty: sensitive artists, angry agents and managers, outraged fans convinced you will fall. And if you do stumble then you, the walker, will hope to hang on with the help of an editor or simply your own strength and determination. In this chapter we will look at the impact of critical judgement in a 360-degree setting – on the makers and producers of art, the productions and projects they represent, the public, the brands the reviewer is writing for and even the effect on the critics themselves.

For much of the time arts criticism goes about its business without incident. Projects are experienced, critics evaluate them and publish or broadcast and everyone survives until the next time, in part because the bulk of reviewing is underpinned by a five-star system (where one is terrible and five truly exceptional) and most of *these* fall into the three- or four-star category. As we discovered in Chapter 5, three stars indicates a solid or fairly good experience with some reservations and, even when stars are dispensed with altogether, we can often read between the lines in surmising how many would be awarded if the critic were to employ them. A four-star recommendation is clearly good news for all involved and would have genuine value for the future life of a project, but this chapter is most concerned with matters at either end of the spectrum, the glowing tributes or the dire warnings to avoid something at all costs.

The impact of criticism continues to be felt nowadays just as it ever has. While the means of publishing that information may have stretched beyond the wildest dreams of twentieth-century critics and the power of an elite few may have been diluted across many additional voices, the weight of a bad review is still keenly felt. I will be looking at exceptional cases where artists react in extreme ways to what is written about them. Also under the spotlight will be art that was immune to negative press.

Tradition would have it that reviewers saw the work of art, went away to write with what Olivier described as their 'inky swords' (Olivier 1987) and the poor wreck of an artist would be left to ponder his fate. If this seems a somewhat romanticised version of events, then Michael Caine's memory may have us think again, for he shares with us the feeling that that sense of trepidation was *exactly* how it was. The signs were not good. Following the Leicester Square premiere of *The Ipcress File*, Sidney J. Furie's 1965 film in which Caine starred, the actor had been recognised outside the cinema by a stranger who had been in the picture house and who yelled at Caine that the film was 'crap'.

Caine went home, he writes, drank a lot and awoke at dawn 'not with a start but a tremor of fear, as I knew I would have to face the day of the critics'. He went out and bought all the papers from his nearest news-stand and brought them home.

> The first review I read was a stinker. My future sank over the horizon. But miraculously, the next one was good, and my future started to dawn again almost immediately. The one after that was marvellous – and so on and so on.
> As I was reading the critics, a strange thing started to happen to me. I suddenly found myself sobbing uncontrollably … the years of stress, anger and pent-up frustration started to flow out of me in the form of tears.
> *(Caine 1992)*

In 1965 Caine was not yet a household name so, why would a rising star of the British cinema care two hoots what a critic says? And more than 50 years later, why do these things still matter in a media saturated world? 'I could never understand why someone would care if I criticised their performance. Why would they care about what I said?', Nina Myskow told me, omitting the small detail of a readership running into many millions.[1]

Context is everything. Some artists are genuinely able to shrug off negative reviews. It may be an unshakeable belief in what they are doing, it may even be tempered by the hefty cheque they have pocketed. Professional artists at all levels in terms of fame, talent and pay scale are at work, and most of us know how it makes us feel if something is said or written about us at work that is critical. It stings. It can be embarrassing or even humiliating. Even if the criticism is justified, it can be hard to take.

In the firing line of the critics

It is striking to see how individuals react to negative criticism ranging from the mild observation to the harshest, cruellest jibe. Staying with Myskow, she remembers one of her reviews taking aim at Bob Monkhouse, the television star as much noted for presenting game shows like *Opportunity Knocks* and *The Golden Shot* as he was as one of the wittiest stand-up comedians around. Monkhouse was greatly admired, especially by comedians themselves, who appreciated his quick mind, but he never won unanimous approval from the British public. 'Bob Monkhouse once sent me an ironic bunch of flowers', she revealed. 'I'd said in a piece that he was unnecessarily smarmy – so that was his response!'[2]

Sadly, Stephen Fry reacted quite differently after opening in the 1995 West End production of *Cell Mates*, a spy drama by Simon Gray. The play opened at London's Albery Theatre for what should have been a 16-week run but closed early after poor reviews and Fry's departure after just three performances. Fry's walkout, citing stage-fright and his failings as an actor, took a further twist when he suddenly disappeared, fleeing – as it turned out – to Belgium and attracting a storm of media attention. Years later he would reveal he had seriously considered suicide during this horrid episode and that his eventual return from Bruges would result in his being diagnosed bipolar.

The thrust of those poor reviews was to ponder why Gray had bothered to write the play at all and how Rik Mayall was proving to be a more dynamic actor than his co-star. Writing in the *Guardian*, Michael Billington (1995) argued that 'Mayall proves himself much the better actor', adding that Fry's character study of 'lofty, smiling superiority' was both predictable and difficult to believe in. Fellow critic Michael Coveney (1995), for the *Observer*, went even further: 'Each time I see Fry, I assume he is trying to sell me something. Or tell me something such as: "I don't read newspapers, they're all toilet paper" … His acting, to put it generously, makes no further inroads on our sympathies.'

A few days after Fry had taken flight, the *Guardian* claimed that Coveney's toilet paper reference was in response to a comment the star had made in the run-up to opening night, saying that insensitive journalists made celebrities cry and that reading a newspaper was 'like opening a piece of used lavatory paper'. The same article (Chaudhary & Ellison 1995) offered a psychologist's perspective that bad reviews for the play and for his television show, *A Bit of Fry and Laurie*, were 'a shock, a double whammy' before reporting the contents of the recording Fry had left on his answering machine at his London flat: 'Please leave a message – unless you are a journalist, in which case you can fuck off.'

If the letters page of *The Stage* (2 March 1995) was anything to go by during Fry's disappearance and what was quite clearly a serious health issue, it was that the theatrical community was undecided on how to respond. One writer felt great sympathy for Stephen Fry, another cited how he had been spotted smiling in a queue for refreshments in France and another rather cruelly taunted, 'did those nasty little critics upset the poor dear!'.

In May 2016 an enormous fuss surrounded the relaunch of BBC Two's global phenomenon *Top Gear*, said to pull in £50 million a year through worldwide sales when controversial presenter Jeremy Clarkson was behind the wheel. But Clarkson and his pals had gone to make another show for Amazon Prime, instead leaving the engine running for Chris Evans to clamber into the car.

Evans, an inventive broadcaster and self-confessed car nut, would have known better than most what to expect but even he must have been taken aback by the intensity of coverage even before the show was aired. Rumours had escalated of behind-the-scenes bust-ups, pointing increasingly to a narrative that this version of *Top Gear* would not measure up.

Television critics had their say on the new-look show in the hours following transmission of the first episode on Sunday, 29 May 2016 and in the next morning's newspapers. 'Rarely has a debut attracted such great expectation, indeed hope, of failure', Andrew Billen's two-star review began in *The Times* below a page 3 headline that read 'New-look *Top Gear* treads too hard on the loud pedal'.

The *Daily Mirror* asked, 'So was it *Flop Gear*?' in its front-page promotional panel, supported by a picture of Evans with the words, 'The verdict on L-plates Evans'.

Page 13 of the *Mirror* had the best of both worlds – a news story headlined 'Bump start: Revamped *Top Gear* takes a battering from loyal viewers' (Watts 2016) and a review by Ian Hyland (2016). While Hyland's take is largely a positive one, the news story written by assistant showbiz editor Halina Watts is essentially a round-up of what viewers like 'Ali' and 'Angela' said on Twitter. 'Poor man's Clarkson' and 'I can't stand Chris Evans' are two of the four negative tweets reported, ahead of a couple of complimentary tweets at the end of the story.

The *Sun*'s approach was similar – an 'exclusive' news story on page 11 (Farrell & Kisiel 2016) featuring six tweets bashing the show along with a quote from 'a source' claiming co-presenter Matt LeBlanc will not return for another series, plus a seven-paragraph review by its in-house television critic Ally Ross – but went further with the puns, opting for '*Plop Gear*' as its headline.

Oddly, while the *Guardian* in print published its verdict on *Top Gear* in the following morning's issue, Sam Wollaston (2016) relied on 'access to a couple of sections of it pre-transmission' rather than wait for the show to be aired and write about it in full.

The same cautious approach was not afforded by the *Daily Mail* or *Daily Telegraph*, which both published reports and reviews across the whole of page 7 and page 3 respectively. Content borrowed from social media again provided the impetus for the reporters. Newsdesks like the convention of a Twitter round-up because it does what the traditional vox populi did, but with many advantages – the reporter does not have to leave the building (vox pops required a journalist to stand on a busy street corner until they had bagged half a dozen quotes or whatever their news editor instructed); the reporter can begin writing their story while the programme is still on air; hundreds or thousands of tweets suddenly become potentially of use. Tweets from the public are not restricted by an embargo, either.

In terms of reviewing, Quentin Letts did the honours for the *Mail* (2016) and Gerald O'Donovan for the *Telegraph* (2016). Letts was the less impressed. 'The motoring show, as you may have heard, has changed its three former presenters', he quipped, in a nod to the aforementioned media meltdown surrounding the new series. 'It all felt a little middle-lane and underwhelming', he went on, while O'Donovan's piece was labelled a four-star review but read like a three-star review in tone ('this relaunch was actually much too cautious and unimaginative').

Five weeks after the opening episode had culminated in disappointing reviews and viewing figures that had dropped from 4.4 million to around 1.9 million, Evans announced he was standing aside and would not be making another series.

The dud, the bad and the ugly

News reporters do not sit at their desks wishing for nothing to happen. Their professional well-being depends on the misfortune of others, as 'motorway traffic moves smoothly' and 'shoppers queue without incident for goods at knockdown prices' is not going to get hits on their website, and so it is the same for critics. Reviewers will require a 'car crash' every so often, if only for purposes of variety.

Film critic Mark Kermode wrote a whole book – *Hatchet Job* (2013) – whose premise was the cause and effect of publicly judging a movie, while *Daily Mail* critic Christopher Tookey produced *Named and Shamed* (2010), a compendium of savagery in the film writing business resplendent with a photo of a turkey on the front cover. Kermode writes: 'For all the movies I love and praise and try to get people to be enthusiastic about, it's the ones I hate that people remember ... Sometimes listeners to the BBC Radio 5 Live *Film Review* show actually get disappointed if I don't get angry enough', he writes, adding that 'being entertainingly negative can help a critic build their career and make a name for themselves in what remains a cut-throat profession' (2013, 4, 15).

Readers expect to trust critics, and part of that contract is to be told directly when the art isn't working.

Spats, attacks and threats of violence

Of course, all of this so far supposes that reviewers deliver their 'judgements' and the artists they have written or spoken about simply accept this without reply. As we will see in Chapter 8, the Internet has changed the game when it comes to engagement between artist, critic and consumer, and its importance cannot be overstated in relation to an artist defending his work or launching a counter-attack of his own. The capacity for emotional reactions has always been there, it is just that the technology makes it so much easier. Compare the following: an author spends two years writing a book which is, in his eyes, unfairly represented in a critic's review. A twentieth-century outcome may have been a telephone call of complaint or a letter to the reviewer or their editor. Both require some degree of effort and can be abandoned right up to the point of hanging up the receiver or stopping short of putting that brilliant letter in the post box, whereas now – in the heat of the moment – an email can be fired off and an angry outburst can be tweeted or shared on his Facebook page.

Critic Neil Norman has adapted to the instant engagement which comes from digital media but, having written professionally since the early 1970s, remembers the cut and thrust of a pre-digital journalism. He has been threatened with legal action, been verbally attacked and has had a punch thrown at him by an irate recipient of one of his reviews (he ducked), but advises always stay cool under pressure. He said:

> On another occasion I ran into the director of a movie I had described as 'watching a Rolls-Royce collide with a tower block', or something like that. He recognised me and said: 'I was the driver of the Rolls-Royce', to which I replied: 'Well, I am glad to see that you are healing nicely.'[3]

None of this is to suggest that threats of violence are, or were, the norm for your average reviewer, but the rock 'n' roll antics of rock 'n' roll writers at the *NME* along with a book blogger whose 'wronged' author drove hundreds of miles to attack her do stand out – and not for the right reasons. Pat Long's deliciously atmospheric history of the *NME* is quite clear on the rock and pop community's way of settling differences. Long (2012) reports how a music manager and two heavies turned up at the office to chastise a journalist for writing a negative review, while Charles Shaar Murray told her how he was threatened by an affronted band, was thrown out of the Rolling Stones' dressing room on the orders of Mick Jagger and, in another episode, sent rotting pig brains in a brown-paper parcel having been critical of two record producers and their work on a pop song.

Book reviewer Paige Rolland was given no chance to avoid the physical attack on her after she criticised an author's efforts. Paige, from Scotland, was just 18 years old when the astonishing assault on her made headlines across the world. She had been uncomplimentary about a book, *The World Rose*, posting on a website called *Wattpad* which invites writers to upload their work in return for its members being able to read and critique the work.

Her attacker, Richard Brittain, the author of the book, had already made a name for himself by winning on *Countdown*, a long-running quiz show on British television which tests a contestant's ability to solve word and number puzzles. But a Glasgow court was told in December 2015 that in October of the previous year, Brittain traced Miss Rolland via Facebook and drove 400 miles from his home near Bedford to Glenrothes in Fife, specifically to the Asda supermarket store in which she worked. Brittain took a bottle of wine from the alcohol section and, without speaking, smashed it over the head of Miss Rolland who was kneeling down beside a shelf in the cereal aisle. She was knocked unconscious and treated in hospital.

Brittain, who had apologised to his victim and who pleaded guilty to assault, was jailed for 30 months. Miss Rolland told the *Daily Mirror*, cited in the *Daily Mail* (McAnally & McLelland 2015) following Brittain's guilty plea, that she had been changed by the attack, and complained of feeling fearful and nervous of meeting new people.

While he did not take out his frustrations on any one individual, Turner Prize-winning artist Douglas Gordon had a unique response to a poor reception to the play he directed as part of the Manchester International Festival, *Neck of the Woods*, which was loosely based on the *Little Red Riding Hood* fairy tale. Gordon swung an axe into the walls of the HOME Theatre in the city before doodling the outline of a large clawed hand, signing his name with a kiss and recording the time and date of his actions – '22:28' on '11/7/15'. The *Guardian*'s two-star review (Gardner 2015) was not an untypical reaction, calling it 'all style and no fangs: no wonder I felt like howling'.

Across the Atlantic, there are many episodes featuring American critics in the eye of a storm resulting from their judgement. *Time* magazine called John Simon the owner of 'the most poisonous pen on Broadway'. Simon spent nearly four decades writing reviews for *New York* magazine until he was eased out of the door approaching his eightieth birthday. He has been variously unkind about Liza Minnelli and Kathleen Turner, and 'in 1973 aggrieved actress Sylvia Miles dumped pasta on his head in a restaurant', reported the *Los Angeles Times*, looking back at his career (Reynolds 2005). But in an interview for *Paris Review* with Davi Napoleon (1997), Simon explained that the dish was actually steak tartare, though, over time, it had been twisted into everything 'from lasagne to chop suey'.

Only two years before that, heavyweight writers Norman Mailer and Gore Vidal began a feud that would last 13 years, sparked by the latter's review of Mailer's book, *Prisoner of Sex*. Vidal's biographer, Jay Parini, writing in the *Guardian*, says the pair famously had a bust-up as guests on the *Dick Cavett Show* – millions have watched it on YouTube, it is a most compelling example of verbal jousting – but had also clashed backstage, with Mailer headbutting his fellow writer. At a party some years later the tensions between the two showed no sign of abating, Parini (2015) goes on to say. Mailer 'threw his drink in Gore's face, right in his eyes, then he hit him in the mouth with a punch, a kind of glancing uppercut. Gore was stunned, and he stepped back. He wiped a dribble of blood from his mouth with a handkerchief. Then Gore said, "Norman, once again words have failed you".' Their bitter rivalry, until a truce was brokered in 1984, was 'emblematic', Parini argued, 'of an age when literary lions roared at each other'.[4]

Mailer and Vidal are both now dead, but one can imagine how they might have sparred with one another in the highly public arena of the Worldwide Web. Quite what their spats via Twitter might have been is anyone's guess. Indeed, it is to the Internet that we turn when discussing more recent high-profile fall-outs between critic and artist. Rather than resorting to the use of the fist, artists are tooled up with a more likely modern option – Twitter. They can use it, or other platforms of social media, to contradict, clarify, deflect, challenge or as a way of garnering support. However, once the artist's grievance is out there, it can be costly, as the novelist Alice Hoffman discovered.

In the summer of 2009 Roberta Silman, writing for the *Boston Globe*, reviewed Hoffman's novel, *The Story Sisters*, and was mildly critical, offering positives along with an observation that the book did not have the spark of her earlier work.

Hoffman immediately tweeted that Silman was a 'moron' and asked her readers to tell 'snarky critics' like her exactly what they thought. *New York* magazine reported that 27 tweets were sent in all (now deleted). To help them in the act, Hoffman published Silman's telephone number (incorrectly, as it turned out) and her email address. But rather than collecting an army of supporters who would enliven this virtual prosecution, the plan backfired and Hoffman herself was pilloried, one tweeter branding her a 'psycho', which of course is a disproportionate response but nonetheless demonstrates the point that anyone can join in. Hoffman's publicist stepped in and conveyed a statement from her where she felt the situation had been 'completely blown out of proportion'. She apologised, wished she had not responded 'in the heat of the moment' and reminded us that reviewers were 'entitled to their opinions'. Silman herself said she had a total of nine emails in response to the tweet, all of them supportive, as reported by Carolyn Kellogg (2009) in the *Los Angeles Times* books blog *Jacket Copy*.

The next day (either coincidentally or not) writer Alain de Botton went even further after a negative review of his new book *The Pleasures and Sorrows of Work* appeared in the *New York Times*. It resulted in an extraordinary reaction. Posting on the critic's personal blog, *Steamboats Are Ruining Everything*, de Botton (2009) told Caleb Crain, the reviewer, that he should grow up and act responsibly as a critic: 'You have now killed my book in the United States ... So that's two years of work down the drain in one miserable 900-word review ... I will hate you till the day I die and wish you nothing but ill will in every career move you make.'

Powerful stuff, and a debate that Crain allowed to live within the comments section of his blog, fuelled by de Botton's 200-word complaint. The publicity generated for both men was in all probability a useful tool, given the coverage it received online and in the upmarket press on either side of the Atlantic.

Fellow New York reviewer Ben Brantley has found himself embroiled in similarly explosive disputes. As chief theatre critic of the *New York Times*, he has run into trouble with, among others, the actor James Franco, who in 2014 pushed the boundaries with his response via Instagram to Brantley's take on his Broadway performance in *Of Mice and Men*. New York website *Observer.com*'s Matthew Kassel (2014) reported on Franco's post that the 'theater community hates him [Brantley], and for good reason'.

A year earlier, Alec Baldwin used his *Huffington Post* blog to compose a stinging attack. In his sights were tabloid journalism, but Brantley in particular, whose review of Baldwin's own Broadway production of *Orphans* was less than glowing but hardly an assassination. And yet Baldwin (2013) took great exception, blaming the critic for the play closing early by about six weeks, labelling him a 'bitter, shrivelled Dickensian clerk' and – turning the tables – saying Brantley did not stand comparison with his predecessor Frank Rich. Baldwin's blistering attack – a criticism of the critic – ran to almost 800 words. The legal and ethical ramifications of both episodes will be looked at later in the book.

Brantley's colleague on the paper, *New York Times* film critic A.O. Scott (2016), essentially used a spat with movie star Samuel L. Jackson as the starting point for his book *Better Living through Criticism*. Matters came to a head in 2012 following Scott's assessment of *The Avengers*, which he referred to as 'a snappy little dialogue comedy dressed up as something else, that something else being a giant ATM for *Marvel* and its new studio overlords, the Walt Disney Company'. This would seem to be a valid observation, certainly worthy of debate and certainly one man's balanced view of what he saw, yet Jackson was having none of it and he proclaimed on Twitter: 'AO Scott needs a new job! Let's help him find one! One he can ACTUALLY do!' While a deafening silence greeted Alice Hoffman's similar request as explained earlier, *Marvel* fans came running to Jackson's rescue, 'retweeting [the] outburst and adding their own vivid suggestions as to what I was qualified to do with myself', Scott writes. The film was a box-office smash, selling $1 billion worth of tickets worldwide in near-record time and, as a minor aside, enabling Scott to pick up a few hundred followers on Twitter to boot. Everyone wins, then? Jackson was angry at Scott's attempts at what he – Jackson – called the 'intellectualisation' of a mass-market movie; Scott's point was that just because something was popular, it did not mean we should not think about it, which is at the core of arts criticism.

Mark Lawson, as a writer of fiction and non-fiction in addition to his criticism, sees the situation regarding attacks in print as thus:

> Because I've published books and written TV and radio plays, I try to avoid casual cruelty or abuse, or at least be aware of its possible physical and psychological consequences. James Corden once rang me up and screamed at me over a review of his TV comedy sketch show, but we had a mature conversation and, in his memoirs, he was gracious enough to acknowledge that the piece had, in retrospect, been fair in questioning creative choices he was making at the time.[5]

How to punish a critic

We have noted how the impact of criticism can start long-running arguments or even deeply personal attacks or physical violence. Public slanging matches are best avoided in these circumstances, but they will continue to happen as digital media makes it so terribly easy. Other than revenge, what options are open to the artist feeling miffed that his new work was not received in the way he would have liked?

Probably few episodes are as extreme as that which featured Wilbur F. Storey, editor of the *Chicago Times*, who in 1870 was ambushed on his way home from work one evening and horsewhipped – not by mobsters but dancing girls. The aggressors were British women, as it transpires, more precisely the British Blondes, whose 'display of legs', as it was reported (Kelley 1919), had 'scandalised' the city. Storey's punishment had come about due to the unfavourable report which had appeared in his newspaper. One of the attackers was Pauline Markham, a burlesque star of the day, originally from England. She and others confronted Storey, hitting him about the head and shoulders with a short whip until pedestrians ran to his rescue.[6]

More typically following criticism felt to be unjust, a complaint may be made by the artist or his representative, usually his management or publicity agent, but not always. The singer-songwriter Tom Odell found himself the source of a now legendary complaint in the music business in 2013 when, after *NME* rated his new album zero out of ten, his father rang the magazine to complain – news of which was publicised on Twitter by a senior member of staff (Rawlinson 2013). While the story may have created extra publicity for the *NME* brand, the reviewer, Mark Beaumont (2013), was accused by some of showboating. 'I wish I could say there's a place in Hell reserved for Tom Odell', he wrote.

Theatre website *WhatsOnStage* covers the length and breadth of the UK, postings its reviews soon after curtain call or at least the following morning. (As pointed out earlier, I am one of its many contributors in the regions, responsible for Leicester.) The website enjoys a strong relationship with the acting community, but there will be moments when a performer or creative is unhappy with what has been written, as editor Daisy Bowie-Sell explains:

> If someone objects to something on the grounds that it's not good for them … we have a duty to the *WoS* readership. We need to inform and tell them about actors and shows they might be excited about, and if that occasionally pisses off a star then that is the lie of the land.[7]

Occasionally arts critics will have upset an artist and will be told they are no longer welcome to review subject X. In practice such a stance is very difficult to carry out. Even if the restriction is successful in the short term, it very rarely works as a long-term strategy because critics find ways of circumnavigating the ruling and, put to the test, they tend to stick together.

Neil Norman recalls being 'banned from the remaining press performances of a certain visiting ballet company after my unfavourable review of their opening show. Thanks to protestations from my colleagues in the Critics' Circle who said they would boycott the entire season if I wasn't reinstated, I was allowed back in for the rest of the shows.'[8]

A similar situation befell *Daily Mail* critic Quentin Letts in 2015 when management of the West End production of *The Queen* chose not to invite him following an article he wrote (not a review) about the play's new star, Kristin Scott Thomas, and what he saw as her limited talent for acting. Letts (2015) merely paid for a ticket and went anyway, albeit in a seat way back in the gods. Aside from raising the obvious question how any *Mail* reader would trust his judgement having remembered this article, Letts's sense of triumph was plain to see for anyone who read his review headlined 'The man they couldn't gag'. He rather confusingly awarded the play four stars but rubbished its leading lady. 'I am not saying she is bad', he wrote, 'but my two neighbours did not return for the second half.'

Lyn Gardner picked up the story in her excellent blog for the *Guardian*, saying that while she often disagreed with Letts's reviews, the ban was a step too far.

> While producers of any show might argue that as it's their party they can invite whoever they want, the principle of extending invitations across the board is a sound one. Trying to exclude particular reviewers is not – if for no other reason that it makes that individual critic seem more important than they are and hints at, if not outright censorship, then at least an over-developed desire to manipulate coverage and ensure good reviews all round.
>
> *(Gardner 2015)*

In terms of attempts to ban individual critics from attending certain productions, there is probably none more significant than the extraordinary events surrounding Hilary Spurling, theatre critic at *The Spectator* from 1964 to 1969. The consequences of her work could be felt by senior decision-makers at one of Britain's most influential theatres, by editors, by other critics and by those in charge of distributing public money to the arts. Now a successful biographer, Spurling in her twenties was, by her own admission (Laity 2010), 'the most dreadful, swingeing, destructive critic, a battleaxe'.

But what could she have possibly done to create such turmoil? In 1969 the English Stage Company (ESC), based at the Royal Court Theatre in London, attempted to ban Spurling from reviewing its work, a decision three years in the making. Tensions had been simmering following an article she had written about the company in 1966, which, in the year of its tenth anniversary, had taken on an extra dimension. The ESC's radical interpretation of *Macbeth* and – a year earlier – its notorious new play, *Saved*, by Edward Bond, had received bruising notices but, as Graham Saunders points out (Saunders 2010), 'it could be argued that the Court not only expected wounding notices for plays such as … *Saved*, but actually gained a self-righteous masochistic pleasure from the critical hostility'. However, he goes on, the fact that Spurling ridiculed the Court by calling it 'touchy' and 'inflexible' at such a sensitive time, and that she questioned why the Arts Council was funding it, meant that her article 'would not be forgotten'.

William Gaskill, joint artistic director at the ESC, wrote to newspaper editors shortly after *Macbeth* opened in October 1966, pointing out that the company's subsidy from the Arts Council was being 'constantly endangered by the flippancy of the theatre critics', before going on to threaten a withdrawal of complimentary tickets (Saunders 2010) as 'the present level of criticism is so low'. Three years later the company was as good as its word, singling out Spurling and, in a press release, offering the following as a quite remarkable explanation (Browne 1975, cited in Saunders 2010): 'There is no question of our banning Mrs Spurling: we are simply not inviting her to review our work. We do not find Mrs Spurling's attitude to our work illuminating, and we do not believe that it furthers our relationship with the public.'

Spurling's predicament quickly found support among the London circle of critics, who felt intimidated by the action, and in a show of unity declared Royal Court productions off limits until the decision was reversed. In the end it was only the weight of the Arts Council stepping in that brought about a proper resolution.

The body decreed that supported theatres could not choose which individual critics wrote reviews and threatened to withhold the 1970–71 subsidy unless *The Spectator*'s arrangement for complimentary tickets was restored.

The publicity machine

The need for control as displayed by theatremakers in the Spurling Affair is notable not just in their vocalising what we might assume to be something they had rather be kept quiet but also in the way it chimes with what is happening 50 years later in modern culture. If ever there was a need for greater control of the publicity stakes it is now, with costs rising and with changes in the way we consume arts and entertainment. A similar situation can be observed in elite, professional sport where, driven by sponsorship and further huge sums thanks to the selling of television rights, the influence of a communications strategy can be felt by all involved: players, managers and of course the press, who are charged with challenging the bland rhetoric coming from the mouths of those they interview. Effectively, public relations teams seek to maintain a narrative invented by owners and sponsors which gives fans/journalists just enough of what they want, often through the vehicle of the after-the-match press conference, but actually says very little. While nobody would want this sort of extreme in arts and entertainment coverage – imagine compulsory interviews post-show: 'Tell us how you saw it, Mike' – it is perhaps understandable that the pressure placed on arts reporters and critics is turned up a few notches.

Gardner (2015) worries that the censorship of any credible critic is part of a wider picture in arts journalism where interviewers are preferred for the expected sympathetic coverage they will provide, where copy approval is requested and where major stars – presumably big enough to look after themselves – are babysat during interviews. The issue, she says, 'is the insidious, creeping desire on the part of producers and their PR agencies to control all press coverage by feature writers and critics'.

A similar worry was voiced by Neil Norman, who said that one of the frustrations of being a critic was 'the increasing pressure brought by PRs who believe that critics are an integral part of their publicity campaigns – they are not and never should be'.[9]

There are numerous examples where the lines have been blurred, or even ignored.

Note the furore surrounding a West End adaptation for the stage of the popular Hollywood film *The Shawshank Redemption*. Publicity teams will seize upon those so-very-quotable words or phrases that are just asking to be picked up and lifted from an expertly crafted review. That is exactly what happened with this production at the Wyndhams Theatre in 2009, which utilised a critic's comments on its billboard outside the theatre. 'A superbly gripping, genuinely uplifting drama', were the words attributed to *Daily Telegraph* critic Charles Spencer. What could be wrong with that? Answer: Spencer was referring to the film. Sadly, he was not keen on the play ('in almost every respect the stage version is inferior to the movie') – and that's what landed the Wyndhams in trouble.

And how must music writers have felt when, in 2008, representatives of rock band Metallica allowed a select few journalists from *The Quietus* and *Metal Hammer* among others to listen to tracks from the group's new album, only to go into shock when said writers started posting their reviews online? Non-disclosure agreements were not signed, and nor were they mentioned. To add insult to injury, the reviews were positive, but pressure to take down the 'offending' material was immediate – only resolved, in fact, when band members got to hear of the situation and quickly saw there was no problem (Van Buskirk 2008).

While examples of poor decision-making still exist, public and media relations in the arts and entertainment business have improved beyond measure. The idea used to be that a PR officer knocked out a press release and checked that the journalist had got it, and that was about it. Nowadays – certainly at the higher end of the market – publicists are involved in the planning and delivery of a strategy that will aim to achieve maximum engagement with the product being sold, whether that's a comedian's nationwide tour or a controversial art exhibition. These campaigns are not only concerned with how much coverage Project X should receive, but where that emphasis should be. The team will think about print, online and broadcast coverage. Social media will feature heavily. The team will know where the natural spikes are for maximum exposure, for example just before tickets go on sale or when a product such as a book or a box set can be bought.

I have experienced dealing with publicists in the fields of television, theatre and books with the intention of writing either a review or a feature previewing the art (normally an interview with a star performer or writer). Good publicists provide a press pack in an easily accessible form, either as Word or pdf attachments or as something to download from a website, especially the latter where high-resolution photographs are required. Normally included in the words are a background and biographies, while images are now often complemented by video trailers as well. In summary, a campaigns team will have a supply of story ideas at its fingertips which give the brand the best chance of exposure but also enable a key message to be put across – for example, 'a true story that will challenge your preconceptions'. Publicists representing agencies or those working in-house, such as for the BBC, will be responsible for arranging press conferences where a product/production is being launched, and sometimes critics will go to these, especially those reviewers who double up as feature writers. In many ways the preview/interview has become just as important as the review.

In terms of live performance like theatre, the PR team will manage the press night. Responsibilities here include ensuring critics are invited, greeting them and making sure they have access to a free programme and interval drinks. When the wine has been sipped and the reviews have been published, the impact of that criticism is now being felt by publicists, whose job includes reporting on what was written or said. Theatres rely, of course, on box-office activity. What effect, if any, did those reviews have? How many reviews were there in print, online or discussed on television or on the radio? How was that coverage packaged – with photos, with links to ticketing information, with that promotional video embedded? What proportion of the reviews was positive? What was being said on social media?

As power shifts into the hands of the publicity people, hovering over their client like a worried parent, critics should be mindful of the PR's motivation but not be distracted by it. The deal should be: here's a book through the post, here's a ticket for the show, now can we have that review, please? Publicity departments should reasonably expect a prompt review, in print or online or broadcast as outlined in your discussions. They should not necessarily expect a *kind* review; that is *not* part of the deal. For you, the critic, your responsibility is to your readers, not to those nice people in PR.

Despite what the critics said…

Critical approval is a potentially powerful tool for anyone involved in the arts, if only to add the words 'critically acclaimed' to any publicity surrounding the work of art. Unanimous or majority support can boost reputation, provide a springboard for other (even bigger) opportunities and can be helpful to those individuals or organisations reliant on subsidy. But despite allegations to the contrary, critics are human. They may misjudge an experience, they may be at odds with the rest of the world. Provided theirs was an honest response, it cannot be *wrong*. All of the arts disciplines can offer countless examples where a work of art was poorly received at the time but the negativity mattered not one jot: readers, viewers, listeners, audiences waved away the doubting voices and loved it anyway. Mark Kermode, the film critic, author and broadcaster, believes there is little evidence (2013) to prove that 'critics can actually affect the box office or movies and, if they do, the result is rarely to the film's financial detriment'. If that is the case for film, it is difficult to argue that any other art form would be an exception.

An interesting exercise might be to separate the bad reviews into two distinct groups: negativity towards artists largely unknown to a mass population or negativity towards established artists producing something new. The degree of risk involved is different in each case. The latter addresses the critic's own taste and preconceptions and also asks questions to do with the trajectory of an artist's career (we've loved everything up to now but at what point do we start getting bored?).

Steve Race, writing for *Melody Maker*, was spectacularly wrong in his assessment of Elvis Presley's *Hound Dog* (1956), but at least he was brave enough to later admit it, and could not have been clearer in his distaste for the singer. In other words, he was coming at the song from the point of view of hating everything so far, what about the new one? 'The fact I can't make out a word he says is of no importance to anyone, least of all to the Boy himself.' Presley was by now the world's highest-paid entertainer, but that was not going to derail Race (1956), who continued: 'These many times have I heard bad records, but for sheer repulsiveness, coupled with the monotony of incoherence, "Hound Dog" hit a new low in my experience.' The critic was sure that this would be the record to finish Presley's career – perhaps it was wishful thinking on his part – but at least acknowledged his misjudgement on that score when it rocketed up the charts a couple of weeks later.

Television situation comedy is one of those areas where shows take time to settle – audiences need to familiarise themselves with the world and to warm to the characters. Given that some jokes are required and a story told in just half an hour, it may go some way to explaining why sitcoms get a bumpy ride from the critics. In the USA, *Friends* was not universally praised, while in the UK there were doubts over *Are You Being Served?*, *Minder* and *Fawlty Towers*, among others. *Minder*, admittedly a comedy-drama with a 60-minute running time, reminded *The Stage and Television Today* of a programme put together in a hurried panic, while Nancy Banks-Smith at the *Guardian* (1979) gave herself a talking to, willing herself to like the show but concluded that the effect of the series on its stars, led by George Cole, was 'oddly unhappy'. *Fawlty Towers* (1975–79) is now widely considered an all-time comedy classic with its eccentric characters and watertight plots but *The Spectator* found it 'unpleasant' – the 'sound of a man shouting at the top of his voice for half an hour is bound to become boring'[10] – and *The Stage* (Dyason 1975), acknowledging John Cleese was funny, reckoned viewers unfamiliar with his style would be left cold.

A similar feeling was experienced by theatre critics having seen *We Will Rock You*, the London jukebox musical based on Queen songs with a story and book from Ben Elton. 'Where did it all go wrong?', Caitlin Moran (2002) wondered in her one-star review for *The Times*, weighing up the fusion between one of the world's best rock bands and a man who co-wrote *Blackadder*. Awarding two stars in the *Guardian*, Brian Logan (2002) felt the musical has a 'sixth form premise'. The comments had zero effect on audiences, as the show notched up some 4,500 performances at the Dominion Theatre over a 12-year period, complemented by dozens of international versions all over the world.

For its dramatic shift in fortune though, it is hard to match *Les Misérables* when it comes to a theatre production disliked by so many critics but universally loved by the paying public. *Les Misérables* has played uninterrupted in London since 1985 and international versions pop up at a rate of knots, underpinned by a new respect from journalists that quash the original critical bashing as if it never happened. Producer Cameron Mackintosh has spoken many times of the rapturous reception the audience gave the show on press night, and yet the downbeat tone of many of the next morning's reviews shocked. Frances Ruffelle, who played Eponine in the original cast, told the *Daily Express* (Edge 2010) of the shock the notices caused. 'It was horrible actually. We couldn't believe it because we could see from the audience that they absolutely loved it and it was absolutely packed at the Barbican.'

Among the critics unconvinced and unimpressed – strengthening London's reputation as a hostile territory for new musicals – were those from the *Guardian*, the *Observer*, *Daily Mail*, *Sunday Telegraph* and *City Limits*, though a handful saw something different, such as the *Sunday Times*, *The Stage*, *Financial Times* and *Punch*.

More than 30 years after the event, it may be convenient to say that the first-night reviews for *Les Misérables* truly were shocking. It helps writers of nostalgic pieces. It helps the *Les Mis* super-fans who can gloat that those so-called critics really didn't know anything at all. It helps Sir Cameron Mackintosh tell a very compelling story. In many ways, it would help the writing of this chapter as well if the narrative were crystal clear: professional critics unanimously loathed *Les Misérables* but it has brought joy to many millions of theatregoers. Awkwardly, the truth lies somewhere between: crushing reviews were written, yes, along with a few nice ones and ones that displayed an accommodating stance with an undertone of negative noises. What it tells us in part, I think, is that art is not static, and neither is our response to it.

And what about the critics?

So far we have completely ignored one area nearly always overlooked when it comes to thinking about the impact of arts criticism and that is the effect on the critics themselves. Writing the nice things is hardly likely to have any long-term psychological effect, but what about the opposite? Does being 'mean' eventually weigh them down? Benedict Nightingale, formerly theatre critic at *The Times*, once wrote that he wished he was in 'a kindlier trade, such as whaling or seal-culling'. And Charles Spencer, on announcing his retirement as number-one theatre critic at the *Daily Telegraph*, wrote movingly about the toll the job had taken on him since suffering serious depression in 2012. 'I no longer enjoy writing knocking copy', he wrote (Spencer 2014), which was striking, suggesting both that the illness had changed him but clearly at one point he *had* enjoyed twisting the knife. 'Why make other people feel miserable? But a critic who is reluctant to put the boot in when it's required is doing his readers a disservice.'

Similarly, how do reviewers cope with bitterness or anger directed at them as a result of their professional criticism? I wondered if it was ever a source of regret, or whether they had developed a way of blocking out the negativity.

Nina Myskow, probably Britain's best-known television critic of the 1980s, was adamant when I asked her if she now regretted any of her reviews – even the most eye-catching ones of a very honest selection. 'No. They were my honestly held opinions at that time and so I can't regret them. I value honesty above anything else and if they are my opinions then they will be expressed robustly.'[11]

Ben Brantley, chief theatre critic at the *New York Times*, told me:

> I don't regret reviews. They are always written at a moment in time, from the perspective of the person I was when I wrote them – and my job is to create as honestly as I can what I felt watching that show at that time. I may return to the play and it may seem different. Of course, since it's live theater we're talking about, it will be different. I'm happy to contradict what I might have said earlier, if a show has changed, but for me that doesn't invalidate what I said the first time around, if that makes sense.
>
> People may say whatever they want to about what I've written. That's only fair, since I have such a visible platform from which to express myself.

I've been fairly openly attacked, via Twitter or Instagram or in print – almost always by movie stars who have felt I have underappreciated their stage work, and for whatever reasons, they have invariably been men. It's kind of fun when that happens. It gives a certain old-fashioned, 'All About Eve'-style crackle to theater coverage that the subject usually lacks.[12]

Notes

1 Myskow, Nina (24 June 2016), interview with the author.
2 *Ibid*. Nina Myskow said she later worked on TV with Monkhouse and saw him on stage, and she liked him enormously.
3 Norman, Neil (27 July 2016), interview with the author.
4 Jay Parini's biography of Gore Vidal, from which he drew for the article, was *Every Time a Friend Succeeds Something Inside Me Dies: The Life of Gore Vidal*, Little Brown (2015).
5 Lawson, Mark (30 August 2016), interview with the author.
6 The 1870 attack by the British Blondes was written about in the *Chicago Daily Tribune*, 22 March 1919, after the death of one of the Blondes, the burlesque star Pauline Markham. She and her fellow attackers were arrested.
7 Bowie-Sell, Daisy (25 April 2016), interview with the author.
8 Norman, Neil (27 July 2016), interview with the author.
9 *Ibid*.
10 See John Cleese, 'The real reason I had to join *The Spectator*', *The Spectator*, March 2009. www.spectator.co.uk/2009/03/the-real-reason-i-had-to-join-the-spectator/.
11 Myskow, Nina (24 June 2016), interview with the author.
12 Brantley, Ben (11 August 2016), interview with the author.

References

Anon. (17 May 1956), 'Critics who stab the theatre', *The Stage*.
Anon. (17 December 2015) 'Author Richard Brittain jailed for "bad review" attack', BBC News, www.bbc.co.uk/news/uk-scotland-edinburgh-east-fife-35128139.
Baldwin, Alec (5 July 2013) 'How Broadway has changed', *Huffington Post* blog, www.huffingtonpost.com/alec-baldwin/broadway-orphans_b_3229873.html.
Bank-Smith, Nancy (20 November 1979) 'George Cole, *Minder*, review', *Guardian*, www.theguardian.com/tv-and-radio/from-the-archive-blog/2015/aug/06/george-cole-minder-review-nancy-banks-smith-1979.
Beaumont, Mark (15 June 2013) 'Tom Odell review, *Long Way Down*', *NME*, www.nme.com/reviews/album/reviews-tom-odell-14533#MckyYSovvfwzV017.99.
Billen, Andrew (30 May 2016) 'New-look *Top Gear* treads too hard on the loud pedal', review, *The Times*.
Billington, Michael (18 February 1995) 'Prisoners of conviction', review of *Cell Mates*, *Guardian*.
Bingham, John and Willgress, Lydia (30 May 2016) 'Evans' changes of gear leave show's viewers in a spin', *Top Gear* news story, *Daily Telegraph*.
Browne, Terry (1975) *Playwright's Theatre: The English Stage Company at the Royal Court*. London: Pitman Publishing.
Chaudhary, Vivek and Ellison, Mike (24 February 1995), 'Fry's flight put down to newspaper fright', from *Guardian* archive, *Guardian*, www.theguardian.com/culture/2015/feb/24/stephen-fry-cell-mates-1995-archive.

Caine, Michael (1992) *What's It All About?* London: Century, Random House.
Coveney, Michael (19 February 1995) 'Spies who've come in from the cold', review of *Cell Mates*, Observer.
de Botton, Alain (29 June 2009) 'Review of Alain de Botton's *Pleasures and Sorrows of Work*', comments section of Caleb Crain's blog *Steamboats Are Ruining Everything*, www.steamthing.com/2009/06/review-of-alain-de-bottons-pleasures-and-sorrows-of-work.html.
Dyason, Jackie (25 September 1975) 'Too much of a one-man show', *The Stage*.
Edge, Simon (4 October 2010) '*Les Misérables* celebrates 25 years on the stage', *Daily Express*, www.express.co.uk/expressyourself/203425/Les-Miserables-celebrates-25-years-on-the-stage.
Farrell, Ally and Kisiel, Ryan (30 May 2016) 'Plop Gear', *Top Gear* news story, *Sun*.
Gardner, Lyn (7 May 2015) 'Quentin Letts "banned" from *The Audience*? Why you can't – and shouldn't – freeze out critics', *Guardian*, www.theguardian.com/stage/theatreblog/2015/may/07/quentin-letts-the-audience-banning-critics.
Gardner, Lyn (11 July 2015) '*Neck of the Woods* review: All style and no fangs', *Guardian*, www.theguardian.com/culture/2015/jul/11/neck-of-the-woods-all-style-and-no-fangs.
Hyland, Ian (30 May 2016) 'Even Clarkson fans must admit that Evans didn't crash and burn', *Top Gear* review, *Daily Mirror*.
Hughes, Tammy (30 May 2016) 'Now it's *Flop Gear*', *Top Gear* news story, *Daily Mail*.
Kassel, Matthew (17 April 2014) 'Ben Brantley doesn't think "little bitch" qualifies as libel', *Observer.com*, http://observer.com/2014/04/ben-brantley-doesnt-think-little-bitch-qualifies-as-libel/.
Kelley, John (22 March 1919) 'Showgirl who horsewhipped editor here dies', *Chicago Daily Tribune*, archives.chicagotribune.com/1919/03/22/page/4/article/showgirl-who-horsewhipped-editor-here-dies.
Kellogg, Carolyn (29 June 2009) 'Alice Hoffman strikes back – and strikes out', *Jacket Copy*, *Los Angeles Times* books blog, http://latimesblogs.latimes.com/jacketcopy/2009/06/did-alice-hoffman-strike-back-or-strike-out.html.
Kermode, Mark (2013) *Hatchet Job: Love Movies, Hate Critics*. London: Picador.
Laity, Paul (17 April 2010) 'A life in writing: Hilary Spurling', *Guardian*, www.theguardian.com/books/2010/apr/17/hilary-spurling-biographer-pearl-buck.
Letts, Quentin (14 March 2015) 'Sorry Kristin, you don't deserve a gong just for having fab cheekbones', *Daily Mail*, www.dailymail.co.uk/tvshowbiz/article-2994240/Sorry-Kristin-don-t-deserve-gong-just-having-fab-cheekbones-writes-QUENTIN-LETTS.html.
Letts, Quentin (6 May 2015) 'The man they couldn't gag … *Mail* theatre critic gets his audience with Queen Kristin: Quentin Letts's first night review of *The Audience* (despite being banned)', *Daily Mail*, www.dailymail.co.uk/tvshowbiz/article-3069598/The-man-couldn-t-gag-Mail-s-theatre-critic-gets-audience-Queen-Kristin-QUENTIN-LETTS-night-review-Audience-despite-banned.html.
Letts, Quentin (30 May 2016) 'It's lost the spark of genius … pass the jump leads', *Top Gear* review, *Daily Mail*.
Logan, Brian (15 May 2002) 'Review: *We Will Rock You*', *Guardian*.
Long, Pat (2012) *The History of the NME: High Times and Low Lives at the World's Most Famous Music Magazine*. London: Portico.
McAnally, Ashlie and McLelland, Euan (10 November 2015) '"I could have died": Asda shelf-stacker, 18, tells how she was bottled by Countdown champion … after she gave his book a bad review online', *Daily Mail*, www.dailymail.co.uk/news/article-3311558/Countdown-champion-travelled-500-miles-Scotland-bottle-teenager-gave-book-bad-review.html.

Moran, Caitlin (15 May 2002) 'Without Freddie this is nothing but theatre ga-ga', *The Times*.
Napoleon, Davi (1997) 'John Simon. The art of criticism, no. 4', *Paris Review* (Spring), issue 142, www.theparisreview.org/interviews/1282/john-simon-the-art-of-criticism-no-4-john-simon.
O'Donovan, Gerard (30 May 2016) 'Slick fun with a classic moment, but this revamp is just too cautious', *Top Gear* review, *Daily Telegraph*.
Olivier, Laurence (1987) *On Acting*. London: Simon and Schuster.
Parini, Jay (14 August 2015) 'A life in feuds: How Gore Vidal gripped a nation', *Guardian*, www.theguardian.com/books/2015/aug/14/gore-vidal-gripped-a-nation.
Race, Steve (20 October 1956) 'Rock and roll on record', *Melody Maker*.
Rawlinson, Kevin (19 June 2013) 'Hello, *NME*? I'd like to complain about your Tom Odell review. Why? I'm his dad', *Independent*, www.independent.co.uk/arts-entertainment/music/news/hello-nme-i-d-like-to-complain-about-your-tom-odell-review-why-i-m-his-dad-8665499.html.
Reynolds, Christopher (11 May 2005) 'Fiery theatre critic John Simon ousted', *Los Angeles Times*, http://articles.latimes.com/2005/may/11/entertainment/et-simon11.
Saunders, Graham (2010) 'Tickets, critics and censorship: The Royal Court, *The Spectator* and the Arts Council of Great Britain', *Theatre Notebook* 64(3), 160–73.
Scott, Anthony Oliver (2016) *Better Living through Criticism*. London: Jonathan Cape.
Spencer, Charles (14 September 2009) '*Shawshank Redemption* at the Wyndham's Theatre', review, *Daily Telegraph*, www.telegraph.co.uk/culture/theatre/theatre-reviews/6187874/Shawshank-Redemption-review.html.
Spencer, Charles (20 September 2014) 'Thank you dear readers, and goodbye', *Daily Telegraph*, www.telegraph.co.uk/culture/theatre/11107255/Charles-Spencer-Thank-you-dear-readers-and-goodbye.html.
Tookey, Christopher (2010) *Named and Shamed*. Leicester: Matador.
Van Buskirk, Eliot (6 September 208) 'Metallica kills early review of upcoming album', *Wired*, www.wired.com/2008/06/metallica-kills/.
Watts, Halina (30 May 2016) 'Bump start', *Top Gear* news story, *Daily Mirror*.
Williams, Stephen (24 May 1956) 'Stabbing the theatre', *The Stage*.
Wollaston, Sam (30 May 2016) 'Struggling in the shadow of that other bloke', *Top Gear* review, *Guardian*.

7
LEGAL AND ETHICAL BOUNDARIES

Sometimes a student will produce copy under the misapprehension that they can use their review as a launchpad to say whatever they like about an artist and his work. The grenades and rockets they fire may seem like harmless fun but they can all the same have serious consequences. On one occasion I remember a student's review suggesting that an actor was 'clearly not bothered' about this particular role she was playing on stage, given that she was better known for a regular and bigger role in a television series. Alarm bells immediately rang. 'But it's my opinion', argued the student. No one was denying that he held this belief. As an exercise only, it was contained within the safety of the class but think of the problems had the review been published.

In this chapter we look at the framework surrounding media law and journalism ethics in practice. Perhaps more so than in other chapters, the critic in this context – regardless of the platform used for his content – must be seen as a legitimate journalist. Wriggling out of it by claiming 'but no, I'm a writer' will fail to impress the court. Reviewers may not busy themselves with uncovering negligence or corruption – two areas where there is much to think about from a legal perspective – but they do nevertheless need a working knowledge of media law, not least because at the core of what critics write about is creative work produced by people who rely on their good reputation. Misunderstand that and you have a critic who is a danger to everybody, including himself.

Protecting reputation forms the basis of British libel laws – in a moment we will look at them in more detail, along with international differences. Copyright and other journalistic regulation also form part of the picture.

The second half of the chapter centres on journalism ethics. This may involve spoilers, breaking embargoes, anonymously talking up your own work online or – the reverse of that – trashing the efforts of your rivals. It is to do with perceived or real agendas on the part of the critic, the expectations built in when you see a work of art for free and on drawing or overstepping the line when personal interest comes into play.

Defamation: a victory for the lawyers

Back to our student who wanted to stick the boot in concerning what he perceived as a distinct lack of effort on the actor's part. If I have already stressed the importance of an opinion in arts reviewing, then why would such a comment be a risk? Quite simply because the remark is potentially defamatory, and central to defamation is the idea that what is said or written is false and would harm the reputation of the person in question. With words published in some permanent form it is libel (and yes, the Web does count), and with words spoken it is slander.

Confusion arises, however, in the field of broadcasting. Logic might suggest that defamatory remarks made as part of a broadcast must be slanderous but television and radio reviews fall under the banner of libel in British law because the programmes they are a part of are seen as being in a permanent form (an argument strengthened by the catch-up generation watching television or facilities like Listen Again on BBC radio). Some variations to this law exist in North America and Australia, depending on the state in question, but the principle applies nonetheless. In Australia, as Martin (1998) identifies, some states require that the controversial remark must be true and other states go further to want it to be in the public interest as well.

Wherever the programme is made, live broadcasting is of course potentially hazardous where an arts review is concerned. A damage limitation strategy is best summed up by a paragraph in Channel 4's Producers' Handbook which offers the following advice: 'In live programmes, presenters must take swift and effective action to distance the programme and the broadcaster from any potentially libellous remark, which must not be repeated.'

So, whether you are a broadcaster, a print journalist or a YouTube reviewer, let us explore in more detail how a claim for defamation might unravel.

Libel laws are concerned with the impact of what is written on right-thinking members of society; how it makes them feel towards the subject of the allegation. If the words cause the person to be shunned or avoided, if they face hatred or are ridiculed then those responsible for those words – legally the publisher but in practice this is real bother for the writer and editor as well – will have a libel claim on their hands. All the subject (the plaintiff) has to determine is that those words were published to a third party, and this is where it gets interesting, because that can range from a handful of people who, say, are recipients of a village newsletter to millions of readers of a market-leading global brand.

Further complications potentially arise with online publications. Let us conjure an example of an artist working in Dorset, someone who has immersed herself in the community and whose paintings take their inspiration both from the natural landscape locally but also from her homeland of New Zealand. A review in a local magazine says a number of nice things about her work, but it is that throwaway remark that stings, the one suggesting she has obviously copied painter X when we study painting Y and what a shame she had to do it. To make matters worse the review has gone online – promoted by Twitter – and has been seen by hundreds of people back home in New Zealand, people associated with her professionally, along with friends and family. Her reputation has clearly been harmed.

The magazine reviewer suggesting that a painting has been copied is defamatory, though a far more measured view that painting Y 'reminds me of the work of Z in its atmosphere and use of characterisation' would not. In fact the poor, victimised painter may even like the comparison!

In our classroom setting, the student theatre reviewer may have been minded to say that the actor was going through the motions or did not look particularly engaged. (Be careful to avoid what has become a cliché, saying that so-and-so 'phoned in her performance'.)

It all comes down to truth: can the reviewer (the defendant) prove what has been written? For truth is the complete defence for alleged defamation. Those libel claims that reach court will be decided upon by a jury under the direction of a judge. Their job is not to consider what the defendant intended by the words published, merely to establish their effect.

Many libel claims are settled out of court and, while that may seem like a small victory for the publisher, it is not. Lawyers are usually the only true winners when it comes to libel. The moment even a *threat* of libel is suggested, the lawyers are like taxi drivers with the meter ticking the moment you climb into their legal 'cab'. Big players in publishing will be insured against incurring libel costs, but in reality it is far better to avoid the problematic review in the first place.

The critic, the actress and other stories

It is rare that actions are brought specifically against reviewers in the wake of criticism that goes too far, but that is not a recommendation to be complacent. News stories, feature pieces and opinion columns are more likely to attract trouble as they can cross the line – sometimes unfairly – between an artist's public and private lives: unfounded rumour, assumptions or a failure to check the facts. Indeed, it is this sense of things 'getting personal' that can be applied to some of the examples we are about to examine when it comes to reviewing.

One of the best-known episodes of all involves television critic Nina Myskow and the actor Charlotte Cornwell, famous in the 1970s for her role in groundbreaking drama *Rock Follies*. A few days before Christmas in 1985 Cornwell won £10,000 in damages brought against the *Sunday People* for comments made two and a half years earlier by Myskow, who wrote that the performer could not sing, lacked stage presence and her 'bum is too big'. The actor complained that the article had been a 'vulgar and vindictive attack', as the *Guardian* reported (Anon. 1985). In labelling Cornwell as 'Wally of the Week' in her column, the judge said he believed Myskow wrote such things 'to enhance her own standing'.

The newspaper and Myskow, who by now was working for the *News of the World*, denied libel and pleaded fair comment on a matter of public interest but a jury of 11 men and one woman found in the actor's favour. Ms Cornwell told reporters after the verdict that she 'believed the article went far beyond fair critical comment'.

More than 30 years later the case is still widely documented in media law books and in articles assessing discourse on the landscape of criticism, which probably suggests two things. First that it perfectly illustrates the fine line between a comment that is personal and one that could damage reputation, and second that high-profile libel cases involving mainstream arts critics are few and far between, such is the frequency that this particular case is discussed. Despite this, what is much less visible is the concluding tale that in February 1987 Ms Cornwell was ordered by a Court of Appeal to repay the damages and the estimated £30,000 costs of the appeal. The court heard, as reported in the *Guardian* (Anon. 1987) that inadmissible and prejudicial evidence had been presented at the original hearing, and that the trial judge had misdirected the jury.

Myskow, in an interview with the author, acknowledged that her opinions were always 'robust' but this was her trademark. 'As far as I know, what I wrote would now not be judged as libellous. It was an opinion in an opinion column. If I had started it off with the words "In my opinion", it would not have gone to court.'[1]

At least Myskow saw the show she wrote about. In one of the more unusual showbusiness claims for defamation, the American actor and singer David Soul, star of the 1970s cop series *Starsky and Hutch*, won £20,000 damages and £150,000 legal costs against columnist Matthew Wright and the *Mirror* newspaper.

The case, heard at the High Court in London in December 2001, followed a review in Wright's column three years earlier about a West End production of the play, *The Dead Monkey*, of which Soul was the star and co-producer. Wright asserted it was the worst play he had ever seen. Legally there was nothing wrong; the columnist can exercise his freedom to state an opinion, but in fact he had sent a freelance journalist on his behalf. Using 'facts' supplied by the freelancer, Wright was incorrect on the (small) number of people in the audience, that they were laughing derisively at Soul and that ushers had been instructed not to let anyone leave. Wright, now a respected presenter of his own live daytime television show, apologised to the court.

According to the BBC, Soul said afterwards: 'I stand really strong on the side of fair comment and opinion about the theatre. I think it's a cornerstone of the theatre but you have to see the play, you have to be there, you have to have the facts' (Anon. 2001).

If ever a lesson was needed in the importance of checking facts then look no further than the claim for libel made by Zaha Hadid, one of the world's leading architects. Rooted in reviewing is the concept of opinion based on a set of facts, something one critic failed to do when referring to her in his piece for the *New York Review of Books*, as Reuters reported (Stempel 2014). In 2014 the critic used quotes made by Hadid but in the wrong context, giving readers the impression that migrant workers were dying while constructing the new stadium she had designed for the 2022 World Cup in Qatar. To make matters worse, the book review suggested Hadid, who died in 2016, showed no concern for these deaths but – crucially – Hadid's comments were made in the context of other construction projects where deaths had occurred and building work on *her* stadium had not even started. Five months after the lawsuit was filed, Hadid settled out of court. The architecture critic in question, Martin Filler (2014), showed great dignity in his apology – it must have been the most awful moment for him – as did the *New York Review of Books*, which, under the terms of the settlement, donated an undisclosed sum of money to a charity supporting labour rights.

Sometimes a libel lawsuit is threatened but it rarely materialises. Amy Taylor, the Scottish-based drama critic, has written a compelling account of her clash in 2012 with a theatre company at the Edinburgh Festival Fringe, a company which took great exception to her perfectly valid – albeit negative – review. 'Threats of legal action, and the intimidation, bullying and harassment of journalists simply because someone disagrees with what they have written, are immoral, unethical and odious', she wrote on her blog (Taylor 2012).

But in terms of threatening letters that do amount to something and in terms of the size of the payout, the Australian case with science writer Lennard Bickel centre stage takes some beating. The dispute concerned a book review. In 1980 Alan Roberts, a physicist, reviewed for the Australian weekly newspaper, the *National Times*, a book written by Bickel, who died in 2002, called *The Deadly Element: The Men and Women behind the Story of Uranium*.

Australian academic Brian Martin takes up the story:

> Bickel was especially upset by Roberts's comment that 'I object to the author's lack of moral concern'. Bickel sued the publisher. After a trial, an appeal, another trial, another appeal, the two parties reached a settlement. The publishers paid somewhat less than the amount awarded in the second trial: $180,000. That was in 1980 dollars – it is more like half a million today. That was one expensive comment to make in a book review. Apparently, according to the law, the cost to Bickel's reputation was greater than the cost of literally losing an arm and a leg, for which compensation under the law would be considerably less.
>
> *(Martin 2011, 14)*

A number of excellent media law books are available which go into greater detail about defamation and other matters of concern to writers and journalists. With a good grasp of this important law coupled with the experience you can only get from writing and publishing, you should be equipped to put your work in the public domain. Supposing a complaint does come your way, then there are various avenues you can take, depending on the severity of the allegation. Clear thinking is required here because a claim for libel will not necessarily reveal itself straight away – in other words, your response could help to alleviate or, more worryingly, exacerbate the problem.

Factual errors, though sure to spoil the critic's day once pointed out, can be put right via a correction added to the end of your blog or web page or in the next available issue if printed. Where it gets trickier is if an apology is called for or – worse – if there is a whiff that the wounded person is taking legal advice. Your response is now vital. You should:

- inform your editor/line manager/publisher. Established brands will have their own in-house legal team or, more likely, be able to call on media lawyers;
- keep emails or any material relevant to this complaint.

Further to this second point, let us imagine you have reviewed a variety show to mark the re-opening of a refurbished theatre in your town. Top of the bill was a comedian and host of a popular daytime television quiz show: let's call it *Ring My Bell*. But our funny man is known in showbusiness circles for his temperamental nature and, true to form, cut short his allotted 30-minute spot by half, allegedly citing a lack of competence on the part of the local musicians designated to accompany him while he sang his signature song. He stormed off, possibly swore and got straight into a waiting car, having insisted on being paid in cash up-front.

What can you write? Obviously the facts – his early departure, the audience's disappointment, the grand opening of a building fondly loved. Your editor hears of the drama and now wants this as a news story as well, putting even more pressure on you to hit the right note with your review. The editor is pushy. He wants news that sells papers, gets hits on his website.

Can you write about his 'temperamental nature'? No, not unless there is evidence, such as previous run-ins where his attitude has been questioned. Far safer to say what you know that 'this is not the first time X has failed to finish his act'. The swearing? You would need to have heard it, or at least have a credible witness that would enable you to write 'allegedly swore'. And what about the band? Again, caution is required, especially if they are professional musicians whose reputation would be tarnished by any suggestion they were not up to the job.

One tip for writing a contentious review, or indeed any piece of journalism, is to break it down line by line. Is that comment fair? (It does not *have* to be fair.) Can I justify it? If it's really near the knuckle, can I prove it if called upon?

Assuming your review is published, X or his manager telephones and shouts at you. Do not panic, do not promise anything you cannot deliver and do not bury the complaint – it will *not* go away! You will need to refer the problem to your boss if your boss does not already know, and legal advice must be sought if a claim for defamation is being brought. In these circumstances lawyers will advise that you cease any contact with the comedian or his representative with immediate effect.

All of this is from the perspective of a newspaper, but what if you are independent? Bloggers or writers running their own websites or niche magazines ought to seek out friendly advice from someone they know and trust in the media. If in any doubt, seek legal advice including that via membership of the National Union of Journalists.

You might offer the aggrieved the right of reply. As it suggests, this option would give them the platform to respond to what they felt was unjust in your review without involving lengthy and costly legal proceedings. You might offer to take down the offending line or passage. This is not ideal, as you have your principles, and yet … Wealthy individuals or at least people with access to wealthy individuals are more likely to sue. This is a fact. Even if the threat of libel proves to be idle, a lawyer's involvement will mean time and money you can ill afford.

Admitting your mistakes

No one seeks to make a mistake on purpose, but it can happen to the best of us. Neil Norman has an interesting perspective on errors. He said:

> The big thing is that critics – unlike artists – are not allowed to make mistakes. We all do it from time to time – a mistaken attribution here, a wrong date there – and it irks me beyond measure whenever I have slipped up but I will always put my hand up and try to correct it.[2]

Mark Kermode takes the same pragmatic approach. In 1996, writing for *Sight & Sound*, Kermode (2013) says he 'carelessly penned' a review of a film he had seen in the cinema and now on video under a different name. 'Having been dumped in the UK cinemas, [film title] suffers a perfunctory title change on video.'

Fourteen words – possibly harmless at first sight – but they were enough to incur a serious complaint from the film's distributors, who immediately banned Kermode from further press screenings. Their objection was nothing to do with whether the film had been appreciated or not, it was the suggestion they had been unprofessional in their marketing and distribution of it, at once providing evidence for the promotional spend and the time taken to ensure it got exposure. A correction was printed. 'I learned a very important lesson that day: in the worlds of both film criticism and film distribution, opinions are ephemeral but professional conduct is sacrosanct.'

Equally critics should stick to their guns when false accusations are made. Neil Norman recalls clashing with the director, Michael Winner, over a review of his film *A Chorus of Disapproval*, a star-studded adaptation of Alan Ayckbourn's play, and their fall-out centred on Norman's late arrival at the London press screening by about ten minutes.

> Having trashed it fairly comprehensively he tried to sue me as he claimed I had only seen half the film. I was able to tell my editor that, yes, I was a little late for the screening but that it was my second viewing of the film which I had seen in total in Edinburgh the week before. I just wanted to remind myself how bad it was. Mr Winner went away.[3]

Copyright

Words can occasionally get you into trouble, but let us not overlook what can happen if you use an unauthorised photograph to accompany your review. The most likely background to such a scenario is material published on the Web, involving not-for-profit websites or blogs. It may be the case that a reviewer does not have access to official images supplied by the press team working to promote the play or concert, and the lifting of a photo was just too tempting. The reviewer may be ignorant of the possible consequences or may think the Internet is such a big place, their one little act of dishonesty was just a one-off and nothing much to worry about.

British copyright law exists to protect ownership of words, music, images and so on. While there is a legal dimension to this example, it asks ethical and moral questions, too, about denying (in this case a photographer's) right to earn a living from their work. Because, especially online, the words can often be read for free, it does not always follow that a photo can be 'borrowed' along the same lines. Here the photographer would be well within her rights to seek compensation and to insist that the offending photograph is immediately taken down. She may acknowledge that she has already been paid to deliver official photos for this event, that the website involved is a modest set-up and to punish it further would be harsh. She may waive her rights for a three-figure fee and simply insist that she is credited for the picture, that a link is included to take readers to her website. But 'may' is the key word; she does not *have* to do any of it as her copyright has been infringed.

The only way is ethics

When Kelvin Mackenzie, the former editor of the *Sun* newspaper, famously pretended not to know what ethics was – it's 'to the east of London where people wear white socks', he quipped – it revealed much in a single line about the state of British journalism. Historically Fleet Street has not worried itself too much on how a story was obtained, as long as it *was* obtained, and preferably well ahead of the opposition. In the post-Second World War glory days, the combined sales of Sunday newspapers in 1955 was a staggering 30 million copies a week (Seymour-Ure 1991), dropping to a still very healthy 18 million a week in 1980. Over the same time period daily papers sold 16 million copies and only fell by a further 1 million sales 25 years later. Power was in the hands of ruthless editors, star reporters and smart headline writers who could bring the story alive in a handful of words or less.

We might be forgiven for thinking that the comparatively gentle art of reviewing is some distant cousin of the political scoop or celebrity sex scandal, yet the foot-in-the-door journalism that framed the British press from the 1970s through to the early part of the twenty-first century did at least remind critics that competition affected everyone. Newsrooms were macho, male-dominated spaces where aggressive tactics were used to get the story. Indeed, such newsrooms have been described by a number of female journalists in recent years as being sexist and intimidating, or sometimes both. I have seen numerous incidents that would confirm this view.

Inevitably, a competitive workplace that pushes beyond what is healthy competition will affect people's behaviour. We saw this to devastating effect in 2011 over the phone-hacking scandal involving journalists and editors at News International and Mirror Group newspapers, which led to the Leveson inquiry examining the state of the nation's press and the dismantling of a famous Sunday newspaper, the *News of the World*.

Negative headlines about the journalism industry have cumulatively had a corrosive effect on its reputation – a reputation that was hardly worth bragging about at the best of times. Nicknames like the Gutter Press have to start somewhere. Nina Myskow, though best known as a television critic at the height of her career, had been a rock and pop reporter at the *Sun*. 'Fleet Street has always been a cut-throat place', she told me. 'The pub that the *Mirror* used to drink in was known as The Stab – short for "stab in the back".'

Journalism – and specifically newspaper journalism – could not continue on a reckless path without casualties. It had to change, or at least give the public the impression it could change. The resulting Leveson inquiry led to a number of outcomes, including new regulations of the press. In September 2014 the Independent Press Standards Organisation (IPSO) replaced the discredited Press Complaints Commission, accused by many of being too soft: the example often used being that adjudications on errant editors were made by other editors.

Ultimately the scandal has firmly put ethics into an ongoing conversation the industry is having with itself, its regulator, the public and even with providers of journalism training and education.

Traditionally the training ground of the newspaper industry was the regional press. Young reporters would be given a chance on weekly and evening newspapers where they would combine on-the-job learning with a fast-track residential course held at one of a handful of journalism colleges up and down the country. But profit-hungry news groups realised this was an expensive way of training a reporter – editors would start to see some progress from their new trainee and then sigh as they waved them goodbye for the next 20 weeks: not only a large bill in college fees and accommodation, but an empty desk to boot. In the early 2000s we began to see a transformation, with editors gradually turning to university courses for their entrants to the profession, and specifically accredited courses.

While institutions will often say, quite legitimately in some cases, that they have always highlighted the importance of ethics (historically universities have been liberal in outlook and the importance of how we behave is embedded in their teaching and learning), there has been a clear shift in making this provision more visible. The National Council for the Training of Journalists (NCTJ), which awards accreditation to university and college courses in journalism in the UK, said in 2013 it wanted the teaching of ethics to be given far greater attention, arguing that provision was 'too patchy, random and implicit'.

Strikingly, in its major survey of the industry in 2002, the NCTJ had not even asked journalists about their views on ethics, either the way it had been taught or its practical application. Ten years later, undertaking its next and most recent survey, the landscape had entirely changed.

Writing the foreword to the most recent report, Ian Hargraves (Spilsbury 2013) states: 'In 2012 these questions [about ethics] were judged inescapable. More than 80% of journalists report that they do not consider themselves under personal pressure to transgress ethical boundaries, but a quarter say that such pressures do exist in newsrooms.'

Ethics has long been an integral part of North American journalism, including the training of journalists. In his book *The Invention of Journalism Ethics*, Stephen J.A. Ward identifies the First World War as a turning point for the management of information. Post-war there was in the 1920s a determination from American reporters and editors to create what he calls a 'code-directed profession'. President Woodrow encouraged such adoption of ethical codes, observing how journalism was lagging behind medicine and law. 'By the early 1940s', writes Ward (2005), 'the idea that a free press had social obligations was common in journalism textbooks.'

Fast forward more than 70 years and the City University New York (CUNY) Graduate School of Journalism is offering a Master's programme in what it calls social journalism, explaining that it will 'recast journalism as a service that helps communities to meet their goals and solve problems'. There is clear evidence of ethics as a core component of learning in other American universities, as vital as the more obvious practical skills like news writing.

No such tradition has existed in the UK. Instead a culture of dismissiveness has been allowed to creep in where ethics is concerned or has even, in some quarters, been encouraged. Reporters were admired for their ability to manipulate people or situations, and pushing them all the way were editors who could quickly climb the career ladder if their bright and forceful thinking translated into newspaper sales. Distorting quotes and intrusion into grief and other matters of privacy were common-place. In his chapter 'Efficks – Or ethics?', Richard Keeble (2001) in *The Newspapers Handbook* offers an anecdote of a Fleet Street editor laughing at the very suggestion of ethical conduct in a classroom packed with journalism students.

It is fair to say that the phone-hacking scandal has shone a light on what it means to be ethical in *all* forms of journalism in a way that would never have happened before.

Add to it the rapid influence of the Internet and we have ethical dilemmas on a scale hitherto unseen. Arts journalism, including criticism, is a part of these changes, too.

The secret reviewer

The critic has a responsibility to record and evaluate what he has experienced on behalf of the reader but there is another important transaction at work, and that is his commitment to the people producing that work which he has seen or listened to free of charge. Nothing upsets a maker of art more – and yes, that probably includes a bad notice – than the breaking of an embargo or wilful attempt by the reviewer to allow spoilers into their copy.

Legally, the writer has broken no law and the producers of the work are powerless, but in terms of ethics and morals it is as bad as it gets. In the period spent writing this book, summer 2016 to spring 2017, and the year that preceded it, there were flashpoints over these issues on a scale never seen before. I would argue this was no coincidence.

December 2015 saw the release of *Star Wars: The Force Awakens*. Much of the discourse surrounding the film centred not only on the special effects and character development, but the reaction of fans as they sought to discuss plot points or avoid plot spoilers. Some online journalism played on the fears of fans, who practically had to switch off all media until they had seen the movie. Other websites, in the run-up to the film's release, had devoted all of their energy to speculation on what the new story might contain, and others wanted to engage with filmgoers who had seen it and wanted to discuss the ending. Striking the right note proved difficult for responsible reviewers. As the *Observer* critic Mark Kermode pointed out, 'even revealing the cast list runs the risk of providing potential spoilers'.

The reach of a movie will of course be greater than that of a play but if one were ever to give a film a run for its money at the box office then London in the summer of 2016 provided an interesting test. In fact the impact of *Star Wars* was even cited by Sonia Friedman, co-producer of the Harry Potter play that opened to an extraordinary fanfare. Making the point to Mark Lawson (2016) in the *Guardian*, in a quote that went round the world, she made this comparison:

> Imagine *Star Wars* opening in one cinema in one city and that was the only place you could see it. That's sort of what's happening with this.

A near-hysteria greeted the world premiere of *Harry Potter and the Cursed Child*, a five-hour play in two parts which moved the action of J.K. Rowling's novels on to show her eponymous hero now a father to his own family and working at the Ministry of Magic. Preview performances began on 7 June 2016 at the Palace Theatre in London's West End, but an embargo remained on any review until after the official first night on 30 July. For the record that is a full seven weeks of previews. So why the fuss?

Let us backtrack slightly. An embargo is a journalistic convention designed to ensure that the news reporter – or, in this case, critic – does not publish until it suits the party which has issued it. In arts and entertainment terms the practice is linked to the introduction of previews, an idea imported from New York in 1968 largely, as Michael Billington points out, to offset the problem of a reduced touring circuit which, in the past, would have given shows more time to fix any problems. Preview performances are open to the public but come before the official 'first night',[4] usually a few days or perhaps a week later.

In the run-up to the opening of *Cursed Child*, arts journalists and reporters wrote of an unprecedented level of excitement for a single production. Three themes featured heavily: the rush for tickets, the casting of a black actor (Noma Dumezweni) as Hermione and a campaign to #KeepTheSecrets – banners inside the theatre, badges handed out to audience members and a YouTube video posted by Rowling urging everyone not to spoil the story for those yet to see it.

Fans restrained themselves rather well, but two national newspapers failed the test. While the *Guardian* had a reporter stationed outside the theatre, asking attendees of the very first public performance what they thought and publishing his report at 12.53am, the *Daily Mirror* and *Daily Telegraph* ignored protocol by running reviews written by their reporters, who were among the first-night audience. The *Mirror* gave five stars. The *Telegraph* was equally enthusiastic, though it dropped its usual practice of awarding stars. The move fooled nobody, it *was* a review – 'objects seemed to disappear before our eyes' and there were 'enough shock plot twists to cause pantomime gasps from the audience' – though plot detail was avoided. Its unofficial review (Furness & Horton 2016) was posted at 11.35pm on 7 June and incorporated videos, background stories about the show and screen shots of some 80 tweets and Instagram photos.

Earlier in the evening *Daily Mail* showbusiness writer Baz Bamigboye was criticised after tweeting that 'live owls' were in the show. One disgruntled Potter fan tweeted him at 9.02pm: 'I know your industry is on its arse but you should try and retain some journalistic integrity and respect the embargo.'

Billington, in his *Guardian* piece the next day, sounded weary at the prospect of nearly two months' worth of 'online opinion-mongering before the official first night'. He worried, too, that 'by the time critics get to see the show, they will be reacting as much to the media hype as to what actually happens on stage'.

The inevitable mud-slinging that followed the *Mirror*'s and *Telegraph*'s bending of the rules had previously been seen ten months earlier for the London production of *Hamlet* with Benedict Cumberbatch in the title role. *The Times* sent Kate Maltby into the first preview and the *Daily Mail* dispatched columnist Jan Moir. The flak did not let up for days. Again Billington stepped in, calling *The Times*'s decision 'unethical' but at least applauding the quality of Maltby's review. Actor Eddie Marsan suggested Maltby should let people read a first draft of her work and playwright Roy Williams was angry at what he perceived as the unfairness of it all – 'they are called previews for a reason'. Writer and comedian David Baddiel said on Twitter that previews allowed productions a 'safe try-out space', while Mark Shenton (2015a), lead critic at *The Stage*, was quoted in his own newspaper saying that much could change between a first preview and a first night.

> As critics, it is our job to respect the artistic process; and part of the process is an acknowledgement that they need previews to work on their show before we pass judgement.

In the same edition of *The Stage*, but in the news pages, he was quoted as saying he was shocked that *The Times*, a 'quality newspaper', was stooping so low and believed the *Mail*'s effort was barely a review, its writer guilty of a 'gushing schoolgirl report'.

A part of the debate surrounding the breaking of embargoes concerns not only the fact that some newspapers are ignoring the convention, it's the worry over *what* they might say and, specifically, the inclusion of spoilers. This was clearly the case with *Harry Potter and the Cursed Child* but not for Cumberbatch's *Hamlet*, for obvious reasons when you put on a 400-year-old play by Shakespeare.

Blogger and *WhatsOnStage.com* critic Matt Trueman makes a convincing case for asking all critics to act responsibly when handling juggernaut productions like the aforementioned *Cursed Child*. It is something of a tightrope, he argues, to give a sense of the story for readers who have yet to see the work, without giving the game away, but it is possible nonetheless. Sitting in one of the preview performances perfectly underlined for Trueman (2016) the importance of story. 'When key plot points dropped, there were huge gasps through the audience – gasps like I can't remember.'

The decision, he adds, by Sonia Friedman, the producer, to let critics into earlier performances but embargo their review until a minute past midnight on 26 July was 'a smart move', and it is difficult to disagree.

> Rather than writing at full-pelt then, under pressure to file as quickly as possible, within an hour – max – of the curtain call, we've got a bit of breathing space. Writing at speed, under such pressure, it's only natural to reach for plot – simply to describe what happens; to report it, not to reflect on it. That way spoilers lie. Under the new plan, not only do critics have time for considered writing, we can find subtle ways to skirt key plot points.
>
> *(Trueman 2016)*

Pressure, I would argue, is the number-one factor pushing journalists to disrespect embargoes and the unwritten rule that spoilers are a cheap shot: pressure to hang on to the readers they do have, that loyal band still buying the newspaper several times a week; pressure to drive traffic online. More clicks equals not only a bigger audience and the potential to grow advertising revenue, but the chance to stay relevant to readers swamped by choice. Indeed, it is a theme we can recognise in the next section, too.

The scandal of fake reviews

A scenario of deception was played out in the late summer of 2012, culminating in the naming and shaming of authors who were caught out fabricating both glowing reviews and more general enthusiasm for their own work. Crime author Jeremy Duns, in a case worthy of one of his stories, spent great energy proving that two high-profile writers were creating fake comments online. They were not alone, he told the *Guardian*, in Flood (2012b), as the practice was 'absolutely rife'.

One of them, Stephen Leather, admitted at the Harrogate crime festival (Flood 2012b) that he had online conversations with himself to create a buzz around his work. The method of the other writer, R.J. Ellory, was to hide behind pseudonyms to talk up the quality of his own books while being derogatory about those of his rivals in the genre. He later apologised for his 'lapse of judgement'. Flood called the summer of 2012 bad 'for the credibility of authors and online book reviewing'.

The business of fake reviewing, or sock puppetry as it has become known, has ranged from one-off misdemeanours to the systematic abuse by bestselling novelists who should know better, to large-scale purchase of positive write-ups written by 'readers'. It reached a peak in 2012 with claims and counter-claims, and at the heart of this scandal three things emerged: the exploitation of writers desperate to do well in a highly competitive arena (often pressured to engage with social media); the apparent ease with which it could be done; and a willingness by the vast majority of the writing community to stamp out illicit practice.

Leading novelists Mark Billingham, Val McDermid, Ian Rankin and Joanne Harris were among 50 writers, who, via the letters page of the *Telegraph*, urged fellow professionals to resist the temptation to misuse 'new channels in ways that are fraudulent and damaging to publishing at large'. They added: 'These days more and more books are sought, sold and recommended online, and the health of this exciting new ecosystem depends entirely on free and honest conversation among readers.'[5]

The Society of Authors was watching closely, its spokesperson told the *Guardian*. 'It [sock puppetry] is in every respect wrong. It is misleading about the book it praises, it is worse than misleading about the work it disparages. And because the truth is increasingly likely to come to light, it is also entirely counter-productive' (Flood 2012a).

Is this something for reviewers to be worried about? Aware of, certainly. Many critics in this field of reviewing double up as novelists, biographers and writers of other kinds of non-fiction. Their ethical and moral compass comes into question if asked to review something by a writer who has reviewed *them* – regardless of whether that piece was positive or negative. Flood cites the example of crime author and *Guardian* books critic Laura Wilson, who believed she had been the victim of sock puppetry following a less than favourable review she had written.

In October 2015 *Sunday Times* journalists reacted to increasing concern within the publishing industry with regard to fake reviewing by writing an e-book over a single weekend and then seeing if they could propel it to the top of the charts. Their book, *Everything Bonsai!*, was deliberately strewn with errors and they set about finding online scammers willing to dishonestly review the book. One reviewer in the USA, they reported, was willing to write five-star reviews for $5 a go and said they had access to more than 70 accounts. Not only did the investigation (Henry 2015) raise this important ethical question about the integrity of what is sometimes being written online, but highlighted how names and photographs were being harvested from Facebook and other sites to give the comments integrity. In other words, any agencies suspicious about the validity of the remarks would see that these people were genuine. Those whose identities were being misused in this way were unaware of the scam until journalists approached them. Carried along by a wave of fake admiration, the book promptly went to the top of the gardening category of Amazon UK's Kindle chart.

A week after their findings, Amazon announced (Gani 2015) it was taking court action against more than a thousand people suspected of publishing fake reviews, stripping them of their anonymity and ordering them to pay damages for the 'manipulation and deception' of Amazon customers. In a separate development in June 2016, the UK Competition and Markets Authority began its own independent inquiry into the murky underworld of false reviews.

Reviewing friends and enemies

Literature lends itself more easily than any other art form to personal testimony. Each book cover has the potential to be a mini-commercial for what is inside, often attributed to other writers we associate with this style of book. There is no real equivalent in other art forms: television shows do not feature a five-second slot before transmission where the director of another television show tells us to keep watching because we are in for treat.

In any case, a little research quickly shows book-cover testimonials often come courtesy of writers signed to the same agents or publishers as the writer whose work you have bought. For some time media commentators have poked fun at this practice, believing it cements a view that publishing – or at least publishing in the traditional sense – is somehow an exclusive club. Ethically it might be fuzzy, but it is not a crime; arguably it is a game which regular readers are familiar with and at least it helps them, especially with new authors, to identify the type of book they might enjoy.

Consider the ethics of your next reviewing job. What if you know the artist or one of the artists involved in the work? What if they are your friend? Or *were* your friend? What if you have clashed with this person before, either over something you wrote or in ordinary life? How about if you were at school or university together? Can it be ethical to review if your spouse or partner is related to them?

Though it will shock some people, critics are human too, with relationships past and present. Steering clear of evaluating work by anyone you know or have ever known may be the ideal response, but it may not be possible, particularly the older and more experienced you become in your field.

But think about how the person being reviewed is feeling. They may well dread the idea of their old university chum knocking out 500 words on their latest television project. Will they be too harsh (an attempt to avoid accusations of favouritism) or too kind? Should the association be declared? Even if the matter is handled faultlessly, someone somewhere will know of the connection and may feel the need to share the 'revelation' online.

Critics respond to the challenges of these dilemmas in different ways. Some are endlessly sociable, free from worry that a drinks party here or there attended by makers of art will somehow infect their ability to think. This is especially true, I think, when critics combine roles as profile and feature writers as well, for that kind of journalism fuels the need for good contacts. These critics might argue that being a part of an artistic community, rather than removed from it, is ultimately beneficial to everyone involved – including the reader – because the writer gets insight into that world. Others suggest a much simpler way is to avoid all personal contact with artists for fear of being compromised.

Like many critics, Nancy Durrant, at *The Times*, would not avoid social engagements with practitioners in her world (visual arts) but neither does she seek them out, she told me. She sits somewhere between the two and would rather not review if she was friends or friendly with someone involved in the making or presenting of the work, instead passing the job to someone else.[6]

But that is not always possible, especially with staff writers in smaller teams, as *WhatsOnStage* critic Matt Trueman, a former actor himself, pointed out in a column for *The Stage*:

> Some of my best friends are artists, to coin a phrase. Next month, I know I'm reviewing a couple of them, and they like that idea even less than I do … The best way to review friends is to treat them as you would anyone else: carefully, considerately, ethically.
>
> *(Trueman 2015)*

In the same newspaper Mark Shenton observed how a West End producer had cooled on their friendship after his review of her show. '"But we're friends," she said. I didn't think of the right answer till later: "Friends tell each other the truth"' (Shenton 2015c).

Other conflicts of interest

At the risk of portraying the critic as some poor outsider, constantly wrestling with her own conscience, checking in the mirror for cracks in her commitment to ethical practice, two further challenges come into view on a frequent basis. Pressure from employers or peers is one of them, so is the complexity of moving from criticism to features and back again, or even shifting from one medium to another.

Mark Lawson is one of the UK's best-known arts journalists and broadcasters, effortlessly switching between television essays, reviews and profile pieces for the *Guardian*, to theatre criticism for *The Tablet*. Millions know him as a former chief presenter on Radio 4's arts programme *Front Row* and for his in-depth interviews on BBC Four with leading lights from television and theatre.

He cites the difficulty of presenting BBC programmes which are widely respected for their objectivity and insight, yet fighting against interference behind the scenes. He explained to me:

> My worst experiences in this area came when presenting BBC arts programmes – *Late Review* and *Newsnight Review* (BBC Two) and *Front Row* (Radio 4) – which could, as part of their remit, criticise programmes produced by the BBC. In many cases, producers complained to me, my editors or senior managers that the BBC should be 'getting behind' its own programmes, rather than criticising them. A version of this tension arises often now in arts criticism, when a particular newspaper has sponsored a play, film, or art show, or run a special ticket offer.

Had working on radio and television for so many years impacted on what and how he writes in the medium of print, I wondered.

> As mentioned before, it confirmed for me the importance of being objective, even if it annoys your employer. Although I don't minimise the difficulty of this, imagine being a *Times* or *Sunday Times* reviewer of a documentary about their owner Rupert Murdoch, or, indeed if I were asked to cover an observational documentary called *Inside the Guardian*. The disadvantage of my other life is that I sometimes can't write about a television show because I have worked closely with the producer or other crew-member in the past.[7]

A similar dilemma cropped up in my conversation with another critic, Nina Myskow, whose tabloid television columns and appearances as a judge on ITV talent show *New Faces* turned her into a household name. She told me that Marti Caine, the entertainer and host of the show, predicted that Myskow would not be able to combine both roles in the long term. It helped her to decide to quit Fleet Street on a full-time basis. 'I was appearing more and more on television and I was compromising myself on what I was writing about – hesitating.'[8]

Notes

1 Myskow, Nina (24 June 2016), interview with the author.
2 Norman, Neil (27 July 2016), interview with the author.
3 *Ibid*.
4 Even the nineteenth century provides evidence of controversy surrounding first-night criticism. *The Stage*, on 1 November 1880, published a plea for critics to be kinder, pointing out the difficulty for an actor being judged on opening night 'when he has the least chance of being at his best'. The newspaper toyed with the idea that a 'first night audience' should come three or four days after opening but ruled it out. Michael Billington suggested that showbusiness reporters should be invited to first previews, 'not to deliver a verdict but simply to describe the occasion' (2016).

5 www.telegraph.co.uk/comment/letters/9518322/Authors-condemn-fake-internet-reviews.html.
6 Durrant, Nancy (7 September 2016), interview with the author.
7 Lawson, Mark (30 August 2016), interview with the author.
8 Myskow, Nina (24 June 2016), interview with the author.

References

Anon. (19 December 1985) 'Actress wins £10,000 libel damages', *Guardian*.
Anon. (14 February 1987) 'Critic wins new trial in Cornwell libel suit', *Guardian*.
Anon. (11 December 2001) 'David Soul wins libel case', BBC News, news.bbc.co.uk/1/hi/entertainment/1703894.stm.
Anon. (12 October 2015) 'Amazon fake reviews bought for £3', *The Bookseller*, www.thebookseller.com/news/true-extent-paid-reviews-scams-revealed-undercover-investigation-314272.
Billington, Michael (8 June 2016) 'Harry Potter and the cursed previews: The opening of plays has become absurd', *Guardian*, www.theguardian.com/stage/2016/jun/08/harry-potter-and-the-cursed-child-previews-opening-plays-system-absurd.
Filler, Martin (25 September 2014) 'A letter correcting and apologizing for a statement about Zaha Hadid', *New York Review of Books*, www.nybooks.com/articles/2014/09/25/apology-zaha-hadid/.
Flood, Alison (3 September 2012a) 'R.J. Ellory's secret Amazon reviews anger rivals', *Guardian*, www.theguardian.com/books/2012/sep/03/rj-ellory-secret-amazon-reviews.
Flood, Alison (5 September 2012b) 'One of the most talented authors of today…', *Guardian*.
Furness, Hannah and Horton, Helena (7 June 2016) '*Harry Potter and the Cursed Child*: "Spine-chilling and stunning": Fans give their verdict plus an owl escapes backstage', *Telegraph*, www.telegraph.co.uk/theatre/what-to-see/harry-potter-and-the-cursed-child-opening-night-of-part-one–li/.
Gani, Aisha (18 October 2015) 'Amazon will sue 1,100 fake reviewers', *Guardian*, www.theguardian.com/technology/2015/oct/18/amazon-sues-1000-fake-reviewers.
Henry, Robin (11 October 2015) 'How to fake a bestseller', *Sunday Times*, www.thesundaytimes.co.uk/sto/news/uk_news/National/article1618237.ece.
Keeble, Richard (2001) *The Newspapers Handbook*. London: Routledge.
Kermode, Mark (2013) *Hatchet Job: Love Movies, Hate Critics*. London: Picador.
Lawson, Mark (21 July 2016) '*Harry Potter and the Cursed Child*: It's extraordinary the story still isn't out', *Guardian*, www.theguardian.com/stage/2016/jul/21/harry-potter-and-the-cursed-child-west-end-palace-theatre.
Martin, Brian (1998) *Information Liberation*. London: Freedom Press, www.uow.edu.au/~bmartin/pubs/98il/il06.html.
Martin, Brian (2011) 'Defending dissent', in *Media and Social Justice*, eds S. Jansen, J. Pooley and L. Taub-Pervizpour. Basingstoke: Palgrave Macmillan.
Royal Commission on the Press (undated) Press Council Annual Reports, cited in Seymour-Ure (1991).
Seymour-Ure, Colin (1991) *The British Press and Broadcasting since 1945*. Oxford: Basil Blackwell.
Shenton, Mark (13 August 2015a) 'Previews should be critic-free zones', *The Stage*.
Shenton, Mark (13 August 2015b) 'Outcry after *The Times* and *Daily Mail* breach review protocol', news report, *The Stage*.

Shenton, Mark (17 September 2015c) 'Reviewing friends is a risky business', *The Stage*.
Spilsbury, Mark (2013) *Journalists At Work Survey*. Saffron Walden: National Council for the Training of Journalists.
Stempel, Jonathan (21 August 2014) 'Top architect Hadid files defamation lawsuit over book review', Reuters, www.reuters.com/article/us-hadid-lawsuit-idUSKBN0GL29420140821.
Taylor, Amy (9 September 2012) 'Trash and the libel case, or how to piss off a theatre critic', *thetaylortrash.com*, https://thetaylortrash.com/tag/national-union-of-journalists/.
Trueman, Matt (3 September 2015) 'It's best to review friends as you would anyone else', *The Stage*.
Trueman, Matt (25 July 2016) 'Why should critics #KeepTheSecrets of Harry Potter?', *WhatsOnStage*, www.whatsonstage.com/london-theatre/news/critics-keep-secrets-harry-potter-reviews-trueman_41355.html.
Ward, Stephen J.A. (2005) *The Invention of Journalism Ethics: The Path to Objectivity and Beyond*. Montreal: McGill-Queen's University Press.

8
EVERYONE'S A CRITIC

At some point in any discussion on the future of the printed press, somebody will make a perfectly reasonable argument that we have buried it before it is dead. Look at radio, they say. Radio came along with its news and information at national and local levels and newspapers survived. Then television. The television put pictures with sound, creating anxiety in radioland but still radio survived – as did newspapers and magazines. This is proof, the argument goes, that newspapers and magazines will also shake off the threat of the Worldwide Web; changed forever but able to sustain the surge.

The problem with this argument is twofold. On one level, the scars and injuries from previous fights could eventually leave the printed page battle-weary and unable to resist another attack. Second, the Web – or the attacker if you want to keep the image going – has a distinct difference from previous threats. Whereas newspapers, radio and television communicated directly with its audience, allowing zero or very minimal interaction (a letter to the editor, perhaps a request for a signed photograph of your favourite presenter), publishing on the Web allows users to not only consume and respond to content but add to it.

Steve Hill and Paul Lashmar in *Online Journalism: The Essential Guide* (2014) credit Jay Rosen, of New York University, with coining the phrase 'the people formerly known as the audience' and describe it a useful explanation of the 'changing producer–consumer relationship between journalist and audience'. Rosen (2006) wrote, they point out, that the media system 'ran one way', with providers 'competing to speak very loudly while the rest of the population listened in isolation from one another – and who today are not in a situation like that at all'.

At the time of writing I have spent ten years as a journalism lecturer at De Montfort University and, with each passing year, have seen a shift in the way students get their news and information. Ten years ago I asked them, who buys a newspaper? I would break that down into 'regularly' or 'twice a week' or 'never'. Some would say not at all but a significant proportion out of a class of 24 mostly 18-year-olds would say they bought a paper once or twice a week. In the intervening years I have, with new cohorts, adjusted the question to who *reads* a newspaper on a regular basis? With a rare exception, no student now buys a printed newspaper at all and, as an interesting sub-plot, it would appear their parents are also reluctant to buy one. Some students may engage with websites operated by national newspapers but they are just as likely to seek news online from the BBC, Sky, Fox or myriad alternatives far too many to mention. They never see their local newspaper. While it is no shock that 18-year-olds do not rush out to buy the local paper, it is telling they never engage with it on any platform. Of course, my colleagues and I encourage students to read a broad range of media, including quality newspapers for depth and insight, red-top tabloids for sharp writing, but instinctively they are drawn to the Web and the sites that best fit their world, their needs.

Why would we kid ourselves that in a few years' time these 18-year-olds will suddenly start picking up a copy of the *Telegraph* on their way to work?

As discussed, arts critics as much as any kind of newspaper journalist or writer – and more than most – have found themselves vulnerable to the digital transformation of the media. Where there *is* work to be had, this seismic shift has signalled a greater reliance on freelance reviewers. Additionally, it has created increasing difficulty in getting paid for the words written or at least paid a fair rate, and in the UK heralds the end (or perhaps the beginning of the end) of the professional critic living outside London.

Now there are potent alternatives to the arts journalism served up by the legacy media. They come in the form of online expansion created by those brands and by websites, blogs, podcasts and videos posted on YouTube. Their rise, along with the fall of traditional media, has been well documented in books, in journal articles, in newspapers and magazines and (naturally) online for the best part of 20 years. The feelings expressed in these pieces include fear, hope, anger, excitement or a combination of all of them. Running through much of this writing are debates about the implications of the democratisation of the Internet and the legitimacy of the amateur critic pitted against the experienced professional. As Haydon (2016) points out, the word 'professional' became 'a frequent stick used to beat the "amateur" unpaid critic, blogger or website reviewer'.

This chapter will consider how the Web gave a possibility for everyone to become a critic, and what effect it has had on readers and writers.

Background

Newspaper and magazine publishers grew curious about the potential of the Web in or around 1997 and 1998, in turn emboldened by the newest, fanciest conference presentation their managing directors had attended or in some cases making tentative steps because their boss had insisted it should be done. For the most part these slow, clunky websites bore little relation to the quality of what was happening in print; furthermore, as bizarre as it remains true, some parts of the UK regional press online were even branded entirely differently from their printed, more glamorous sibling. Editors, nervous that free content would disrupt all that they had built in terms of circulation stability, ticked the box by allowing inferior material to be uploaded or – as became the norm – short summaries of the story with a promise of more as long as you bought the hard-copy version. It cannot be overstated that newspaper sales figures were what kept editors awake at night. Essentially it worked like this: achieve good sales figures and it could be explained by a combination of factors working favourably, even down to the weather; bad figures and all eyes were on the editor who had better have a solution.

What newspapers failed to do though on a large enough scale was provide interesting content unique to those communities or audiences that complemented the print version. Daisy Bowie-Sell, now editor at *WhatsOnStage* but who began her career at the *Daily Telegraph*, said:

> I think print should have adapted much, much earlier than it did to the Internet. Newspapers have taken too long to do this and it has caused a lot of trouble down the line. Some of them are now turning it round in terms of getting copy in so that it's not just print-focused, which is how it should be.[1]

Nationally the *Guardian* in the UK was by some distance first off the blocks in embracing the idea that a digital-first strategy could work. It had begun experimenting in the mid-1990s with technology and football websites and launched its *Guardian Unlimited* site by 1999. Elsewhere the *New York Times* introduced its website to the world in January 1996, promising immediate access to most of the daily newspaper's contents plus bonus material. In a telling vision of what was to come, it summarised that television networks and computer companies were among those embracing Web technology and 'even individuals [were] creating electronic newspapers of their own'.

Le Monde in Paris had launched its website the previous year, as did the *Sydney Morning Herald*.

Specifically in the arts, the aforementioned *WhatsOnStage* and the *British Theatre Guide* (*BTG*) sprang up in 1997, 'two major players in British online theatre reviewing', as Haydon describes them. I have written for both of them and for many years worked for publishing company Emap, founders of *WhatsOnStage*. The *BTG* was founded by Peter Lathan initially as a resource for drama teachers and *WhatsOnStage* was, as launch editor Terri Paddock tells Haydon (2016), first a host for basic listings which developed an e-commerce element – essentially 'if someone wanted to buy tickets they could hit a button which would send an email to the office and someone at Emap would call the box office'.

In the USA the film reviews aggregator site *Rotten Tomatoes* began life in 1998, two years ahead of the highly influential music site *Pitchfork*. It is of course impossible to chart the beginnings of every important arts website across the globe, but we can signpost the mid-to-late 1990s as a turning point, though not the whole story – the user-generated content (UGC) sites which sprang up as a result of the

Web 2.0 explosion cranked things up a notch and brought into sharp focus the idea that the professional critic had a younger, hungrier breed snapping at its heels.

Traditional media players, despite many of them making some attempt to engage with their readers online from 1995 onwards, would, in some cases, take another 10, 12 or even more years to fully embrace a digital-first strategy. Even as recently as 2014 there was a high-profile opposition to the change. Natalie Nougayrède, editor-in-chief of *Le Monde* in Paris, felt she had to resign following, as the *New York Times* (2014) reported, 'staff resistance to her efforts to push the paper faster and more fully into the digital era'. History of media professor Patrick Eveno was quoted as saying this kind of upheaval in France was similar to what American newspapers had experienced years before. 'It has taken French journalists time to understand that it wasn't just an economic crisis, but a crisis in social habits, that the information as a product had to be transformed' (2014).

France was not alone in struggling to adapt to new market forces where readers expect content for free. British national newspaper the *Independent* closed in 2016 along with its Sunday edition, and regional papers have taken a battering with the closure of weeklies, while some smaller evening titles reinvented themselves as weeklies. Research by *Press Gazette* (2015) estimated there had been a net reduction – that is, closures offset by launches – of around 180 local titles since 2005. *Press Gazette* also reported that around 6,000 jobs had been slashed in a two-year period from 2013 (Ponsford 2015). We can add to that other factors designed to stem the tide, which include pay freezes, sharing staff and content, losing or limiting freelance photographic cover in favour of supplied pictures or reducing the size of the newspaper (even shaving a centimetre from the depth of a newspaper will, across a publishing group, across a year, mean massive savings given that the advertising rates will stay the same).

By the time the *Guardian* positioned itself as a digital-first brand in 2011 – again ahead of the curve in the UK – three things had become abundantly clear. One, the digital revolution was changing the way people consumed all media, not just newspapers but music and television, for example; two, readers were not only accustomed to commenting on stories 'below the line' but were using smartphone technology to generate and complement news stories; three, blogs were very much part of the media furniture.

Democratisation of the Internet

Academics often refer to what is happening to arts criticism and to journalism more generally as being part of the democratisation of the Internet, and agreement cannot be reached on whether it is a good thing that reviewing is now receptive to so many different kinds of voices. Voices, it has to be said, that for the most part would not have been heard in a system of values driven by newspapers. Of course, with pleasing symmetry, those very battles about whether there should be room for Web-based criticism are now being played out – on the Internet. But as Radosavljevic points out, something unexpected is happening as well:

> The paradox is that, despite this apparent openness of access [to the Internet], the actual hierarchies of opinions in the digital realm might become even stricter. The way I see this is through the shift of power from an editor (deciding on the publishability value of a text) towards the reader (deciding on the readability value of the text), and the latter being more difficult to discern or standardise.
>
> *(Radosavljevic 2016)*

Why has this shift occurred? First we should remind ourselves why criticism exists in the first place – a record of experience, a personal response, a way of understanding why an artwork can be linked with something else we have encountered or even wish to encounter either thematically or by the people responsible for the work. But also, as is evident with the checks we make about hotels or holiday cottages on Trip Advisor, we want assurances from people like us. We may question the validity of some of these reviews, but we read them all the same.

As a result of these changes the professional newspaper or magazine critic will have adapted to this change if their career is to continue. Mark Kermode, in *Hatchet Job*, reminds us that the late Roger Ebert was an early adopter of online film reviews. 'Today every print journalist has an online presence whether they like it or not', he says, adding that 'we're all bloggers now' (2013).

He points out that the Internet has almost certainly prolonged his career. Twitter and Facebook alerts drive readers to the online version of his *Observer* reviews, while in April 2013 (the example he shared) more than 2 million people downloaded as a digital podcast the film review shows he presented alongside Simon Mayo on Radio 5. 'Stranger still, a significant proportion of the audience choose to watch the programme online, either live via the 5 live website, or later on the Kermode and Mayo YouTube channel.'

But what do mainstream critics really think about the shifts that have changed their careers or, in some cases, threatened to end them? Neil Norman said:

> Probably the greatest challenge to the critic today is the sheer number of outlets for anyone who wants to express an opinion, however well – or ill – informed. Thanks to the democratisation wrought by the Internet and social media everyone can be a 'critic' and bang out their thoughts on just about anything they have read, heard, tasted or seen. This has raised the bar for professional critics who have spent a career and much of their lives studying and thinking about work in their selected field as they are now competing with neophytes and fans whose literacy and critical powers range from the impressive to the imbecilic.[2]

This suggestion that a crowded virtual space of critics has forced the old school to up their game is an intriguing one. Music writer Dave Simpson recognises it as well, that 'the modern day critic is less an opinionated voice, and more a consumer guide to help people through the labyrinth'.[3] It is not necessarily a bad thing, he argues. This happens in two distinct ways. First, because publishing online makes a traditional critic's work potentially available to the world (leaving aside for now the notion of paywalls or other such restrictions for a printed title), it leaves the review – and therefore its reviewer – exposed to criticism himself. Most obviously this works in factual errors. Given that there is always someone, somewhere who knows more than you do, a wrong date or name can be seized upon by an eager fan, as can an opinion that does not sit easily with a reader who sets to explaining why you got it so badly wrong. Second, influenced by the breadth of work written about online, there is clear evidence of reviewers being more open to different styles, genres and artists, and even different towns, cities and nations with which they may not have ordinarily engaged.

One of the accusations often thrown at the critic is that he is out of touch, set in his ways. The dead white male label referred to earlier in the book is rolled out as evidence that the business of arts criticism needed shaking up anyway – they had it coming – and Web-based citizen criticism was great timing. The emergence of twenty-first-century criticism in the UK especially was a reminder that younger writers from more diverse backgrounds offered a compelling alternative to what was seen in some quarters as safe, predictable reviewing from middle-aged or older men, most of whom would have been educated in elite universities. Indeed, the conveyor belt of men as reviewers was formed even a hundred years ago – a 1923 Critics' Circle newsletter reported how 'it means much for the future that Oxbridge, Cambridge, London and other universities are definitely preparing some of their most promising men to become critics'.

It is not the complete picture, though. Theatre criticism has certainly been dominated by this kind of profile, as have – to varying degrees – such other art forms as film, literature, dance, classical music and visual art, though popular music – with its reputation for rebellion anyway – has steered clear of such stereotypes.

In negotiating this new wave of citizen criticism and all that it brings – the real chance that much of it will be unpaid, that press reviews will be cut both in terms of their volume and length – Mark Lawson made the point to me that traditional newspaper reviewers have gone on the defensive, 'forced to argue their right to existence, or at least any special claim to be heard within the democracy of opinion'.[4]

There is good and useful Web-based criticism published by accomplished individuals knowledgeable about their area, and then there is other material thin in argument and bedevilled by problems with style, tone and consistency. Not everyone appreciates the work of this kind of critic.
Lawson again:

> Some of my more belligerent colleagues argue (privately) along the lines that you wouldn't want a 'citizen surgeon' taking out your appendix, and so should no more submit to a self-appointed critic, but I think it's risky to compare complex medical procedures with two opinions on whether *Are You Being Served?* should have been revived.[5]

In his essay 'Between journalism and art: The location of criticism in the twenty-first century', *Sunday Herald* and Scottish critic for the *Daily Telegraph*, Mark Brown (2016), goes public with his belligerence, concluding that the citizen critic is 'an amateur, a mere dabbler', though it is a view tempered somewhat by a clear rebuke for the 'many established critics, both in academe and the popular press, [who] are wallowing almost masochistically in such subjects as the remorseless rise of the internet, the decline of the printed page (particularly newspapers and magazines) and the much-vaunted "death of the critic"'.

But if these old-school reviewers needed a boost then they got it in the summer of 2016 with comments made by Sonia Friedman, co-producer of *Harry Potter and the Cursed Child*, which opened at the Duke of York's Theatre and had already sold enough tickets to play to full houses for the next year at least. Although bloggers and tweeters could react in an instant to what they had seen, Friedman went on the record to say that the impact of traditional critics should not be underestimated. In comments pouring cold water on the idea that digital media was in the driving seat, she told Richard Morrison (2016) in *The Times*:

> Without question the moment that really matters for any new piece of theatre, but particularly one of this size and complexity, is when the critics give their verdict. Not in commercial terms, but in terms of 'did this piece of theatre work?' It's true that social media has changed the game, but the tweeters and bloggers aren't the experts. To take Harry Potter to the next level we need to attract not just Potter fans but general theatregoers, and they wait for the critics' verdicts. They aren't looking at social media.

It would seem, then, that not everyone is convinced by the power of amateur commentators for all eventualities. Television critic Mark Lawson said that in his experience, citizen criticism was well informed and had value but was too often aimed at other (sometimes obsessive) viewers of the show in mind and so relied on being 'exhaustively detailed or statistical'.[6]

Often central to the objection to the citizen critic is a question mark regarding authenticity. Thinking of this as merely an amateur versus professional grudge match rather misses the point: established critics have a bank of memories, a consolidated view and in many cases a loyal readership. But Web-based amateur writers (unpaid: strictly no other meaning intended) can have all of that as well, it can be suggested, but what they do not always have is accountability to an editor ultimately responsible for what they have written. Validity comes about, Kermode argues, by the risk involved – for the writer it is her next commission, for the publisher it is readership and reputation. 'The problem with many social media reviews', Kermode (2013) observes, 'is that they carry no weight because the people who write them have no track record, and therefore have nothing of value invested in their accuracy or honesty.'

Logically, however, that argument will fade in time (he published it in 2013) as non-traditional critics accumulate experience and followers. Perhaps revenue as well in the future, though being paid for their review is not necessarily the prime motivation for some writers.

What can be concluded is that a digital response to arts criticism has had a huge effect in three key areas: the speed of publication both after and even while the art is in progress, the sheer breadth of art being covered and the creative way critics have embraced it.

An instant response

Online journalism and social media have opened up wider possibilities to respond quickly to a work of art, in a sense replicating the urgency of a news environment to win the 'race' to review first. In turn, readers are able to challenge or support those reviews almost as they are published. The motives for comments below the line differ enormously. For every measured, constructive stance against what the critic believed there comes a rant, a wholly disproportionate attack on the writer who must surely be covering up the fact that (a) they're taking bribes, (b) they're related to the artist or (c) they didn't even read the book in question. For every smart, insightful remark designed to encourage genuine debate, there is another boasting of how you, too, can earn $400 a day.

Refreshingly, Neil Norman is one of those critics who sees the positives in those below-the-line comments. He told me:

> Readers' comments are always welcome – whether favourable or unfavourable. At least it shows that somebody out there is reading the stuff! I am happy to engage in a debate if occasion and time allows. Social media has made this much easier, of course.[7]

If some critics begrudgingly dragged their heels into twenty-first-century journalism, many have rather enjoyed – as Norman points out – the attention the comments bring. While the practice is not without risk (a critic lazy on research, sloppy on fact-checking will quickly get caught out by knowledgeable readers), it does at least demonstrate to editors that their critic is hitting the mark. These new terms and conditions between writer and reader forced reviewers to up their game, not least the notion – once unthinkable – of critics engaging with their readers. Most obviously this involved responding to points in the comments section but also developing their skills on different platforms like Twitter, video and podcasts.

For some critics, speed of publishing went to a whole new level thanks to the smartphone, but it has also enabled Twitter users to effectively start a conversation while the art is still in progress. Television, in particular, allows this instant critical reaction from the public. While we no longer watch shows in quite the same way as we did, Twitter does at least give a nod to the idea that we are all crowded around the television set in the corner of the lounge. On Monday, 29 May 2016 BBC Two launched its rebooted version of motoring show *Top Gear*, fronted by radio presenter Chris Evans and American actor Matt LeBlanc following the controversial sacking of its original star Jeremy Clarkson. Within eight minutes of the opening credits, one viewer had had enough and tweeted: 'No no no no no no no. Chris Evans is trying too hard to be @Jeremy Clarkson in the new #TopGear. I cannot take his explanations seriously.' Exactly a minute later another viewer saw it entirely differently: '#TopGear loving it so far … Seems a more classy upmarket version … In your face Clarkson.'

News providers reacted to this reaction with equally impressive speed, though analysis and depth were not particularly their targets.

Clearly some arts disciplines require quick turnaround more than others and lend themselves more readily to the experience. This can be determined by the limitations of time and by the minimum standards we require of others while sharing the same art experience. More precisely, readers who read the same book published on a certain day will engage with it differently, they will not all finish the last page in unison. Plays, however, along with opera, concerts and other live events, begin at a certain time of day and enable the reviewer to respond afterwards as soon as possible. Even within the live event, a critic writing his review on his phone at a rock concert is going to be less of a distraction to the audience than a critic tapping away in the fifth row of a theatre.

Iain Shedden, music critic at the *Australian*, told me it was now normal to file reviews very quickly at the end of a gig. He gave as an example a festival in New South Wales where he was writing his account of The Strokes and The Cure gigs while they were still in progress.

> This happens often in Sydney too if I'm reviewing something of the calibre of Bruce Springsteen or U2. It has to be online as soon as possible. I still write reviews of concerts for the paper as well, but opportunities to spend a day or two musing on an artist's nuances are becoming less frequent.[8]

Daily Telegraph critic Neil McCormick uses the same principle for his live work – both his Coldplay and Adele reviews from Glastonbury 2016 were written this way.

> Both those reviews were written in a field of mud, tapping into my phone whilst the artist was on stage, filed at the encores and ready to be read online before I got back to the hospitality bar. So I wouldn't say they are amongst my most considered works but that is very much the way of modern music journalism.[9]

Blogging and being creative

Earlier in the chapter we talked about the democratisation of the Internet, and it is clear that one of the most powerful forms of writing to emerge from a digital landscape is blogging. Across the globe writers passionate about the arts have, in the last ten years particularly, shared their enthusiasm and knowledge with the rest of us. Blogs span the full range of arts disciplines and differ widely in their levels of accomplishment. Some bloggers see their remit as being to entertain (themselves perhaps as much as anyone else) while others view their published work as a starting point for a career. In the chapters to follow we will look at specifics involving bloggers who have managed to earn money from their writing.

Free from the shackles of editorial control and limitations surrounding the publication cycle of print (when to publish) and how to print (a set number of pages), bloggers have provided a refreshing alternative to mainstream journalism. Indeed, some bloggers have so many followers and are so influential that we might deem them to be *part* of the mainstream.

Where arts blogs work well they have some or all of these characteristics:

- a clear target audience
- an interesting/different viewpoint
- a compelling writing style
- news and interviews in addition to reviews
- a strong presence on social media
- a sense of community
- links to other relevant websites or blogs
- video or audio to complement the content.

To settle on just one of those points – the audience – the blogger does not have the weight of a powerful publishing brand behind her which will open doors for her, but what she does have is the scope to go deeper, more niche with her journalism than mainstream titles can. Notice how many successful blogs are not just about a subject but explore areas within that subject in greater detail. In fact some of them actually celebrate and perpetuate the idea that their blog is best for geeks.

On the question of viewpoint, I asked Megan Vaughan, the influential theatre blogger behind *Synonyms for Churlish*, what she believed her blog had brought to the table that was an alternative to criticism in print. She began by saying this was a difficult question to answer, but added:

> The profile and power of critics writing for mainstream publications is still disproportionally large, and I still get frustrated when I read a review on a newspaper website and I know I am both a better writer and a better thinker than the person who wrote it. But there is a sense that some online-only publications, like *Exeunt*, are growing into major players now. While there is still a distinction to be made between the economic structures that hold these publications together (*Exeunt* will be an 'alternative' to *The Times* for as long as its editorial policy remains untainted by commercial interests), I'm not sure that we should be thinking about the style of individual writers or websites as 'alternative' to anything more established. I prefer to think of it as a spectrum, or a landscape.[10]

Vaughan's chatty writing style is deceptive, it has you in its grip before you have realised, but her style of course is not the only way. In theatre alone Matt Trueman writes convincingly in print and online – interviews and reviews for newspapers, websites and his blog – all crafted with the help of his many years working in theatre. Andrew Haydon's blog *Postcards from the Gods* is similarly arresting, as is *theatreCat* from Libby Purves, the former theatre critic at *The Times*. But offering a completely different perspective is *A West End Whinger*.

With fabulous self-deprecation, this blog uses as its motif an apparent jibe once made about it by the theatre critic Michael Coveney, who said it was 'full of trivial opinions'. Penned by 'Andrew' and 'Phil', the blog promises to 'help you decide between the Merlot and the Marlowe'. Humour is at the core of their reviews, involving camp put-downs, theatreland in-jokes and even a great twist on the ubiquitous five-star rating system: here 'Andrew' and 'Phil' have opted for pictures of glasses of red wine instead, demonstrating how personality can shine on the Web in ways not always possible in print (at least not in newspapers; magazines can sometimes offer more leg-room to stretch out).

The playful tone is carried into the viewpoint as well – no standard first-person approach here. Instead reviews are written in the third person: 'When Phil told his mother he was going to see *Our Ladies of Perpetual Succour* she asked, in all innocence, "What are they sucking?"' Or try this for a London production of *Jesus Christ Superstar*: we are several paragraphs in before we learn what *A West End Whinger* thinks of the show. Prior to that we learn that it was the Phil's first experience of the West End and how, with the help of his friend, he taped the original album on to a reel-to-reel machine. 'He typed out the entire lyrics using his sister's Brother typewriter, bound the sheets with Sellotape and created a cover reproducing the album artwork using felt tip pens. Quite an achievement for a 25-year-old' (West End Whinger 2016a and 2016b).

Hill and Lashmar (2014) identify that two key elements are at the core of social media, and both of these can be applied to *A West End Whinger* and thousands of other blogs worldwide. Participation, they observe, is important; here users not only read the content but can create it as well. Then the idea of community is equally vital. Communities of course are not restricted by geography; far from it. Instead, on the Web, a community is a reference to a shared interest. The 'Whingers' may refer to a location (London) but readers will be scattered throughout the UK and further afield. The community is strengthened when content is shared and, as the authors suggest, 'a story or a funny video can act as social capital when shared among a group of friends who find the content significant'.

Videos and podcasts

User-generated content can be shared at astonishing rates. In 2012 alone, Hill and Lashmar report (2014), on average 60 hours of video was uploaded to YouTube every minute. One of the reasons arts reviewing is popular on YouTube is because the reviewer is able to convey a clear emotional response to the work. Saying something is terrible is one thing, *showing* how you feel adds another layer to the review and this may be done with facial expression, body language, tone and volume of the voice, even using a sound – for example 'Aaaaaaagggghhhhh!' or a noise suggesting dread – which may not work so well as a published word. Purists may not approve, but the noises *they* make and the rolling of *their* eyes are unlikely to have any effect; the video reviewer is here to stay.

One popular film reviewer using YouTube in the USA is Chris Stuckmann. As an indicator of his reach, his take on *The Girl on the Train* was seen 148,000 times only three days after he posted it. With introductory music and credits in the style of a blockbuster movie, Stuckmann talks straight to camera interspersed with fast cuts and still photography of scenes from the film.

Discussing his work, Stuckmann says: 'When I moved over to doing video reviews I found that I was able to enthuse so much more energy physically into a video than I was able to into my writing, and that's one of the things that appealed to me most' (2014).

His website lays bare a hope that YouTube reviewers will 'continue to gain more respect as legitimate film critics', a point amplified in one of his postings in which he shares disappointment that film critics *writing* about the art – some of whom are 'decidedly hostile' – do not see the video equivalent as being 'for real'.

Stuckmann is one of hundreds, if not thousands, of video reviewers creating content about films. The standard, it will come as no surprise, is variable and the style and subject matter equally diverse. Some reviewers pitch themselves as serious film 'critics', others make no apology for the simplistic language, the mimicry of actors or scenes, or reviews presented as comedy characters. Doug Walker's *Nostalgia Critic*, for example, fits into the character category and has a huge following – views between half and three-quarters of a million are not unheard of, while the number of comments on his site regularly exceed 100 (even a posting that 'Doug was unwell' and unable to show anything garnered 60 get-well messages). Alicia Malone, meanwhile, sits on her sofa or her bed to tell us what she thinks of a trio of film choices in any one posting. *Malonesmovieminute.com* is an example of a journalist spanning news, reviews and celebrity interviews.

The voice of the people

Momentum is firmly behind the 'amateur' reviewer who wants to share her experience of an artwork with the world, and there have never been more platforms on which it can happen. A nervous collective of critics has stood and watched (and read and listened) as millions of Internet users post, blog, tweet, write and talk their way through millions of books, movies, songs, video games and more. Who needs reviewers if film distribution companies are happy to display posters on the London Underground or take out advertisements in national newspapers, quoting the tweet that Louise, 23, sent moments after seeing that new romcom. Who'd need reviewers if Simon Mayo's Radio 2 Book Club was rolled out across other art forms? That is not to say it is not a clever idea or an entertaining show – not at all, it clearly works. Essentially an author is interviewed by Mayo and his co-presenter about his/her new book. The presenters have their say and then open it out to pre-recorded messages – effectively short reviews – from listeners. Mostly these are very positive comments, with one or two thrown in with just a hint of negativity, perhaps a concern about the ending or a complaint that there were too many characters to have to keep track of – in other words, nothing too heavy, for the author is there in the studio. Still, it is good radio and helps stimulate discussion about reading and about stories.

Online, the engagement with amateur reviewing is on a different scale altogether. Amazon book reviews, for example, have extraordinary reach and from the comments posted, suggest huge numbers of people genuinely find them useful. Real concern was expressed, though, when in 2013 Amazon announced the acquisition of *Goodreads.com*. Launched in 2007, it is, according to its website, 'the world's largest site for readers and book recommendations', with a mission to 'help people find and share books they love'. It holds awards ceremonies, interviews with authors and has other features designed to keep its 55 million members feeling as if they are part of a community. With an eye-watering 50 million reviews notched up, we begin to understand the potential power of the brand allied to the distribution clout of its parent company.

Kermode (2013) says Amazon has become the 'world's largest market-place for film products' with its ownership of Internet Movie Database (information), *Lovefilm.com* (rental/streaming) and more recently Amazon Studios to develop its own television shows and movies. The *Goodreads* purchase 'provoked howls of outrage about monopolistic practices in the book trade', he says, with a warning of how that might affect the future of film criticism.

Despite the negativity, it would appear to be having no effect on the website. At the time of writing this chapter, I followed the level of interest from members on dozens of books. Members rate the book and an average rating is taken from those scores based on a five-star system. Books with fewer than 100 ratings are unusual; indeed often they score well in excess of 300 ratings. Sometimes the books smash the 3,000 mark, while one publication stood out by a distance – Jack Thorne's playscript for J.K. Rowling's *Harry Potter and the Cursed Child* brought about an astonishing 200,000 ratings.

But what to make of the integrity of these reviews on sites like this, and others like them? For all the grinding of teeth from the 'professionals', a 2012 Harvard Business School study challenged perceived wisdom with a lengthy research project over several years analysing 100 non-fiction reviews in 40 major media outlets. It compared reviews on Amazon with *metacritic.com* on reviews in titles like the *Washington Post* and the *Guardian* and came away with a headline finding that experts and consumers agreed in aggregate about the quality of a book. The authors (Dobrescu, Luca & Motta 2012) found that professional critics were 'less favourable to first-time authors', suggesting that consumer reviewers were 'quicker to identify new and unknown books'.

Meanwhile in the UK, former publisher Peter Crawshaw has come up with a business model for book reviews that marries expert professional guidance with knowledgeable amateurs. *Lovereading.co.uk* formed in 2006 as an online bookshop underpinned by reviews from a nucleus of about ten book experts alongside a 600-strong reader review panel. Crawshaw accepts there is a point to the 'wisdom of the crowd' that is driven online but believes there are other factors at play. He says:

> Some people do know more about things than you do. These people have lived and breathed books their entire life and if they rate a book then it's going to have more value than that said by Mrs X of Arcacia Avenue. It's a curated approach from experts with real provenance. It's not trying to be anti-net but in truth these people do know more about books than the general public.

It is not an open-ended invitation for reviewers to write in the way that Amazon works. They are asked to apply. 'We do know these people, it's not a sock puppet issue.'[11]

Notes

1 Bowie-Sell, Daisy (25 April 2016), interview with the author.
2 Norman, Neil (27 July 2016), interview with the author.
3 Simpson, Dave (27 July 2016), interview with the author.
4 Lawson, Mark (30 August 2016), interview with the author.
5 *Ibid*.
6 *Ibid*.
7 Norman, Neil (27 July 2016), interview with the author.
8 Shedden, Iain (27 July 2016), interview with the author.
9 McCormick, Neil (17 October 2016), interview with the author.
10 Vaughan, Megan (17 July 2016), interview with the author.
11 Crawshaw, Peter (29 July 2016), interview with the author.

References

Brown, Mark (2016) 'Between journalism and art: The location of criticism in the twenty-first century', in *Theatre Criticism: Changing Landscapes*, ed. Duska Radosavljevic. London: Bloomsbury Methuen Drama.
de la Baume, Maia and Rubin, Alissa J. (14 May 2014) 'Editor of *Le Monde* resigns amid discord', *New York Times*, www.nytimes.com/2014/05/15/world/europe/editor-of-le-monde-resigns-amid-discord.html?_r=0.
Dobrescu, Loretti I. Luca, Michael and Motta, Alberto (26 April 2012) 'What makes a critic tick? Connected authors and the determinants of book reviews', Harvard Business School, http://hbswk.hbs.edu/item/what-makes-a-critic-tick-connected-authors-and-the-determinants-of-book-reviews.
Haydon, Andrew (2016) 'A brief history of online theatre criticism in England', in *Theatre Criticism: Changing Landscapes*, ed. Duska Radosavljevic. London: Bloomsbury Methuen Drama.
Hill, Steve and Lashmar, Paul (2014) *Online Journalism: The Essential Guide*. London: Sage.
Kermode, Mark (2013) *Hatchet Job: Love Movies, Hate Critics*. London: Picador.

Kirk, Ashley and Chang, Nicole (16 January 2015) 'Some 48 regional newspapers have closed since 2012 – but 39 have launched', *Press Gazette*, www.pressgazette.co.uk/some-47-regional-newspapers-have-closed-2012-39-have-launched/.

Morrison, Richard (29 July 2016) 'I think it might be the biggest project that any theatre producer has done', *The Times*.

Ponsford, Dominic (9 September 2015) '6,000 drop in number of UK journalists over two years – but 18,000 more PRs, Labour Force Survey shows', *Press Gazette*, www.pressgazette.co.uk/6000-drop-number-uk-journalists-over-two-years-18000-more-prs-labour-force-survey-shows/.

Radosavljevic, Duska (ed.) (2016) *Theatre Criticism: Changing Landscapes*. London: Bloomsbury Methuen Drama.

Rosen, Jay (27 June 2006) 'The people formerly known as the audience', *Press Think*, http://archive.pressthink.org/2006/06/27/ppl_frmr_p.html, cited in Hill & Lashmar (2014).

Stuckmann, Chris (8 June 2014) 'On film criticism', YouTube channel, www.youtube.com/watch?v=wJdfJVyDEQE.

A West End Whinger (9 August 2016a) 'Review: Jesus Christ Superstar', https://westendwhingers.wordpress.com/2016/08/09/review-jesus-christ-superstar-regents-park-open-air-theatre/.

A West End Whinger (26 August 2016b) 'Review: *Our Ladies of Perpetual Succour*', https://westendwhingers.wordpress.com/2016/08/26/review-our-ladies-of-perpetual-succour-national-theatre/.

9
BREAKING INTO THE BUSINESS

Unlike a lot of professions where a set pathway of learning bolstered by qualifications will in turn lead to a career, journalism looks hazy. The days where an eager, aspiring reporter could finish their school exams one week and land a job on their local paper the next, are long consigned to history. Now the rich array of choices facing the young journalist is to do with how and where to train or study rather than which job to go for. On the one hand, these exciting, inventive programmes offer an invaluable insight into the job and are increasingly specialised (an undergraduate degree in football journalism is a case in point). More negatively, they baffle as much as they inspire.

Research is vital, therefore, if the aspiring journalist is to stand any chance of navigating her way through the detail of accredited and non-accredited courses. British journalism training is broadly broken down as follows: pure journalism courses targeting print and multi-media would often seek accreditation from the National Council for the Training of Journalists. Aspiring radio and television reporters may sign up for a course accredited by the Broadcast Journalism Training Council before starting their first job, while the Periodicals Training Council offers recognised qualifications for the magazine industry.

But specifically for the arts journalist-in-the-making, the picture is less clear. In this chapter we will examine why that is so and what the options might be in terms of training and education, unpaid and paid work – as well as highlighting important concerns like the lack of diversity among arts writers. Is this a problem restricted to the UK? Why is it the way it is? What might be done about it to encourage non-white critics to find their voice? Worth flagging up, too, is a worrying notion that a formal training in journalism becomes the preserve of those able to afford it.

As already discussed, free content online has threatened and – in some cases – virtually ended the careers of established arts critics working in the medium of print. Publishers looking to make savings have turned to the arts desk as an obvious solution by cutting jobs, putting staffers on freelance contracts, reducing word counts and frequency, and reducing or freezing rates of pay. Talented writers speak of scratching around for a living or somehow being cornered into working for nothing, either in the hope of securing a paid gig or because writing is – well, what they do. And yet – and *yet* – there are more opportunities now than ever before for an arts critic to showcase her skills.

While no training or education in journalism guarantees a job, while no blog or podcast can be a sure-fire way to earn money, certain personal qualities will always be key – a curiosity about people and things, a willingness to work hard, read widely and write. Then write some more. Of the many critics I spoke to in the writing of this book, all of them had – and have – an insatiable appetite for writing, closely followed by a compulsion to watch, read, listen, learn, experience and question. They want to evaluate, inform, record; to tell stories. So how did they get to where they are now? Perhaps there was luck involved to add to their obvious abilities. Perhaps they knew the right people. In asking how the next crop of arts critics can break through, what can we learn from the past?

Starting out as a critic

Careers advisers are not usually known for their expert guidance in identifying the 14-year-old version of the arts critic and channelling that interest into a life of work. Instead, chance and circumstance are a more likely explanation for how some of our best-known arts writers achieved success. Neil McCormick, rock critic at the *Daily Telegraph* and author of books including the U2 biography, is regarded as one of the finest in the business. Leaving school as a 17-year-old punk in Ireland, McCormick zig-zagged his way into reviewing via art college and a spell in the graphics department of *Hot Press* magazine. He recalled:

> I began as a music writer completely by accident, it certainly wasn't a career plan, though I always felt I would be a writer of some kind. I loved books all my life and, in my teens, started to love journalism too, coinciding with the explosion of rock music in my life. I read music papers voraciously, with a fascination for the worlds they opened up, and the space they gave for the writer's expression. I wolfed down *NME* (it really had the best writing by a large margin), *Sounds*, *Melody Maker*, *Record Mirror* and *Rolling Stone* when I could get it, and, of course, the *Hot Press*, keeping Ireland safe for rock and roll. But I wanted to be a rock star, not a rock writer.

After his promotion a couple of years later to art director – McCormick stresses it was not as grand as it sounded – he got an opportunity to write as well.

> As an opinionated youth, I asked to do some reviews, and they would indulge me, tutor me, edit me … the only thing they didn't do was pay me. It was years before I realised how much work I was doing for nothing (on top of all

the graphics and layout work that earned me £60 a week, cash, in a brown paper envelope).¹

By now McCormick balanced working on the magazine with 'a wonderful bunch of maverick lunatics' and playing in a band. The journalism only began in all seriousness when he had moved to London as a musician but the band fizzled out at the end of the 1980s. 'I really didn't want to be a music journalist', he said. 'It felt too close to the painful failure of my own music career.'

But his entry into the business was nothing short of spectacular – associate editor of *GQ* within a year and later editor-at-large, which involved commissioning as well as writing. In 1996 McCormick was offered the chance to double his salary and replace Tony Parsons (who would go on to become a bestselling novelist) at the *Telegraph*.

> I knew that once I started writing about music, I would be stereotyped as a music critic, and that has really been the case. It is all I am asked to do now. At the same time, it was an incredible pleasure to come back to it, because I came to realise it was my life degree subject. I plugged into something I had been thinking about and participating in since my earliest years and when I surrendered to my passion, it became a vocation. It's an odd story, but probably not that odd. I didn't go to journalism school. But I did learn to write. I got good at it with the help of experienced mentors, approached it with focus, passion and all the skills I had mustered and found a place for myself writing about my greatest obsession.²

Both Nancy Durrant, commissioning arts editor at *The Times*, and Daisy Bowie-Sell, editor at *WhatsOnStage*, entered the profession from London university colleges. Durrant studied English literature at UCL before joining *The Times*, first as a critic for about six years before taking on commissioning duties around 2008. In contrast, Bowie-Sell, another English literature graduate, took the journalism MA at Goldsmiths alongside regular work experience at the *Daily Telegraph*. It became a full-time job in 2010 as she was coming towards the end of her course, after the arts editor at the time, Sarah Crompton (now working under Bowie-Sell at *WhatsOnStage*), encouraged her to apply.

Bowie-Sell, whose responsibilities included keeping track of CDs coming into the office and sourcing photographs, says:

> My title was researcher. I was basically a journalist but it involved writing news stories for the website. From doing the MA I could do the online stuff – uploading and responding to stories on the Web – without batting an eyelid.³

Now one of the world's best-known drama critics, Ben Brantley served his writing apprenticeship mulling over the hits and misses of the catwalk. Even as a child, theatre had been his first love, but Brantley would have to wait until he was in his thirties before writing about it professionally for the *New York Times*. He said:

> My first job out of university was at *Women's Wear Daily*, where I wrote features and was (improbably) a fashion critic – first in New York, then in Paris. After that, I was a staff writer first at *Vanity Fair* magazine and then the *New Yorker*. During that period, I was writing film reviews for *Elle*, which was what captured the attention of *Times* editors. I became *The Times*'s second-string theatre critic in 1993, and then moved up to chief critic in 1996.[4]

Influential blogger Megan Vaughan had an unlikely introduction into the world of theatre criticism. Her blog, *Synonyms for Churlish*, was born in 2008 but had concentrated on books, music and general updates about her life. The shift to drama resulted partly from a government scheme to encourage people under the age of 26 into the theatre by way of sponsored tickets and partly because of boredom with the music scene in her home city of Manchester. She said:

> At the time I worked in the office of a commercial receiving house in Manchester, but wasn't engaged in the work there because I didn't really give a fuck about touring musicals. But that ticket scheme meant I could suddenly go to the Royal Exchange or Library theatres for about £4, and I started writing about what I was seeing because I generally blogged about any interesting stuff that was going on in my life.

About a year later she left Manchester, aged 25, to study arts management in Leicester at De Montfort University. With London just an hour away by train, Vaughan took advantage of cheap rail tickets and was able to afford a couple of productions a week in the capital, not worrying too much if it meant a late return home to the Midlands. 'I carried on writing throughout all this. It was always writing first, theatre second.'[5]

Neil Norman has covered theatre as well, most notably for the *Daily Express*, as well as dance, music and film, making him one of the most versatile critics around. Luck has played its part, he freely admits, starting with time at London University's Bedford College. He said:

> One of my friends on the English literature course was Nick Kent, the rock critic. He advised me to write a review of the next gig I attended and send it off to the reviews editor at the *NME*. I went to see the German group Can at Guildford Civic Hall and wrote a 300-word review and posted it to Tony Stewart, who was the reviews editor at the time. They ran it and I got a cheque for £20. That was it. I was hooked. This was the early 1970s and the *NME* had a terrific film review page edited by Monty Smith. Monty loved football and films but hated rock journalists. I kept badgering him to write a film review knowing that I would make a better film critic than a rock critic

as there were loads of great young music writers who were just pouring out of the woodwork and fewer really good writers about film. Eventually he relented and sent me to see *Escape to Athena*, a godawful war film with Roger Moore and Telly Savalas. He read the review and said: 'You're right. You are a better film critic than a rock critic.'[6]

Via a stint at *Record Mirror*, penning a film review column under a female pseudonym (Jo Dietrich; 'quite liberating'), Norman's second big break came in the 1980s when former *NME* editor Nick Logan was about to launch *The Face* and was looking for a film critic. Monty Smith recommended Norman for the role.

I owe Monty big time as it was the beginning of my so-called career. *The Face* was unique at the time and unbelievably influential. It was probably the only magazine I have ever worked for that had the power to 'break' a band or a movie. Consequently I was often invited to see films long in advance of their opening in the hope that a mention in the magazine would kickstart the publicity. The best example I can think of was Jean-Jacques Beneix's *Diva*, which could have been designed for *The Face* readership. I told Nick about it and he trusted my judgement enough to put it on the cover. Bingo.[7]

On the road to reviewing

Lessons from the past are only truly useful if we can make them purposeful for the age in which we live now. Neil McCormick, Neil Norman, Meg Vaughan and the other critics I spoke to may have taken different pathways to reach their destination but what they had in common was a willingness to try. So much negativity surrounds any talk of making journalism a career, let alone arts journalism in particular, that the less determined among us may believe there is little point in trying. Editors exploit eager-to-please young writers into working free of charge, established critics chase fewer openings for paid work in print and are spoiled for choice in what they may produce online for no pay. Frustrating times, yes, but also times rich with opportunity with the right mindset, which must include persistence in large measure. Here are some positive steps you can take if you want to break into arts reviewing.

Read more, write more, build a portfolio

Well, that's obvious, isn't it? Reading and writing. While dedicated, exceptional students soak up information faster than you can provide it and choose to read more deeply into a topic as well as around it, a hefty chunk read as little as they think they can get away with. Any student serious about a life in arts journalism needs to wake up to the cold reality that no natural talent for using language will ever close the gaps in their knowledge. At the University of Kent in Canterbury, Dr Margherita Laera runs a module called Theatre and Journalism. She said:

The advice I give my students who want to pursue this profession is to read newspapers (all sections!), read print and online criticism, practise writing, build a portfolio of reviews and then try to approach blogs like *A Younger Theatre* to publish their first reviews.[8]

There really is no substitute for developing your powers than to read skilled practitioners every day – see how they approach their criticism, how they hook you in and keep you interested. Allied to that is a compulsion to write frequently, preferably every day. Even if you have no intention of publishing the piece, hone your reviewing style. Get someone to read it whose opinion you respect and who is willing to say what does not work as well as it might, not just point out the things you want to hear. Experiment with style and with voice; if you are in your comfort zone writing about film then choose another art form that is a far bigger challenge. Who knows, the points you learn from it could help you to see your more usual kind of review in a way that had never occurred to you before.

They may not want to pay you, but…

In difficult economic times the complimentary ticket, or pair of tickets, coming your way is not to be sniffed at. Getting paid for your work – and paid at a fair rate – is not easy, but the reality is that there are hundreds of people with similar skills to yours. While I was writing this chapter, one of my students was wrestling with the ethics of what has been proposed to her by a magazine editor – as it turns out, another editor trotting out that well-known line 'no budget; we can't afford to pay – sorry'. She has been asked to write a ten-page cover spread on a musician for an up-and-coming title. On the one hand, a great opportunity, but sadly they won't be paying her because they know she will do it and that it is, as they say, an *opportunity*. For the student it does, indeed, present a fine opportunity and she has decided to write this one for free, but there the gesture will stop.

Music journalist Dave Simpson, who lectures in music journalism at the University of Huddersfield, had this to say on the subject of words-for-free:

> Write for free only for a limited period or extent and only as long as it works for you, e.g. gig tickets. There is too much exploitation. Show knowledge and passion. If your writing is good, then there will be someone, somewhere prepared to pay you to do it. Even in *2016*. Hopefully…[9]

Offering your services to write reviews for no pay is beyond the pale for a hardcore of battle-weary journalists and critics. You are being exploited, they say. You are ultimately reducing the value of the work produced by writers who rely on paid work to do the basics like pay the bills and put food on the table, they say. And then they add that you are reducing or, at best, freezing those rates of pay by your willingness to play along with this dubious practice. All of these points have merit but ultimately you are not to blame for the downturn in fortunes of the paid critic and the wish of the world to read online without paying for it. You could dig your heels in, and while you were doing it someone else would have taken your place in the queue. It is legitimate and – arguably – necessary to be prepared to write at least some work for nothing as a way of showcasing your talent. You do not need to do it for ever, but you can at least choose wisely: check websites thoroughly before agreeing to write something. Check the style, depth and range of the work online, preferably over several days. Look at the quality of the writing and editing – if you believe an association with this website would enhance your portfolio, then go ahead.

Some years ago, having given up my career as an editor in the regional press to join academia, I still wanted to write – and especially about the arts, my first love. I did get commissioned by national daily and Sunday newspapers, as well as trade and lifestyle publications to produce both features and reviews, but it took a while to get to this point. I may have had a career in local newspapers, but now I had to prove myself all over again with editors who had never heard of me. I mapped out how it could be done and started by asking a couple of established websites if I could help, initially pitching ideas to interview comedians. One piece I did on a household name got some traction, led to other opportunities and gave me the confidence to believe I was headed in the right direction. I repeated the formula, and it led to commissions.

Be professional

Whether you are being paid or not, your aim should always be to act in a professional manner, and that means writing the review you have agreed to write, doing it on time and with a minimum of fuss. In short, do what you are asked to do. Freelancer Rich Chamberlain once commissioned an experienced writer to review an event at which there were five acts performing.

> On receiving the review all seemed absolutely fine until I reached the closing paragraph, which read: 'Unfortunately, I missed the headline act as I needed to catch the last train home.' Brilliantly bonkers, but I guess it showed that I should have made it one hundred per cent clear in my review commission that I wanted a full review of each and every act![10]

Check the house style for whoever you are producing content for. Ask for their guidelines. Check if it is your responsibility to source approved photographs from PR personnel, and check the email address for sending copy (sometimes this is a central inbox, different from that of the individual you have been dealing with). And finally, feel free to check that they received it if you have not heard, but do not feel dispirited if the reply is only a 'yep'. They are busy, yours is probably a small part of a rather large jigsaw. Occasionally I have had a 'fabulous!' or something similar, but I have come to accept the silence. If editors don't like it, they'll soon tell you.

Enter competitions

They may not be to everyone's liking, but the beauty of a well-organised, well-publicised competition is that if you are shortlisted – or better still, win it outright – you immediately jump ahead in the queue. Editors are always looking out for talent, and your finely crafted review may be just what is needed. Let's face it, the reviewing world is mainly made up of freelance contributors and it is not a static entity: critics move on, change direction, give it up, fall out of favour, die … someone has to replace them and it could be you. Titles in print and online occasionally run competitions to find new voices for their field, and by keeping an eye open for details announced in print or via Twitter or email alerts, you help to create opportunities for yourself.

Theatre newspaper *The Stage* has, for the past two years, run a Critics' Search attracting hundreds of entries from as far afield as the north of Scotland to the south-west of England. Twelve finalists representing British regions are mentored by a professional critic before being whittled down to three grand finalists who are each asked to review the same production. Fergus Morgan, representing the East of England region, won the 2016 final. Along with a £1,000 prize, Morgan and his fellow finalists can expect more chances to write for *The Stage*.

Editor Alistair Smith, in backing the awards at a time when national newspapers were pulling back on theatre coverage, wrote that he saw 'the current situation as both an increased responsibility, and – to be frank – an opportunity' to run more reviews in print and online than other newspapers.

Elsewhere you can keep abreast of opportunities in a number of ways – magazines like *Writing* and its rival *Writers' Forum* which regularly publish competition details, either in the form of email alerts or in print; following your favourite arts writers or websites on Twitter; looking out – if you are a student – for details posted on your university's virtual noticeboard.

Work experience or internships

Increasingly hard to come by, the work experience gig can be a useful way to showcase your talents. but do not assume editors will beat down your door when they know you are on the lookout. To increase your chances of getting a gig, there are a few things you can do:

- write a short, lively email that suggests you'd be a good fit;
- send it to the right person;
- be confident but not *too* confident;
- show the editor you have a connection with his magazine (or equivalent). For instance you've read it since you were 15; the issue that blew you away was the one where…;
- don't give in if you don't get a reply straight away; send a polite follow-up after, say, a couple of weeks; give them a call perhaps (sometimes just speaking

to the right person at a convenient moment means they'll book you in while you're chatting);
- even think about posting an old-fashioned letter to get their attention. But of course they can't hit 'reply'.

Once you're there, do not assume that every smile or compliment necessarily means they want you on the payroll. Magazines, newspapers and websites with any kind of clout will have seen hundreds of students pass through over the years. The success of your stint depends on a number of factors, even down to things you can't control like the morale of the staff and whether the editor specifically tasks someone to liaise with you for your period of time there. There are, however, a number of things you *can* control.

Doing your research is one of them. Remember that any title inviting you to spend time at their organisation is ultimately doing *you* a favour, not the other way round. With that in mind, the least you can do is prepare, like the basics on the title's history, its key features and who it speaks to. Experienced staff journalists will know within a few minutes whether your alleged passion for their publication is genuine.

A bright outlook for the work experience journalist will almost certainly pay dividends. Go along with ideas for features and reviews. Don't pull them out of your pocket only half an hour into the placement, but offer them if you get the chance – ideas are currency in publishing and there's little an editor likes more than strong ideas. It shows you have been thinking about the title, about the placement. More importantly, it sets you apart from the students who sit there sneaking a look at Facebook. Ask for opportunities to show you can deliver. Without being a nuisance, ensure you are busy and useful. If a chance crops up to review something and others are lukewarm, how about if you did it? You're not an expert, though, someone mentions – perfect! From a newcomer's perspective then…

Be curious about everyone and everything. How does stuff work? What jobs and tasks are people doing? By choosing your moments carefully, you can connect with people on the title in a positive way. How did staff get the jobs they're doing? What might it teach *you*? People like talking about themselves, and journalists are no different. In fact, they ask questions for a living and so when the tables are turned, sit back and listen because this may take a while … Make them remember you for the right reasons.

Turn up on time. Treat it as you would a job.

You should do your best to fit in. That does not mean you have to ingratiate yourself or believe your (very) temporary role is suddenly crucial to the wellbeing of the company, but being friendly and open to suggestions are useful traits. Staff – especially in tight-knit teams who spend a lot of time in each other's company – will normally have formed a view on you by the time you have finished your first round of coffees. As an editor, I once asked a student to put the kettle on, thinking she would jot down everyone's preference and come back with a bulging tray about ten minutes later. Ten *seconds* later she returned to her desk from the kitchen, having switched on the kettle and never said another word!

Of course, as someone on a work placement, you deserve respect as much as anyone else. Ideally, you will have the name of a tutor you can contact if there are problems you feel you cannot solve alone.

Once the stint is coming to a close, see if you can arrange more if you want to, either there or perhaps at a sister publication even better suited to your interests. Ask one of the team to send an email to you with brief, positive feedback.

Thank them.

Buy them cake.

Branch out, write features

You can maximise your chances of being offered opportunities in arts journalism by writing features as well as reviews. Just as the modern journalist needs to be equipped to deliver onto digital platforms, so too can you think about extending your flexibility to include format. In professional journalism it is the norm for critics to produce preview pieces on artworks about to launch which are often motored by an interview with a key player involved in the project.

Critics like Mark Lawson and Lyn Gardner regularly produce work which appears outside of the parameters of reviewing. Gardner blogs on the *Guardian* website about the theatrical climate; Lawson is noted for essays which identify patterns or trends within the arts, sparked by the topicality of a theatre production or television series. At *The Stage*, the joint chief theatre critic Mark Shenton not only weighs up the merit of a production but is sometimes tasked with interviewing its leading lady as well. Clearly this can be a delicate arrangement, particularly where a wholly positive interview highlighting an artist's fine reputation is in stark contrast elsewhere in the same edition, where the review is sadly less enthusiastic, but the business of feature writing in addition to reviewing adds value to the critic's worth and it is something he should be practising wherever possible.

Be distinctive

Rather than following the crowd, competing with all the best talents writing about the most obvious things, why not step back from it and do something different. Jude Rogers, live gig reviewer for the *Guardian* and others, suggests being a specialist.

> You don't have to be a specialist in one area – I'm someone who writes a lot about modern folk, but I'm also a huge fan of 80s pop and ambient electronica. Blogging about a genre you know a lot about will make you stand out, though, especially if it's an emerging one. Lots of editors are getting older, and don't necessarily spend every evening in a moshpit. If you do, tell them about it. They still need people like you.[11]

Show your commitment

One of the best stories I have heard that demonstrates someone's commitment to reviewing comes from Rich Chamberlain, one of my former students and a freelance writer who has plied his trade with the likes of *Rhythm*, *Total Guitar* and *Classic Rock*. His breakthrough working for one particular title came about in peculiar circumstances. For a long time he had tried to get a foot in the door with this magazine, but nothing – not even a reply. Then one evening, while travelling home to the Midlands from his magazine job in the South-West he had a voice message from the reviews editor of this title.

> They asked if I was free to review a band in Bristol that night. The band was due on stage at 9pm. It was currently 6pm and I was on a train from Bristol to Birmingham. After a slight panic thinking that I was missing a great opportunity I took the decision to get off the train at Birmingham, buy a new ticket and travel back to Bristol. The fact that it was a 90-minute journey back the way I had come did not matter. Neither did it that the fee for the piece was actually less than the train ticket I had just bought … I realise that I may sound like a total idiot for doing this, but in my mind the short-term pain was worth the potential long-term gain and that is something that helped me to stand out.[12]

Pitch perfect

As a freelance reviewer, do your homework when pitching to titles. Send your email to the correct person or risk having it deleted, unopened. Chamberlain again:

> Do your research, ring the magazine/newspaper's office if possible and speak to the editor or reviews editor. During my time on magazines we received an incredible number of inquiries from prospective writers, so set yourself apart. It is staggering how many people fire off one email asking to become a contributor and then never follow this up. Also, and this is so obvious that it almost goes without saying, but proof-read your emails as if they were cover features. Sending an email to a magazine starting with, 'Dear [insert the name of rival publication here]' will not work out well for you.[13]

Be a reporter

One route into reviewing which can pay off almost immediately is to train as a news reporter. While the number of roles on local newspapers has diminished in recent years, they do crop up – particularly at junior level – and in getting taken on, you not only learn the ropes as a journalist but can become the go-to person in the office when it comes to reviewing live gigs or plays. As we discovered in earlier chapters, not every journalist is going to be as enthusiastic as you are at the prospect of a cold winter's night at the panto (a rock star at your local city concert hall might be a different matter). Either way, enjoying a good training as a reporter will bring benefits to you and your writing for years to come in terms of identifying angles and working to a deadline. One easily overlooked, additional point is that a journalist cannot wait for inspiration to strike; there are stories to write, pages to fill. When it comes to journalism there is no such thing as writer's block. If you like the idea of exploring job opportunities as a reporter, what are the options?

As indicated earlier, reporters' jobs in the twenty-first century almost without exception require a level of experience and even qualification before entering the field. As Lily Canter points out:

> Journalism has become a graduate occupation and it is extremely difficult – although not impossible – to enter the industry without an undergraduate or postgraduate degree. Training no longer occurs systematically on the job as industry increasingly relies upon higher education to provide this service.
> *(Canter 2015, 41)*

In the last 40 years, she argues, the transformation of journalism from a school-leaver's job into a graduate's job has happened at a steady pace, though the shift was felt more keenly in the USA and parts of Western Europe.

While journalism's entry requirements are less rigid than those for professions like medicine and law, the likelihood is that fledgling news reporters in the UK will have trained on an NCTJ-accredited undergraduate programme or at least undertaken postgraduate study. Such courses are typically run at Master's level, supplemented by a diploma made up of NCTJ preliminary qualifications – essentially those you would have done on your undergraduate three-year course like media law and shorthand. UCAS (Universities and Colleges Admissions Service), according to Canter (2015), advertises 100 single honours and joint honours degrees involving journalism, along with an eye-watering 200 courses at postgraduate level.

Such courses, with varying levels of emphasis, introduce traditional skills in journalism – news writing and gathering, sub-editing and so on – with multi-media and digital practice, some of which is underpinned by academic theory. Having identified potential degree programmes to suit your needs via UCAS or the NCTJ websites, study those respective university programmes via their dedicated websites. What is the content of those programmes? How relevant is it to what you want to achieve? Is there room to specialise? Who is delivering the material? All universities want their places to be filled, so don't be shy about asking them questions.

The problem with diversity

Art is for all. The arts on film, on canvas, in sound or on stage should reflect the way we live, smashing through barriers built on the colour of skin, on sexuality, or whether you are male or female, disabled or able-bodied. Yet while the art itself may wrestle with some of these conflicts, the people *writing* about the art find themselves momentarily in the spotlight. Do they represent the communities in which they work? From interviews and from research, it would seem there is much to do.

Picture bylines accompany many reviews published online and in print, and it is clear that white faces are in the majority. Those of us with insight as to who is writing reviews in English-speaking journalism will know that the number of writers of Asian or Black African heritage in no way reflects the diverse populations in which they operate. When I pointed out this inconsistency to an editor, they replied, 'Tell me about it!' In other words, the issue was very much in mind but solutions were thin on the ground.

This lack of diversity is troubling the arts world. Seemingly not a week goes by without an initiative designed to arrest the issue reported, or a new controversy breaks out over stereotyping or decisions involving casting. J.K. Rowling labelled social media users 'a bunch of racists' for their disparaging comments reacting to the choice of a black actress (Noma Dumezweni) to play Hermione in the West End production of *Harry Potter and the Cursed Child*. While most tweets were positive, the play's director, John Tiffany, told the *Observer* in the same interview (Ratcliffe 2016) he was shocked 'people couldn't visualise a non-white person as the hero of a story'.

In the USA in the spring of 2015, speaking at a conference on the future of film criticism, Rebecca Theodore-Vachon, a contributor to *RogerEbert.com*, cited a University of California Los Angeles study which found that 94 per cent of all studio heads were white men. The discussion was reported (Childress 2015) on Chaz Ebert's blog, hosted by *RogerEbert.com*.

Matt Zoller Seitz, Theodore-Vachon's editor at the website, entered the debate with a reminder of what it was like to write television criticism in America in the late 1990s – which he did – saying 'shows which dealt with black themes or black casts were often "ghettoised" to minor networks'. Seitz said one television executive told him that while he himself was not racist, the audience was, and that was why he would not run shows featuring black characters.

American music journalist Jordannah Elizabeth is one of the loudest voices trying to raise awareness of the under-representation of ethnic minorities and attitudes to black writers. A musician and singer as well as a critic and interviewer, Elizabeth carries out public speaking engagements about her work along with penning articles that directly address the challenges faced by writers of colour. Her 2016 piece, 'Black voices in music criticism are essential', for the *East Bay Express*, California, was, she wrote, 'dedicated to all the Black journalists, editors, authors, literary scholars and others who are constantly belittled and overlooked. We are in this together and hopefully will open doors for many.'

She has contributed to many publications and websites including *Vice*, *Village Voice* and *LA Weekly*. Her article goes on:

> I understand that Black readers could view my contribution to predominantly white-run publications as tokenization, or assume that it stems from my personal desire for validation from a white readership. But I would counter that,

through journalism, I have the opportunity to share my frustration with the reality of my oppression with a broad audience, and bring my perspective to newsrooms that often lack diversity.

(Elizabeth 2016)

Change will only come about, Elizabeth argues, by writers such as her being visible. Black critics may feel shut out of mainstream media. 'It is not about fitting in with white writers and editors – or promoting mainstream, white narratives – but about carving out an equal place for Black voices.'

I asked her if in the States there was any concerted effort to improve diversity levels, expecting there to be a positive reply but Elizabeth said not nearly enough was being done to improve things,[14] though, for balance, it is fair to point out that a few weeks after speaking with her, the National Association of Black Journalists in the USA held its annual convention. Several discussions were planned that either directly or indirectly touched on issues relevant to black arts reporters or critics. Listed events included advice on 'How to Land Your Dream Arts and Entertainment Gig before the Age of 30' and another on the challenges facing journalism academics of colour working in American colleges.

Similar obstacles to those facing American writers of colour face their British counterparts. In trying to bring authority to the subject, I wanted to speak to news organisations representative of the Asian and Afro-Caribbean communities in Britain. London-based *Eastern Eye* and *The Voice* were approached for interviews. While *The Voice*, for whom I have written about theatre in the past, chose not to take part, *Eastern Eye* put forward its veteran journalist Amit Roy. In the business for more than 40 years, Roy began his reporting career on the *Hampstead News* before stints at the London office of the *Glasgow Herald*, the *Daily* and *Sunday Telegraph*, *Daily Mail* and *Sunday Times*.

On a freelance contract with the *Eye*, Roy writes a weekly column which includes arts news and reviews alongside his work for the *Telegraph India* as its Europe correspondent. He has free rein to find a dozen stories a week and has discovered that a burgeoning British Asian arts scene over the past 20 years has provided rich pickings for his journalism.

When I met him, it soon became clear how frustrated he felt at being unable to fully immerse himself in the London theatre scene. He spoke highly of his relationships with art galleries and museums (the V&A and the Royal Academy were mentioned), but West End theatre was a tougher nut to crack. In the past 12 months prior to our meeting, he had bought four tickets himself at a cost of around £70 a time to see West End shows so that they could be reviewed for his newspaper. He told me:

> I find it difficult to get press preview tickets for any major show. I have tried to convince people that it can give them two bites at the cherry (*Eastern Eye* and *Telegraph India*). There is a big American holiday market here but I tell them [press offices] that with the economy improving there are a lot of Indian business people and holiday makers in London so they ought to

go out of their way to target an overseas audience when Indian papers are as important as American papers. People want to see the best shows and they can afford the tickets.

I would be invited if it was a mainstream musical like *Bend It Like Beckham* but if it was for anything else then the allocation is finished. Part of the process with making people feel more engaged with this country is that you get to make them feel comfortable experiencing the arts.[15]

Theatres have a set allocation for press tickets, and there is pressure on them to stick to it – especially with demand from the growing army of bloggers. Even on the blockbuster musicals, a decision not to sell a seat but instead give it away for the night has to be justified.

Roy stopped short of suggesting the treatment was racist – pointing out that press officers were always polite – but wondered why room could not be found for publications other than mainstream ones beyond official press nights.

His work – speaking to British Asian readers already in the UK or Indian families planning a trip to London – would surely be useful for a theatre industry in constant dialogue over how to engage with actors and audiences of colour. 'How do you make people more British and create a more harmonious country? We are struggling here and through Europe with the idea of identity, and one way is to make people feel more tuned into this country.'[16]

A city or country may be multi-cultural but it does not necessarily equate to being culturally integrated. As Naseem Khan, author of the groundbreaking 1976 report *The Arts Britain Ignores*, noted in a 2005 article for the *Independent*, 'integration is not so much a matter of a common voice but opportunity for different voices, leading to a shared space'.

Twelve years after Khan's article, ethnic diversity in British journalism remains 'troublingly low', according to a major report by the NCTJ (Spilsbury 2013). Its 98-page study, *Journalists At Work*, further points out the inadequacy of the industry to reverse that trend, given that more than half of the nation's employed journalists are based in the capital and the South-East, namely centres of large populations where the proportion of non-whites is greater. The report's findings establish that 94 per cent of UK journalists are white, while 91 per cent of the nation's workforce is white.

Among measures being undertaken to improve the situation, the NCTJ's own Journalism Diversity Fund – launched in 2005 with a £100,000 donation from the Newspaper Licensing Agency – is 'aimed at people without the financial means to attend NCTJ-accredited Diploma in Journalism courses who can show they are ethnically or socially diverse' and committed to a career in the profession. Current sponsors are DMG Media, Thomson, Reuters and Sky.

Media Diversified is working to highlight a lack of positive representation in journalism, from the content itself to the people making that content. Writing in the *Guardian*, Samantha Asumadu, a Media Diversified co-founder, said: 'As a born and bred Londoner, I only have to walk outside my door to see a wide range of people with a variety of skin colours. Yet, when I flick through the newspapers, all I see is whiteness' (2013).

And in the theatre, Curve at Leicester has won plaudits for its cultural leadership programme, developing eight arts managers from diverse backgrounds in association with De Montfort University in the city and thanks to support from Arts Council England. Furthermore it estimates that 46 per cent of tickets for its own produced work were bought by people from black and minority ethnic (BAME) backgrounds (Stafford 2017).

Sadly the Royal Shakespeare Company's bursary scheme open to BAME arts journalists has been shelved because of a cut in funding, though, at the time of writing, the RSC was hopeful it could be resurrected.

Meanwhile a new study into the lack of diversity in British theatre found it to be an environment that was 'hideously white'. The study (Kean & Larsen 2016), commissioned by the Andrew Lloyd Webber Foundation, urged arts organisations, drama schools, creative teams and others to do more to actively reflect the British population. Report authors Danuta Kean and Mel Larsen said:

> If the situation continues, there is real danger that, not only will black and Asian young people stay away from the theatre as a profession, they will stay away as punters. And without them in the audience, theatres will become unsustainable, as they are forced to compete for a dwindling, ageing, white, middle-class audience.
>
> *(Kean & Larsen 2016, 3)*

Notes

1 McCormick, Neil (17 October 2016), interview with the author.
2 *Ibid.*
3 Bowie-Sell, Daisy (25 April 2016), interview with the author.
4 Brantley, Ben (11 August 2016), interview with the author.
5 Vaughan, Megan (17 July 2016), interview with the author.
6 Norman, Neil (27 July 2016), interview with the author.
7 *Ibid.*
8 Laera, Margherita (27 July 2016), interview with the author.
9 Simpson, Dave (27 July 2016), interview with the author.
10 Chamberlain, Rich (18 November 2016), interview with the author.
11 Rogers, Jude (19 October 2016), interview with the author.
12 Chamberlain, Rich (18 November 2016), interview with the author.
13 *Ibid.*
14 Elizabeth, Jordannah (14 July 2016), interview with the author.
15 Roy, Amit (7 September 2016), interview with the author.
16 *Ibid.*

References

Asumadu, Samantha (8 July 2013) 'It's time to boost ethnic minority representation in the media', *Guardian*, www.theguardian.com/commentisfree/2013/jul/08/redress-ethnic-minority-representation-media.
Canter, Lily (June 2015) 'Chasing the accreditation dream', *AJE Journal* 4(1), 40–52.

Childress, Erik (16 March 2015) 'SXWS panel. The future of film criticism: Diversify or die', Chaz Ebert's blog at *RogerEbert.com*, www.rogerebert.com/chazs-blog/sxsw-panel-the-future-of-film-criticism-diversify-or-die.

Elizabeth, Jordannah (5 July 2016) 'Black voices in music criticism are essential', *East Bay Express*, www.eastbayexpress.com/oakland/black-voices-in-music-criticism-are-essential/Content?oid=4881539.

Kean, Danuta and Larsen, Mel (December 2016) *Centre Stage: The Pipeline of BAME Talent*. Newbury: Andrew Lloyd Webber Foundation, http://andrewlloydwebberfoundation.com/.

Khan, Naseem (22 September 2005) 'We should celebrate diversity, not suppress it', *Independent*, www.independent.co.uk/voices/commentators/naseem-khan-we-should-celebrate-diversity-not-suppress-it-314453.html.

Ratcliffe, Rebecca (5 June 2016) 'JK Rowling tells of anger at attacks on casting of black Hermione', *Observer*.

Spilsbury, Mark (2013) *Journalists At Work Survey*. Saffron Walden: National Council for the Training of Journalists.

Stafford, Chris (2 March 2017) 'Curve to launch leadership programme for BAME artists and cultural leaders', *Curve online*, Leicester, www.curveonline.co.uk/about-us/press-office/curve-to-launch-leadership-programme-for-bame-artists-and-cultural-leaders/.

10

THE NEW REVIEWER

Making it pay

'The comparison is a cup of coffee…' So begins an online appeal by the *Guardian* to ask you to support its journalism. You are looking at its website, engaged with its writing. More people than ever are doing exactly the same, 'but far fewer are paying for it'. Advertising revenues are falling across the media but something has to give if this 'difficult and expensive work' is to continue. The 'small favour' that the publishers ask is that you support this work for £5 a month – 'less than the price of a coffee a week'.

Go to *The Times* or the *Daily Telegraph* and a realisation sets in that content which would have been free a few years ago is now subjected to a more commercial test. Paywalls are here, and it looks like we will have to adapt. Both newspaper groups offer variations on subscription packages. At the time of writing you could sign up for *The Times* at £8 for eight weeks, and £6 a week thereafter. The *Telegraph*'s Premium package, meanwhile, for £1 a week for 13 weeks and then £2 a week thereafter, would signal unlimited access to premium articles, the chance to take part in online discussions and a newsletter pinging towards your inbox. On top, digital access to the *Washington Post* is thrown in.

Both pathways are presented impeccably, though neither has the benefit of the *Guardian*'s back-story – namely Trust status combined with a 'unique ownership structure [meaning] no one can tell us to censor or drop a story'. The *Guardian*'s special set of circumstances has always allowed it the breathing space that its competitors have never enjoyed. It enables the brand to distinguish those who do pay up as 'Supporters' rather than people who merely take out a subscription.

For all the titles that have built paywalls around their websites (the *Daily Mail* remaining free), the perception is that the stable door is being shut long after the horse has bolted. The conundrum of how to stop readers dropping their print products has bewildered publishers for the past 20 years – publishers who expected those very consumers to migrate to their online versions. But it did not happen and nor did the digital advertising rates get anything close to those in print. Additionally, publishers have faced the challenges of advertising budgets being spread more thinly as clients used other platforms like Facebook, Google or bloggers.

Creating paywalls is not restricted to the UK by any means. The *Australian* took the plunge in 2011, reporting in bullish terms in the autumn of 2016 that its strategy was paying off thanks to a combination of pushing purpose-built digital versions of its content and editorial for which the reader pays extra, so-called premium content. It had 85,000 digital subscribers and expected that figure to climb to 100,000 by 2017.

In Germany *Bild* constructed its paywall in 2015, and in the same year in North America (USA and Canada combined) 456 newspapers were charging for content (Van Meter 2015).

The narrative behind the decline of advertising revenues and circulation figures for the UK press does not make for pretty reading, according to media analyst Raymond Snoddy (2016). The average circulation of daily newspapers combined was 12.49 million copies in 1997 but by 2016 that figure had halved to 6.28 million. Within a similar time frame, the share of the UK advertising market enjoyed by national, regional and local newspapers had also taken a nosedive. In 1995 print had 65 per cent of the market, television 27 per cent and online was zero. Skip forward 20 years and television's share of the market had not budged at 27 per cent but newspapers plummeted to 16 per cent of the cake, while online advertising accounted for an impressive 50 per cent.

If anyone really needs convincing of the difficulty of selling copies of newspapers then look no further than the closure of two of them – the *Independent* after nearly 30 years of publication in March 2016 and *New Day*, Trinity Mirror's ill-fated start-up which lasted a mere nine weeks.

Fewer readers paying for what they read combined with a downturn in advertising revenues inevitably created uncertainty – and ultimately cost-cutting – in newspapers and magazines. Lack of investment by owners and the culling of jobs put quality in the crosshairs, and so began a downward spiral of poorer products resulting in worse sales and weaker revenues. Why did it all happen? Former magazine executive Joely Carey says in her chapter in *Last Words?* that 'publishing seemed to lose its nerve':

> The publishing industry failed to understand just how important emerging technology and global competition could (and would) be to their age-old business model. They failed to understand the impact of how digital accessibility to words, pictures and videos would change and, consequently, devastate the glory days of sell-out issues and circulation figures that regularly bust the 1m mark – a week.
>
> *(Carey 2016)*

Arts journalists, unsurprisingly, were not immune to the turbulence both here and abroad, as we have already learned. Ismene Brown (2013) reported in the *Guardian*: 'Astonishingly, New York – one of the two capitals of world dance

(London is the other) – has only one fully employed newspaper dance critic. And London is not lagging far behind.' And in the UK in the same year the *Independent on Sunday* culled its entire arts team in one fell swoop.

Neil McCormick, at the *Daily Telegraph*, had this to say:

> No one really wants to pay for content in the Internet free-for-all and it is killing journalism. Maybe some technological or cultural fix will come along that will resolve the issues of copyright and paid for content that is currently funnelling all revenue towards a few major new media players (Google, Facebook and Amazon, essentially). But in the meantime ... there are a lot of fine music journalists struggling to make ends meet in the present climate. Sometimes I feel like one of the last hacks standing.[1]

No matter how talented, great writing alone is not enough to sustain the arts writer or that of the family they may have to feed and, slowly at first, but now with an increased sense of urgency, an abundance of initiatives has emerged to rethink how a critic may work and be paid for it. Some of these projects have enjoyed success, others have a long way to go before they can be judged as having cracked journalism's biggest ever challenge.

New websites, niche magazines, paid-for magazines that go free and not-for-profit reorganisation are some of the ideas created by editors, publishers and writers to provide engaging arts coverage while trying to ensure long-term survival. Add to that blogging, vlogging and embedded criticism, along with critics branching out into academia and other forms of education – the paths are many but the destination is the same: embrace a digital world in a way that will pay the bills.

Powered by the Web

The Arts Desk

Firmly on the back foot, with shrinking space for coverage and more staff writers forced to go freelance, the arts community of the British legacy press experienced something interesting and inventive happening from within. In 2009 *The Arts Desk* sprang up as the UK's first daily website providing news, reviews and features across the whole of the arts spectrum. The *Daily Telegraph*'s move to cut its arts budget and place all of its critics on freelance terms was the decisive factor in *Theartsdesk.com* becoming a possibility. Former *Telegraph* dance critic Ismene Brown is a co-founder of the website, and she has said the Web opened up a brilliant opportunity to do better, more up-to-date work free from the restrictions on space that the newspaper was imposing on them (Jokelainen 2014).

In his paper for the Reuters Institute for the Study of Journalism, 'Anyone can be a critic', Jarkko Jokelainen, says:

> The group of journalists had a meeting and came up with the basic idea. It was worlds apart from the convention of the legacy media: there would be

no editor, no staff, and no office. *The Arts Desk* would be a collective of equals and all would have a share in the business. Every art form would be treated equally.

(Jokelainen 2014, 18)

A core team of 'Fleet Street' writers was behind the early development of *The Arts Desk* though gradually other critics have been invited into the fold. I was asked to contribute as a television reviewer and found the set-up to be well organised, with ideas encouraged via email. Brown calls it a 'conductorless orchestra' where writers feel they can take ownership of their area; they have become versatile, too, as a result of the shift online, embracing digital skills they would not have used if they had stayed solely as print journalists (they still write for various publications). Other forms of coverage are pushed as well, taking advantage of opportunities that would not be possible in print – long-form journalism including lengthy interviews and photo galleries, to name but two examples.

Voted best specialist journalism website at the Online Media Awards 2012, *The Arts Desk* did not have advertising visible at the time of writing but the project does adopt a paywall. Readers can access four articles for free a month, but for unlimited access they are asked to pay £2.95 a month or £25 a year. It opens up 30 reviews, news stories and features a day along with an archive consisting of 10,000 articles.

Culture Whisper

Things to do in London is the focus for this elegant website, masterminded by ex-BBC programme editor Eleanore Dresch and run by an all-female team. Signing up will cost you more than *The Arts Desk* but there are differences with this site. The former will provide beautifully written pieces about events its reviewers hated as well as loved, whereas *Culture Whisper* is very much a membership scheme.

Time-pressed Londoners get notified about arts and culture events that interest them – even suggestions on where to eat beforehand or afterwards. Frequent updates will arrive in your inbox along with details of a 'free surprise ticket' to a London event each month. Members will also have access to all of the website's content and exclusive invitations, discounts and offers. Premium membership costs £85 a year or £15 a month.

Launched in January 2014 'by a small team of London insiders with a mission to streamline and share their knowledge about the capital's culture', the website has staff working in editorial, design and marketing as well as relying on around 40 contributing writers. The profiles of these writers would suggest a mix of experienced ex-legacy press critics and arts graduates working on other projects as well. Upmarket magazines like *Tatler* and *Bazaar* celebrated *Culture Whisper*'s launch.

Reviews published by *Culture Whisper* stick to four or five stars, nothing less. Logically, as a commercial enterprise, the website is hardly likely to send its members to things it considers sub-standard, though it is unclear how that operates, whether critics only attend plays, for example, that they expect to be good or if they abandon any hope of writing it up if two stars beckon. *Culture Whisper* did not respond to requests to be interviewed for this book.

WhatsOnStage.com *and the* British Theatre Guide

The UK's best-known online-only theatre websites both began life in 1997. *WhatsOnStage.com* (*WOS*) was initially a listings site owned by magazine publishing giant Emap. It added an e-commerce element, as Andrew Haydon (2016) discovered in his interview with original editor Terri Paddock. The system appears crude compared with today's sophisticated set-up, but nonetheless this was ahead of its time: a reader who wanted to buy a theatre ticket submitted a request via the site, which generated an email to *WhatsOnStage*'s office, whereupon a member of staff would buy the ticket by calling the theatre box office. As Haydon observes, 'by the end of 1998, most of the still-familiar elements of *WhatsOnStage* were in place', including reviews, star ratings and discussion forums.

The twenty-first-century version combines reviews, news, videos, interviews and – crucially – a ticket-purchasing facility from which *WOS* receives a percentage from the sale. There is a West End emphasis to the ticket sales, but Broadway is not out of reach thanks to the presence of American-based owner *TheatreMania.com*. On the day I researched its ticket prices, savings were announced for major London shows of between 25 and 45 per cent. Shows in the UK regions are not ignored, either, though here *WOS* will take you directly to the box offices of theatres in 33 towns and cities.

Other important elements contribute to *WOS*'s growing status as an influential voice in the theatre community. Its annual awards show, voted on by its readers, regularly honours some of the leading lights in British theatreland, while its reviews service offers a distinctive feature: not only the thoughts of its professional critics but a summary of what other key critics said along with their star rating. If the reader wants to know even more, then alternative voices in the shape of short reviews by 'confirmed ticket purchasers' who saw the show are also available to see.

Would *WOS* push even harder at the commercial door, I wondered. Was a paywall ever on the cards? Here's editor Daisy Bowie-Sell:

> We would never do that. Part of the reason people love us is because we are so accessible. We make the money through ticket sales and that is doing really well and increasing. Our readers are theatregoers so if you see a show written about that has recently opened or is about to open then you might want to book a ticket, and so it makes sense to have those links on that page.[2]

With its focus firmly on covering as much of the country's regions as possible, the *British Theatre Guide* (*BTG*) is an interesting alternative to *WOS* and labels itself as the leading *independent* website on the scene. Launched by former drama teacher Peter Lathan, who still plays an active role, the website is edited by David Chadderton. Nine British regions are covered in addition to London, with a small army of around 60 reviewers on board. Podcasts are an important part of the mix, along with daily reviews, features and news items. This website attracts advertising and has a ticket-purchasing function, too, thanks to its association with Encore.

Pitchfork, The Quietus, Drowned in Sound

From its festivals to its video site to its quarterly journal and finally a high-profile buy-out by Condé Nast, online music magazine *Pitchfork* has been nothing short of a phenomenon. The Chicago-based brand stepped into the fold while mainstream British and American titles were dithering over what to do (or not to do) online. Its president Chris Kaskie has targeted the team to create 'the largest and most respected music publication in the world' (Cardew 2014).

Evidence of this ambition can be found in what it calls Cover Stories, which 'take inspiration from both physical magazines – using picture-heavy, visually-pleasing layouts – and the interactivity of digital technology'. The stories are noted for their horizontal as well as vertical scrolling, and bold photography and layout. Suddenly a photograph of an artist will shift into view from the left or a pull-out quote will appear from the right. The pictures themselves might be a hybrid of video and still photography. These stories are told in long form, 4,000 words for example. Online reaction to the innovation in comment forums ranges from the viewpoint that it is the work of genius, while others believe it is a gimmick or a distraction.

Kaskie told the *Guardian* that Pitchfork would not be taking advantage of the innovation to simply ratchet up page views – its 45 million to 50 million page views a month globally was enough 'and to interrupt the user experience through extra clicking to the next page cheapens the experience for readers and advertisers'.

Two other websites worth noting are *The Quietus* and *Drowned in Sound*, the latter of which took the step in the spring of 2014 to ask for donations from its readers. The Drowned in Sound Whip-Round, as founder Sean Adams called it, was the first such call in the website's 14-year history and stemmed from a cumulative effect of users activating ad-blockers, Facebook and Google 'lowering the value of advertising' and increased administration costs of staying online – server costs alone were £1,100 a month, he wrote on the *Drowned in Sound* website. One-off payments would be greatly appreciated, as would a £3 monthly donation (Adams 2014).

The campaign had snowballed from an initiative the previous month when readers who regularly used the message boards wanted a number of errors with the site fixed, and also 'felt guilty for using ad-blockers whilst racking up hundreds of page views a month'. More than £1,000 was raised. But, as Adams pointed out, 'This Internet lark isn't quite the goldmine that the headlines about start-ups make out. Last year, despite racking up 28.5 million total page views from 3.5 million music fans ("unique users"), we had one of the worst years for advertising income in our history.'

At *The Quietus*, founder John Doran says financing any online music magazine is a challenge, meaning less money in the jar for good photography, nothing left in it for a sub-editor and barely anything left with which to pay the writers. It is a familiar tune. Online advertising is a slog and should not be relied upon, he says. Sponsorship and innovation are essential. 'To be honest, most ideas have only been marginally successful and some haven't been successful at all' (Jokelainen 2014).

ArtsJournal.com

Curated content is very popular for readers who may have a deep interest in a subject and would want to engage with it online but do not have the time to find it. American scholar and arts writer Douglas McLennan founded *ArtsJournal.com* in 1999. His digest of 'some of the best arts and cultural journalism in the English-speaking world' features daily links to newspapers and magazines with an online presence alongside countless websites and blogs. Some 60 bloggers have their work showcased via the website – *Wall Street Journal* drama critic Terry Teachout and *Sunday Times* critic David Jays among them. As a rule McLennan does not link to stories that are behind a paywall.

A former arts reporter in Seattle, McLennan teaches at the Annenberg School for Communication and Journalism at the University of Southern California, and has 30,000 subscribers signed up for his daily or weekly newsletter.

His website gets 45,000–55,000 readers a day and 250,000 unique users a month, demonstrating a clear commercial potential. There are sponsored posts and banner advertising in addition to classified advertisements. McLennan expands on this when describing the value of classified ads on his site:

> We were shocked. After we redesigned *ArtsJournal* in January 2014, we began displaying a list of the five most-read stories on the site. We were amazed when a classified ad for a job at the Los Angeles Philharmonic showed up in the top five. It confirmed what advertisers have been telling us for some time. AJ readers see our ads as content they want to read. Why? Because we don't accept ads from non-arts advertisers. Our advertisers are part of the arts community we serve, and they know AJ is a great way to reach that community.[3]

The website claims it is 'the leading (and largest) source of arts news on the internet', indeed the depth and breadth of material Mclennan and his deputies curate is exhaustive.

Bloggers provide an alternative

The Movie Blog *and* Flickering Myth

They are separated by the Atlantic Ocean but the editors of UK-based *Flickering Myth* and the USA's *The Movie Blog* are connected by a desire to publish fast, relevant content that makes them distinctive from the countless others doing similar things. It is a given that the best arts bloggers are devoted to their subject but can they make it pay as well? Writer and lecturer Gary Collinson says monetising a website remains a huge challenge, with the practice of ad-blocking being one of the main concerns. He said:

> It's easy to see why people are turning to ad-blockers. A lot of websites have started to include auto-playing videos with their content; these pay well, but do people really want to see them? It's kind of a vicious circle. People are turning to ad-blockers due to intrusive advertising, which hits publishers' revenue and forces them to turn to ever-more intrusive advertising.[4]

Flickering Myth has adopted what Collinson refers to as 'traditional' online advertising and has tried to ensure those ads are unobtrusive but he remarks on a year-on-year decline. The pattern is negated somewhat by enough traffic to ensure that running costs are met, but nevertheless Collinson points out that 'there's definitely a lot of uncertainty surrounding the future of online advertising'.[5]

The Movie Blog senior editor Anthony Whyte also addressed these issues, echoing much of what his British counterpart said:

> People want to consume content in different ways, and we're seeing that now with the increase in the amount of video content, for example. Do they want to read a 600-word article accompanying a poster or trailer for a new movie, when they can scroll through their social media timeline and see said poster or trailer? Do they want to read the thoughts of a critic, when they can do a search on Twitter and read, interact and discuss with fellow fans, or watch someone talking to a webcam on YouTube?[6]

Audiences for blog content would reduce, he felt, though at a slower pace than the decline of print, but online media was 'much better positioned to deal with future developments in media consumption, whatever they might be'.[7]

Megan Vaughan: Synonyms for Churlish

Arts administration graduate Megan Vaughan is widely regarded as one of the most exciting bloggers writing about British theatre in the last few years. *Synonyms for Churlish* – incisive, funny, experimental in form and style – sets her apart from traditional criticism. Her frequent use of Twitter helped bring new audiences to her work. Her most popular posts have had 'several thousand views in a day'.

But where Vaughan becomes even more interesting is in her resistance to getting paid for reviewing and the way she has developed the blog into a source of income through crowdfunding. Her views are controversial. She would undertake freelance work writing opinion pieces for editors, but as far as paid reviewing is concerned she said:

> I refuse free tickets. The traditional transaction of professional reviewing (a review that sticks to a certain format, by a certain time-date, in exchange for

a free ticket from the theatremakers and some cash from the publication) is the absolute worst. It's bad for everybody: writers, artists, readers, everybody.[8]

Fixed on this view, it means Vaughan's criticism is saved for her blog, 'where I could write what I wanted about what I wanted, and never felt obliged to churn out 300 words about a show that was just a load of bollocks. Or not even a load of bollocks – just … nothing. The absolute worst.'[9]

Vaughan's relationship with crowdfunding began with the website *Patreon*. She saw it as an ideal solution, facilitating small but regular donations from her readers without forcing her into writing something specific.

> It got a fantastic response, and has provided me with over £2,000 in the last year, something I'm hugely grateful for. There's also something to be said for the validating effect of this income. I've been introduced to smug luvvie cunts as a 'blogger' and their first question is always, 'Oh really, and do you make any money from that?', delivered with a half-smile that suggests they know the answer already, as if I only do it because I'm not good enough to work for a paper. Being able to tell those people 'yes, actually, I do – about £200 a month' gave me a chance to shut them up, as well as hopefully go some way to changing their opinion of bloggers.[10]

But at the time of our interview in the summer of 2016, Vaughan was wrestling with the principle of crowdfunding, despite its success. It had changed her relationship with writing, she said, and was partly why she had made the decision to take 'a few months out to recharge and rethink'. Her point that being commissioned by one editor to write one piece being simpler than producing content commissioned by 50 people out of their own pocket is a good one. With a career in arts administration alongside her blogging, Vaughan needed the peace of mind to be able to step away from the blog for a week when the day got too busy. 'I'm not quite able to rationalise my way through the crowdfunding guilt, but I'm working on it.'[11]

What to do about print

The Philadelphia Inquirer and other not-for-profit journalism

Serious journalism – and arts journalism is a part of that – will suffer without financial security. Thinking this way has led to more than 150 journalistic enterprises unfold in the USA on a not-for-profit model. Rachel Oldroyd, in her chapter in *The Last Word?* (2016), says a study by the Pew Research Center in 2013 found alternative funding to be 'a healthy, optimistic and growing sector'. Most notable of these examples is the *Philadelphia Inquirer*, its sister paper the *Daily News* and associated website *Philly.com*. Owner Gerry Lenfest in 2016 transferred ownership of the titles to a newly created not-for-profit organisation. Under the new arrangement the titles are now owned by a so-called public benefit corporation which, in turn, is run by a trust, not unlike the British model of the *Guardian* and its Scott Trust status. As *Fortune.com* reported, 'the newspapers and website will remain for-profit companies ... but will have greater access to donations and other philanthropic financing methods'.

Other non-profit projects continue to grow flourish in the USA, notably Propublica and the Centre for Investigative Reporting with its *realnews.org* brand.

NME *goes free*

A collective sigh greeted the news announced in the summer of 2015 that *NME*, the UK's best-known music magazine for more than 40 years, was finally succumbing to the inevitable. No longer able to prop up worryingly low sales (15,000 at the end, with a 20 per cent annual decline) and the downward effect such a situation has on advertising revenues, publisher Time Inc. UK opted to continue publishing weekly but going down the route of free distribution. Other titles including *Time Out* and *ShortList* had followed a similar path, in their case being handed out at Tube stations. *NME* now gives away some 300,000 copies a week via railway and Tube stations, selected shops and university campuses.

Editor Mike Williams told the BBC at the time: 'Every media brand is on a journey into a digital future. That doesn't mean leaving print behind, but it does mean that print has to change, so I'm incredibly excited by the role it will now play as part of the new *NME*' (BBC 2015).

Some five months after adopting the free circulation model, the magazine recorded its highest ever readership figure of 307,217.

In keeping a high profile for the brand's website, *NME.com*, the print publication relaxed its emphasis on music and broadened its coverage to include film, television, politics, fashion and technology. The decision to dilute coverage away from guitar bands to serve more general appeal was met with scepticism by media commentators and by fans in online forums, but, ultimately, it is not something that will worry publishers as long as the magazine turns its fortunes around. In December 2016 Time Inc. UK chief executive Marcus Rich cited the overhaul at *NME* as being a significant factor in the company's excellent end-of-year results.

The part-time critic

Unquestionably, arts critics the world over are realising there are fewer of them earning a full-time living from what they do, or did. Work is still to be obtained but there is not as much as there was, and rates of pay have in many cases been frozen or even chopped back to accommodate such change. In all likelihood reviewers will have to find additional income – the possibilities for which are looked at later in the chapter. This is less of an issue for reviewers who have grown up in the digital age as it is for older critics having to adjust.

Lyn Gardner, the *Guardian*'s senior theatre critic after Michael Billington, considered the point in time when the pair of them are no longer in post:

> When I go, when Michael goes, will those jobs be replaced in the same way? Probably not, but that's part of continual change. At one time there were 12–16 people writing about theatre in the UK and they were largely from the same backgrounds, but now there are many different voices from different backgrounds and that can only be a good thing for theatre, but whether people can turn that into a paying career is probably very questionable. But now people [in life generally] have portfolio careers where they do a bit of this and a bit of that and maybe something similar is happening in criticism.[12]

If it sounds like a return to the past, where critics combined their journalism with teaching, with academic work or with other creative endeavour, then that is a fair comparison. In Europe, for example, it is a tried and tested model. Italian scholar and University of Kent academic Dr Margherita Laera conducted a survey of critics in her homeland in 2014 and produced some eye-catching results: for a mere 5 per cent of critics, arts reviewing is their only profession, while about 65 per cent of those surveyed did so purely on an amateur scale. Laera described the situation in Italy thus:

> The challenges there are very similar to those in the UK: lack of paid jobs for critics and an ever smaller word count for print reviews, which has resulted in the majority of those who practise criticism having to have day jobs, often in academia, theatre making, theatre production, publishing, teaching, etc.[13]

In addition, she says, critics are blogging, they are curating content (*Reta Criticia* being a strong example), they are responding to productions at sponsored festivals and they are writing or editing artist or company websites.[14]

Solutions for the new reviewer

In addition to publishing giants building paywalls in front of their digital content and writers launching their own websites or blogs, many fascinating projects are being tried out in different corners of the globe to ensure that arts journalism can still be produced and enjoyed by millions, and that its producers can be paid for that work. For this final part of the chapter, we take a look at some of these examples.

Embedded criticism or in-house journalism

Washington Post reporter Peggy McGlone interviewed the chief executive of the New Jersey Performing Arts Center in Newark in 2014 who told her that coverage of arts news was now so unreliable that something radical had to be done. 'We can't wait to be written about anymore', said John Schreiber. 'We as arts presenters understand that we can't depend anymore on third parties to tell our stories' (McGlone 2014).

The complaint was triggered by a frustration with traditional media, and it is a familiar grievance. I have heard UK arts press officers or other executives despair that coverage in their city newspaper is not what it once was, or that London-based critics and feature writers rarely look beyond the capital. They realise that the lack of engagement is not because these journalists are not interested, rather that budget cuts, less space with which to play and ultimately reductions in staff numbers are having a detrimental effect.

But as McGlone described, the New Jersey set-up is one of a growing band of American institutions in recent years that have looked at an entirely different model for communicating with their audiences, effectively 'cutting out the middleman' and publishing directly using in-house journalists. Similar projects were launched by the symphony orchestras in Baltimore and Chicago respectively, by the Denver Center for the Performing Arts, the Los Angeles County Museum for Art and by the Geffen Playhouse in Los Angeles.

Many of the writers working in these centres as 'embedded' or in-house journalists are graduates of the University of Southern California Annenberg School of Communication and Journalism, the place most widely credited with originating the idea for embedding arts journalists inside arts organisations. Two journalism professors, Sasha Anawalt and Douglas McLennan, the latter noted earlier in the chapter for his influential *ArtsJournal.com*, drove the initiative. Anawalt said the idea was first developed in 2008, and it had come from an unlikely source.

A year earlier journalism in the USA was being hit hard by the Internet, she said – the impact of *Craigslist*, for example, the Web-based classified advertisements service – and by 2008, half of the nation's arts journalists had lost their jobs. It was at this time that USC Annenberg's masters course in arts journalism was being rolled out.

> I thought to myself, 'What am I doing training arts journalists in this economic climate?' My answer was to give them digital skills and inspire a mindset that could not only adapt to the technological changes, but in the best-case scenario take leadership of them. Drive them. I looked at Human Rights Watch as my model, and saw that when the foreign correspondent reporters covering human rights abuses in Somalia, Iran, you name it, were also being 'let go' by the mainstream press, that HRW was hiring them. Why?
>
> Because if there are no reporters telling the stories of human rights abuses, HRW is much less visible and will have a harder time raising money, operating and functioning as a successful and important organisation. I thought that the same thing would happen to arts organisations. That they, too, would 'miss' the coverage by the press, and that, to compensate, would hire 'out of

work' arts reporters, editors and – yes – possibly even critics to come inside their organisations.[15]

Essentially the 'embedded' journalist has access to all departments within the environment, and is tasked with creating short and longer features, news stories, profiles, video- and data-based content beyond the remit of what a PR would do, and certainly in excess of what traditional journalists have time for on a daily basis.

Unsurprisingly, a culture where the journalist is now on the payroll of the very thing she is charged with writing about may have its doubters, who question the integrity of the scheme, but the fact remains that American arts organisations are turning to it as a viable alternative to telling their stories.

One of the features of the digital age is that public acceptance is so important, to be liked and 'liked', even; to know that your work is available and relevant to the communities we serve. Arts institutions are no different, pressured to make work that ticks a range of boxes if their funding is to continue, so the step towards a new type of arts coverage seems wholly logical if mainstream press is increasingly at a distance from the people who make the art and the people who want to read about it. As Gabriel Khan, professor and co-director of media, economics and entrepreneurship at Annenberg School of Communication and Journalism, says: 'Arts organizations are understanding that there is value in supporting arts journalism because it helps people understand and value the artefacts of that industry' (McGlone 2014).

Up until this point in the section, there has been no mention of reviewing. The Annenberg model steers clear of critical evaluation, instead its participants focus on arts news and features. Consider the implications for an in-house journalist employed or on contract for a dance company, asked to review its latest production. Shower it with praise and find yourself justifying the reaction; give it the thumbs down, then don't expect many smiles in the queue for lunch the next day.

But perhaps there is a third way? Perhaps there is a job that straddles elements of reporting, recording and criticism without compromising the writer. Freelance critic Maddy Costa is the best-known example of a British journalist operating as an embedded writer. Her collaboration with celebrated theatremaker Chris Goode is documented in her chapter in *Theatre Criticism: Changing Landscapes*.

Costa (2016) was approached by Goode in spring 2011. His email said he had a hunch that the company needed a narrator whose job embraced elements of being an archivist, documentary artist and brand manager. 'He knew that I was ready … to write about theatre in a different way: not as a "product" of press nights, but the process of making it in a rehearsal room then remaking it night after night with different audiences.'

The term 'embedded criticism' was coined, Costa suggests, in the UK in April 2012 by the critic and blogger Andrew Haydon following his visit to Kurdistan with a touring company. He had believed that criticism might work if there were closer ties between critic and maker. In fact Costa rejected the phrase for her own job, uncomfortable with its militaristic origin and preferred instead the title critic-in-residence. Her work has become more personal, detailed and freer as a result of the collaboration with Goode. 'Compared with the days when I was confined to writing a 300-word review of Chris's work with a star rating', she writes, 'the possibilities feel limitless and invigorating.'

Artsy

The New York-based online resource for art collectors and galleries shows that the Web can be monetised and opportunities for arts writers can arise as a consequence. *Artsy*'s mission, as outlined on its website (www.artsy.net), is 'to make all the world's art accessible to anyone with an internet connection'. At the time of writing there were 300,000 pieces on its database, about half of which were for sale, from some 4,000 galleries around the globe, including the Louvre in Paris and London's National Gallery. High-resolution images of an artwork lead the potential buyer to contact details for the seller, where it is up to those two parties to negotiate a price. Launched in 2012 and having raised around $26 million in venture funding, according to *Forbes.com*, *Artsy* makes money through a monthly subscription charged to galleries and from a small commission on benefit auctions. Interest in the site is booming, says the magazine. Writers specialising in visual art and design would be needed to join the company's 90-strong workforce, again not wearing a critic's hat but diversifying into news and features. For example the articles editor's job advertised in the winter of 2016–17 pinpointed that someone was required to 'tell stories around art, art-making and the art business' which would include profiles on artists and curators and coverage of international fairs and auctions.

Notes

1 McCormick, Neil (17 October 2016), interview with the author.
2 Bowie-Sell, Daisy (25 April 2016), interview with the author.
3 www.artsjournal.com/about-aj-classifieds.
4 Collinson, Gary (17 October 2016), interview with the author.
5 *Ibid.*
6 Whyte, Anthony (19 October 2016), interview with the author.
7 *Ibid.*
8 Vaughan, Megan (17 July 2016), interview with the author.
9 *Ibid.*
10 *Ibid.*
11 *Ibid.*
12 Gardner, Lyn (19 April 2016), interview with the author.
13 Laera, Margherita (27 July 2016), interview with the author.
14 An in-depth appraisal of Italian theatre criticism can be found in Laera (2016).
15 Anawalt, Sasha (10 February 2017), interview with the author.

References

Adams, Sean (9 July 2014) 'The DiS whip-round: Please donate today', *Pitchfork*, http://drownedinsound.com/news/4147618-the-dis-whip-round–please-donate-today ArtsJournal.com.

BBC (6 July 2015) 'NME magazine to be given away free', *Newsbeat*, www.bbc.co.uk/news/entertainment-arts-33408435.

Brown, Ismene (2 August 2013) 'Only the artists can save the arts critics', *Guardian*, www.theguardian.com/culture-professionals-network/culture-professionals-blog/2013/aug/02/only-artists-can-save-critics.

Cardew, Ben (4 May 2014) '*Pitchfork* has an influential voice – but is it in tune with its readers?', *Pitchfork*, www.theguardian.com/media/2014/may/04/music-website-pitchfork-cover-stories-interactive.

Carey, Joely (2016) 'The magazine market isn't dead, it's different', in *Last Words? How Can Journalism Survive the Decline of Print?*, eds John Mair *et al*. Bury St Edmunds: Abramis.

Costa, Maddy (2016) 'The critic as insider', in *Theatre Criticism: Changing Landscapes*, ed. Duska Radosavljevic. London: Bloomsbury Methuen Drama.

Davidson, Darren (24 October 2016) 'Newspaper paywall successes vindicate Murdoch's strategy', *Australian*, www.theaustralian.com.au/business/media/newspaper-paywall-successes-vindicate-murdochs-strategy/news-story/949e106a024fbb7bf37b08c104042b8c.

Griffith, Erin (22 January 2015) 'A bold, new direction for the fine art industry: Online sales', *Forbes.com*, http://fortune.com/2015/01/22/artsy-galleries/.

Haydon, Andrew (2016) 'A brief history of online theatre criticism in England', in *Theatre Criticism: Changing Landscapes*, ed. Duska Radosavljevic. London: Bloomsbury Methuen Drama.

Jokelainen, Jarkko (2014) 'Anyone can be a critic: Is there still a need for professional arts and culture journalism in the digital age?', University of Oxford, Reuters Institute for the Study of Journalism.

Laera, Margherita (2016) 'How to get your hands dirty: Old and new models of "militant" theatre criticism in Italy', in *Theatre Criticism: Changing Landscapes*, ed. Duska Radosavljevic. London: Bloomsbury Methuen Drama.

McGlone, Peggy (31 October 2014) 'Arts organizations are hiring pros to tell their stories', *Washington Post*, www.washingtonpost.com/entertainment/museums/arts-organizations-are-hiring-pros-to-tell-their-stories/2014/10/30/c999beb6-53c0-11e4-809b-8cc0a295c773_story.html?utm_term=.92a17039bff3.

Oldroyd, Rachel (2016) 'Foundations and the foundation of a new way of funding journalism', in *Last Words? How Can Journalism Survive the Decline of Print?*, eds John Mair *et al*. Bury St Edmunds: Abramis.

Radosavljevic, Duska (ed.) (2016) *Theatre Criticism: Changing Landscapes*. London: Bloomsbury Methuen Drama.

Snoddy, Raymond (2016) 'Print has declined, but the evidence suggests it need not be fatal', in *Last Words? How Can Journalism Survive the Decline of Print?*, eds John Mair *et al*. Bury St Edmunds: Abramis.

Van Meter, Mary (February 2015) 'North American papers with paywalls', *News and Tech.com*, www.newsandtech.com/stats/paywalls.html.

CONCLUSION

Near the end of his book *Year of the King*, Antony Sher's riveting account of a time spent in 1984 preparing for the role of Richard III with the RSC, the actor turns his attention to opening night, seeing the nervous faces of the audience alongside 'the frosty passivity of the critics'. First nights are 'stupid', he thinks in that moment. Afterwards, in The Duck, Stratford's famous theatre pub, he sees something else. Someone

> whispers that the word is good and nods towards the table where they sit: Billington, Coveney, Tinker and others. These crazy evenings in The Duck after an opening night, when we all pretend we don't know one another – us and them.

Sher (1990) highlights two things in this passage – that critics and artists stand together and yet slightly apart. Second, that were three critics to sit in a pub today they would, in all probability, be writing up their reviews on their laptops, ready to post online an hour or so after the fall of the curtain.

So much has changed in the art of reviewing, especially in the last 100 years or so, regarding the profile of the critic and the devices used to communicate the message. Professional critics in print, delivering judgements from on high, have had to make room for other kinds of reviewing from other kinds of critics. The Internet has not only altered the way consumers view or listen to content but given new opportunities to those who want to write about it – unqualified and not an expert, as some traditionalists would see it, but that is to disregard the power (and the talent) of the best bloggers around. While deeply difficult times remain for some brands unable to monetise digital content (and by association those critics writing for them), there are pockets of light to suggest other options may work in the future. To be a part of that, critics will have to adjust their thinking, but history shows us that critics have always done that in any case. Perhaps there is room for all kinds of critics working across platforms – not all of them will do it as their only job, some of them will not even be paid at all. Music writer Neil McCormick sees it thus:

> There have never been more media to sort through than right now, so we need gatekeepers more than ever, to guide our choices, and contextualise the art of the moment. Consumer-generated reviews are all very well, but does anybody really trust them? The best critical voices offer a narrative of art that can be as fascinating as the art itself (I'd much rather read a witty, insightful review of a bad film than waste my time watching it).[1]

At the heart of this book is an attempt to highlight how to write better reviews and point out what the critic actually does, to make clear it is not merely a case of saying what you liked or hated. Here's television critic Mark Lawson:

> I think that a really good review – like the best sports writing – should contain an element of explanatory reportage, bottled for posterity, so that a cultural historian of the future, if finding the piece on Google, should have some sense of why something or someone was such a big deal at the time. So don't write '*Breaking Bad* is just genius' or 'Andy Murray is a brilliant tennis player', but try to tell us why.[2]

The best criticism can explain, challenge or champion obscure art or artists. It can point the reader to something else that is relevant, perhaps something the reader did not even realise was there or would interest them. The best criticism should start a discussion, amuse and entertain. When the critic is working with live art, especially, a clear sense should come through of what it was like to be there on that day.

Good critics are honest and optimistic about what they might find. Here's Lyn Gardner at the *Guardian*:

> Some people talk about critics being jaded but how would you leave the house if you were not optimistic. You want to be able to say 'I am going to go and see something that is amazing and astonishing' but the reality is that you don't. I will see something amazing and astonishing half a dozen times a year. But when you see things that are astonishing it's like falling in love all over again.[3]

Now prepared – and hopefully inspired – what matters most is what *you* think. It's over to you. Write soon.

Notes

1 McCormick, Neil (17 October 2016), interview with the author.
2 Lawson, Mark (30 August 2016), interview with the author.
3 Gardner, Lyn (19 April 2016), interview with the author.

Reference

Sher, Antony (1990) *The Year of the King*. London: Methuen Drama.

INDEX

Agate, James 29–30
Amazon 37, 122, 139, 161
Anarchy in the UK 11, 32
Anawalt, Sasha 170
angles 63–4, 70
Angry Young Men 30
Are You Being Served? 103, 132
arts critics, reviewers and writers:
    discovering talent 19; definitions 5–6;
    diversification 4–5, 132; historical record
    31; job cuts 4, 161, 170; power of 27;
    professional 2; reputation 16; status,
    education and profile of 5–9, 132; on
    television 30
Arts Desk 38, 60, 82, 161–2
Artsjournal.com 165, 170
Artsy 172
Australian 15, 135, 160
A West End Whinger 137

Baker, Danny 32
Bamigboye, Baz 119
Bangs, Lester 28
Banks-Smith, Nancy 34, 103
Barber, Lynn 71
Bartleet, Larry 70–71
BBC 24, 26, 37–8, 53, 62, 78, 84, 91, 93,
    109, 111, 123–4, 134, 162
Beatles, The 28, 30, 32
Beaumont, Mark 52, 98
Bennett, Steve 15
Bild 160
Billboard 32, 34, 55

Billen, Andrew 62, 92
Billington, Michael 6, 13, 27, 40, 61, 74–6,
    91, 119, 169
Birthday Party, The 19, 29
bloggers 2, 8, 17, 52, 54, 128, 156, 160;
    influence of 131, 133, 174; legal
    advice 113
blogging 3, 86, 98, 112, 135, 161,
    165; challenging convention 8, 79;
    commercial and other success 136–7,
    166–7; for fun 38; as a specialism
    13, 151
Boston Globe 95
Botton, Alain de 96
Bowie-Sell, Daisy 39–40, 98, 129, 144, 163
Bragg, Melvyn 30
Brantley, Ben 41, 96, 104, 144–5
British Theatre Guide 129, 163
Brittain, Richard 94
Brooker, Charlie 13, 34
Brown, Georgina 65
Brown, Ismene 160–2
Brown, Mark 133
Burchill, Julie 32, 79
Butterworth, Jez 74
bylines 27, 80

Caine, Michael 6, 90
Campbell-Johnston, Rachel 40
Cavendish, Dominic 27, 55
Chamberlain, Rich 148, 152
Channel 4 33, 63, 109
Chicago Sun-Times 13

Chicago Times 97
Chortle 15
Clarkson, Jeremy 79, 91–2, 135
Collinson, Gary 165–6
Comerford, Frank 33
Cooper, Tommy 55
copyright 115
Corden, James 97
Cornwell, Charlotte 110
Coronation Street 9, 13
Costa, Maddy 171
Coveney, Michael 11, 91, 137
Craigslist 170
Crain, Caleb 96
Crawshaw, Peter 139–40
Critics' Circle 23, 132
Crompton, Sarah 40, 144
Culture Whisper 162–3
Cumberbatch, Benedict 54
Curious Incident of the Dog in the Night-Time, The 66

Dad's Army 11
Daily Express 84–5, 145
Daily Mail 17, 25, 92–4, 98, 119–20, 155, 159
Daily Mirror 92, 94
Daily Telegraph 3, 40, 52, 63, 92, 129, 133, 135, 143, 155, 159; first-night reaction 119; freelance terms 161; generating publicity 100; how critics cope 104; star critics 27; television reviews 1930s 33; using past tense 82
Dallas 34
descriptions 74–5
diversity 153–6
Drowned in Sound 164
Durrant, Nancy 40, 42, 47, 79, 81, 123, 144
Duns, Jeremy 120

Eastern Eye 155
Ebert, Roger 13, 131, 154
Elizabeth, Jordannah 154–5
embargoes 85, 118, 120
embedded criticism 161, 169–71
ethics 108, 115, 117–18, 122, 147
extreme reactions 82–3
Evans, Chris 92–3, 134–5

Face 146
Facebook 38, 58, 83, 93, 122, 131, 150, 160–61, 164
fake reviews 120–1
Fantastic Beasts and Where to Find Them 70–1
Fawlty Towers 103

feature writing 5, 56–7, 148, 150–1
Filler, Martin 111–12
finding your voice 78
first person 79–80
Fisher, Mark 9, 14, 15, 17, 42, 79, 84
Flood, Alison 121
Fox, Laurence 56–7
Frankel, Eddy 60
Friedman, Sonia 118, 120, 133
Front Row 123–4
Fry, Stephen 91

Gardner, Lyn 3, 13, 95, 98; on controlling the Press 100; the future of criticism 169; on optimism 175; reading other reviews 49; responsibility 39; star critics 27; working routine 5, 40–1, 151
Gilbert, Jenny 60, 63
Gill, A.A. 63, 79
Girl on the Train, The 138
Goodreads.com 37, 138
Griffiths, Richard 54
Guardian 5, 6, 13, 14, 16, 34, 47, 49, 52, 121, 123, 139; banning critics 98; covering the regions 39; different voices 156, 169; digital-first/online journalism 129–30, 159–60, 164, 168; on individual performances/productions 74, 91, 95, 118–19; star critics 27, 151; television reviews 71, 84, 92, 110–111; use of language 77

Hadid, Zaha 111–12
Hancock's Half Hour 11
Harry Potter and the Cursed Child 39, 118, 120, 133, 139, 154
Haydon, Andrew 13, 128–9, 137, 163, 171
Hazlitt, William 5, 31
Henry, Lenny 61
Hepple, Peter 25–6
Hobson, Harold 8, 19, 23, 28, 31, 41
Hoffman, Alice 95–7
Hound Dog 32, 102
house style 77–8
humour 75–6
Hunt, Leigh 31
Hytner, Nicholas 7

Impressionists 26
Independent 76, 130, 156, 160
Independent on Sunday 4, 52, 161
Independent Press Standards Organisation (IPSO) 116
intros 70
ITV 30, 38, 71, 78

James, Clive 12, 34
James, Sid 55
jargon 74
Jays, David 58–9, 165
Jerusalem 74
Johnson, Samuel 5, 8
Jokelainen, Jarkko 161
journalism training 117, 142, 153

Kael, Pauline 27
Kent, Nick 19, 28, 145
Kermode, M. 4, 9, 11, 13, 16, 30, 93, 102, 114, 118, 131, 133, 138
Khan, Naseem 156
Kretzmer, Herbert 25
Kinn, Maurice 32

Laera, Margherita 146, 169
language 72
Lawson, Mark 3, 33, 52–3, 84, 97, 118, 123, 132–3, 151, 175
Le Monde 129–30
Leroy, Louis 26
Les Misérables 24, 104
Letts, Quentin 92, 98
Leveson Inquiry 116
libel 108–11
Littlewood, S.L. 23
Long, Camilla 63–4
Logan, Nick 32, 146
long-form journalism 10, 13, 28, 164
Long, Pat 7, 16, 19, 28, 32, 42, 94
Look Back in Anger 19, 88
Los Angeles Times 82, 95–6
Lovereading.co.uk 37, 139
Love Thy Neighbour 33

Mackintosh, Cameron 25, 104
Mailer, Norman 95
Mail on Sunday 60, 62, 65, 81–2
Major, John 25
Manzoni, Alessandro 53
Maxwell, Dominic 81
Mayall, Rik 91
Mayo, Simon 37–8, 131, 138
McCormick, Neil 3, 52, 63, 85–6, 135, 143, 144, 146
McGlone, Peggy 169–70
McLennan Douglas 165, 170
Media Diversified 156
Melody Maker 28, 32, 102, 143
Minder 103
Monkhouse, Bob 91
Moran, Joe 8, 13, 23, 33–4
Morecambe and Wise 34

Morley, Paul 30, 45
Motherland 62
Mrs Brown's Boys 53
Muggeridge, Malcolm 63
Murdoch, Rupert 124
Myskow, Nina 9, 12, 13, 14, 27, 34, 42, 79, 90, 104, 110, 116, 124

National Council for the Training of Journalists 116–17, 142, 153, 156
National Union of Journalists 113
New Journalism 28
News of the World 12, 27, 34, 116
news reporting 57, 152–3
New York Review of Books 111–12
New York Times 34, 41, 62, 82, 96, 104, 129–30, 145
New Yorker 19, 67, 145
newspapers: circulation decline 4, 160; local and regional press 7, 56, 116, 148, 152
Nightingale, Benedict 104
NME 16, 28, 70, 145; controversy 52–3, 94, 98; history of 32, 168; influence of 7, 19, 28; on punk 11
Norman, Barry 30
Norman, Neil 14, 18, 42, 85, 94, 98, 100, 114, 131, 134, 145–6
not-for-profit journalism 167–8

Observer 9, 12, 19, 29, 47, 52, 66, 76–7, 91, 118, 131, 154
Odell, Tom 52–3, 98
Olivier, Laurence 90
Orpheus in the Underworld 26
Osborne, John 19, 29, 88
Outnumbered 62

Paris Review 76, 95
Parker, Dorothy 27
Parsons, Tony 28, 32, 144
Petrusich, Amanda 19, 67
Pinter, Harold 8, 19, 29
Pitchfork 129
points of view in stories 67
Potter, Dennis 44
precise writing 72
Presley, Elvis 30, 103
Press Complaints Commission 116
Purves, Libby 17, 61, 84, 137

Quietus 101, 164

Race, Steve 102
Radosavljevic, Duska 130
Rantzen, Esther 53

Record Mirror 28, 143, 146
reviewing: accuracy 18; admitting mistakes 114; analysing works of art 65–8; angles 63; audience behaviour 53–4; below-the-line comments 134; career choices 168–9; changes in taste and technology 22–3; choosing what to review 37; complimentary tickets 45–6; effect on critics 104; friends 122–3; influence of PR 100–2; intros 57; negative criticism 17, 90, 93, 96; news sense 54; opinions 14, 80, 108; pitching to editors 152; responsibility 15–18; social media 9, 54, 76, 134, 166; starting out as a critic 143; the unexpected 55–6; using knowledge and experience 41; versatility 10, 42; violence or threats of violence 94–5, 97; watching and listening 47–8; without pay 146–8, 166, 175
Rich, Frank 28, 96
Rogers, Jude 47, 58, 70
Rolland, Paige 94
Rotten Tomatoes 129
Rowling, J.K. 63, 71, 118–19, 139, 154
Royal Shakespeare Company 24–5, 43, 78, 157, 174
Roy, Amit 155–6
Rylance, Mark 74–5

Savile, Jimmy 63
Scott, A.O. 96–7
Second World War 7, 23, 33, 115
Sex Pistols 11, 32
Shaar Murray, Charles 28, 32, 42, 94
Shakespeare, William 5, 11–12, 31
Shaw, George Bernard 44
Shawshank Redemption, The 100
Shedden, Iain 15, 47, 135
Shellard, Dominic 23–4, 29, 31
Shenton, Mark 54, 119, 123, 151
Sher, Antony 174
Sherrin, Ned 76
Silman, Roberta 95–6
Simpson, Dave 16, 82, 131, 147
Simon, John 75, 95
Siskel, Gene 13
Smith, Alistair 39, 149
Smith, Sheridan 55
Smith, Monty 145–6
sock puppetry 121
Soul, David 111
Sounds 28, 143
Spectator 99–100
Spencer, Charles 100, 104

Springsteen, Bruce 59, 135
Spurling, Hilary 99–100
Stage, The 5, 24, 29, 33–4, 85, 88, 91, 119–20, 149, 151
star ratings 82, 89, 162–3, 172
Star Wars 2, 118
Steele, Richard 31
storytelling 58, 64, 66
structure (importance of) 70–2
Stuckmann, Chris 138
Sun 92, 115–16
Sunday People 9, 12, 27, 34
Sunday Times 19, 29, 33, 63–4, 79, 82, 121, 124, 155, 165
swearing 76–7
Sydney Morning Herald 129

Telegraph India 155
Thatcher, Margaret 24–5
theatreCat 17, 84
third person 79–80
Times, The 6, 17, 43, 61–2, 81, 92, 104, 123, 133, 136, 144, 159; controversy 25, 119–20; covering regions 40; history of arts writing/reviewing 31, 33
Titchener, Campbell B. 6, 16, 17, 65
Top Gear 91–2, 134
Trueman, Matt 40, 120, 123, 136
Tynan, Kenneth 8, 11, 17, 19, 27–31
Twitter 83, 97, 110, 119, 149; as a conversation 92, 134, 166; to promote content 10, 131; used in retaliation 93, 95, 105

Vanity Fair 145
Variety 4, 25
Vaughan, Megan 3, 9, 18, 46, 52, 145–6, 166–7
Vidal, Gore 95
vox pops 92

Waiting for Godot 29
Waller, Jack 88–9
Wardle, Irving 25
Washington Post 139, 159, 169
Wells, Stanley 12, 31
We Will Rock You 14, 103
WhatsOnStage.com 39–40, 84, 98, 120, 123, 129, 144, 163
White, Cliff 11, 32
Whitehouse, Mary 63
Williams, Gilda 30, 42, 72–4
Wollaston, Sam 71–2, 92
Women's Wear Daily 145

Woods, Frank E. 31
work experience 144, 149–51
Worldwide Web 3; democratisation of the Internet 130; digital explosion 3, 4, 8, 22, 161; digital technology 63; how we consume 14, 127, 129; paywalls 132, 159–60, 163, 169; potential of 128; user-generated content 129, 137
Wright, Matthew 111
writer's block 86

YouTube 84, 109, 119, 128, 131, 137–8, 166

Taylor & Francis eBooks

Helping you to choose the right eBooks for your Library

Add Routledge titles to your library's digital collection today. Taylor and Francis ebooks contains over 50,000 titles in the Humanities, Social Sciences, Behavioural Sciences, Built Environment and Law.

Choose from a range of subject packages or create your own!

Benefits for you
- Free MARC records
- COUNTER-compliant usage statistics
- Flexible purchase and pricing options
- All titles DRM-free.

Benefits for your user
- Off-site, anytime access via Athens or referring URL
- Print or copy pages or chapters
- Full content search
- Bookmark, highlight and annotate text
- Access to thousands of pages of quality research at the click of a button.

Free Trials Available
We offer free trials to qualifying academic, corporate and government customers.

eCollections – Choose from over 30 subject eCollections, including:

Archaeology	Language Learning
Architecture	Law
Asian Studies	Literature
Business & Management	Media & Communication
Classical Studies	Middle East Studies
Construction	Music
Creative & Media Arts	Philosophy
Criminology & Criminal Justice	Planning
Economics	Politics
Education	Psychology & Mental Health
Energy	Religion
Engineering	Security
English Language & Linguistics	Social Work
Environment & Sustainability	Sociology
Geography	Sport
Health Studies	Theatre & Performance
History	Tourism, Hospitality & Events

For more information, pricing enquiries or to order a free trial, please contact your local sales team:
www.tandfebooks.com/page/sales

Routledge — Taylor & Francis Group | The home of Routledge books

www.tandfebooks.com